Top Federal Tax Issues for 2021 | CPE Course

Annette Nellen, CPA, CGMA, Esq.

Greg White, CPA

James R. Hamill, Ph.D., CPA

Jennifer Kowal, J.D.

Klaralee Charlton, J.D., LL.M.

Contributors

Contributing Editors	Annette Nellen, CPA, CGMA, Esq.
	Greg White, CPA
	James R. Hamill, Ph.D., CPA
	Jennifer Kowal, J.D.
	Klaralee Charlton, J.D., LL.M.
Production Coordinator	Mariela de la Torre; Jennifer Schencker;
	Gokiladevi Sashikumar
Production	Sharon Sofinski; Anbarasu Anbumani

This publication is designed to provide accurate and authoritative information in regard to the subject matter covered. It is sold with the understanding that the publisher is not engaged in rendering legal, accounting, or other professional service. If legal advice or other expert assistance is required, the services of a competent professional person should be sought. All views expressed in this publication are those of the author and not necessarily those of the publisher or any other person.

ISBN: 978-0-8080-5532-7

© 2020 CCH Incorporated and its affiliates. All rights reserved.
2700 Lake Cook Road
Riverwoods, IL 60015
800 344 3734
CCHCPELink.com

No claim is made to original government works; however, within this publication, the following are subject to CCH Incorporated's copyright: (1) the gathering, compilation, and arrangement of such government materials; (2) the magnetic translation and digital conversion of data, if applicable; (3) the historical, statutory and other notes and references; and (4) the commentary and other materials.

Do not send returns to the above address. If for any reason you are not satisfied with your book purchase, it can easily be returned within 30 days of shipment. Please go to *support.cch.com/returns* to initiate your return. If you require further assistance with your return, please call: (800) 344-3734 M-F, 8 a.m. – 6 p.m. CT.

Printed in the United States of America

Introduction

Each year, a handful of tax issues typically require special attention by tax practitioners. The reasons vary, from tax legislation, a particularly complicated new provision in the Internal Revenue Code, to a planning technique opened up by a new regulation or ruling, or the availability of a significant tax benefit with a short window of opportunity. Sometimes a developing business need creates a new set of tax problems, or pressure exerted by Congress or the Administration puts more heat on some taxpayers while giving others more slack. All these share in creating a unique mix that in turn creates special opportunities and pitfalls in the coming year and beyond. The past year has seen more than its share of these developing issues.

Top Federal Tax Issues for 2021 CPE Course identifies those recent events that have developed into the current "hot" issues of the day. These tax issues have been selected as particularly relevant to tax practice in 2021. They have been selected not only because of their impact on return preparation during the 2021 tax season but also because of the important role they play in developing effective tax strategies for 2021 and beyond.

This course is designed to help reassure the tax practitioner that he or she is not missing out on advising clients about a hot, new tax opportunity; or that a brewing controversy does not blindside their practice. In addition to issue identification, this course provides the basic information needed for the tax practitioner to implement a plan that addresses the particular opportunities and pitfalls presented by any one of those issues. Among the topics examined in the *Top Federal Tax Issues for 2021 CPE Course* are:

- The Rules on Entertainment, Meals and Snacks in Light of Changes by the Tax Cuts and Jobs Act (TCJA)
- Section 199A Qualified Business Income
- The Federal Tax Consequences of Presidentially Declared Disaster Areas under the Stafford Act
- The Families First Coronavirus Response Act and CARES Act
- COVID-19 Employment Tax Changes for Employers and the Self-Employed
- Tax Issues Involving Troubled Borrowers
- Paycheck Protection Program (PPP) Loans: New Legislation and the Impact on Forgiveness
- Retirement Plan Changes by Congress and the IRS in Response to COVID-19

Study Questions. Throughout the course you will find Study Questions to help you test your knowledge, and comments that are vital to understanding a particular strategy or idea. Answers to the Study Questions with feedback on both correct and incorrect responses are provided in a special section beginning at ¶ 10,100.

Final Exam. This course is divided into four Modules. Take your time and review all course Modules. When you feel confident that you thoroughly understand the material, turn to the Final Exam. Complete one, or all, Module Final Exams for continuing professional education credit.

Go to **cchcpelink.com/printcpe** to complete your Final Exam online for immediate results. My Dashboard provides convenient storage for your CPE course Certificates. Further information is provided in the CPE Final Exam instructions at ¶ 10,300. **Please note,**

manual grading is no longer available for Top Federal Tax Issues. All answer sheets must be submitted online for grading and processing.

Note: The material contained in this publication was current at the time it went to print.

October 2020

PLEDGE TO QUALITY

Thank you for choosing this CCH® CPE Link product. We will continue to produce high quality products that challenge your intellect and give you the best option for your Continuing Education requirements. Should you have a concern about this or any other Wolters Kluwer product, please call our Customer Service Department at 1-800-344-3734.

COURSE OBJECTIVES

This course was prepared to provide the participant with an overview of specific tax issues that impact 2020 tax return preparation and tax planning in 2021. Each impacts a significant number of taxpayers in significant ways.

Upon course completion, you will be able to:

- Identify and explain the tax rules applicable to a company's expenditures on entertainment, snacks, and meals for customers and employees
- Recognize and apply the rules of the proposed regulations under Code Sec. 274 released in February 2020
- Recognize and apply the Tax Cuts and Jobs Act (TCJA) changes and the IRS guidance addressing these changes
- Compute the Section 199A deduction for taxpayers above the threshold income level and for other taxpayers
- Identify planning opportunities to maximize the deduction
- Define a service business as that term is used in Section 199A
- Describe the basic structure of Section 199A
- Recognize how qualified business income (QBI) applies to clients
- Define a trade or business as the term applies to Section 199A
- Identify aggregation factors
- Recognize what is included as a service business
- Identify unadjusted basis immediately after acquisition (UBIA)
- Recognize when a special allocation of UBIA or W-2 wages may be made by a partnership
- Calculate interest and penalties if tax is not paid by the Notice 2020-18 due date
- Identify which clients are best served by filing early
- Recognize the amount of taxes clients must pay by April 15
- Describe the key features of the Families First Coronavirus Response Act and the CARES Act that apply to businesses and individual taxpayers
- Recognize how provisions of these acts apply in common factual scenarios
- Identify how to determine whether taxpayers are eligible for provided benefits under the acts

- Recognize how Pandemic Emergency Unemployment Compensation applies
- Describe what happens to an EIDL loan received before April 3, 2020, for COVID-19 related purposes
- Identify employment tax relief for employers and self-employed individuals in the FFCRA and CARES Acts
- Compute the employee retention credit with and without the employer OASDI tax deferral provision
- Recognize how the payroll/self-employment tax relief interacts with other COVID-19 and general tax provisions
- Explain the difference in tax treatment between cancellation of recourse debt and foreclosures of property securing non-recourse debt
- Identify situations when cancellation of indebtedness income may be excluded under Code Section 108
- Describe which types of debt modifications are treated as exchanges, and the tax consequences
- Explain the tax treatment of claims in bankruptcy and the taxation of the bankruptcy estate
- Identify what is considered first in the order of basis reduction
- Recognize how to compute the amount of debt forgiveness
- Recognize how to compute the limit on nonpayroll expenses
- Develop practical steps for unused funds near the end of the 8-week covered period
- Compute the maximum loan amount for sole proprietors and partnerships
- Identify remaining areas where guidance is still lacking
- Describe the efforts by Congress and the IRS in response to the COVID-19 pandemic
- Describe the retirement distribution changes implemented by the SECURE Act and CARES Act
- Recognize and analyze the options available to employees to use retirement funds for current liquidity needs
- Recognize recommended plan changes to employer retirement plans based on shrinking revenue and employee reductions
- Identify the impact of using government loan proceeds to contribute to retirement plans
- Recommend estate planning techniques to achieve client goals in light of modified withdrawal options

---

Additional copies of this course may be downloaded from **cchcpelink.com/printcpe**. Printed copies of the course are available for $4.50 by calling 1-800-344-3734 (ask for product 10024491-0008).

Contents

MODULE 1: BUSINESS—Chapter 1: IRS Serves Us New Guidance on Food and Fun

¶ 101 WELCOME

This chapter reviews the rules on entertainment, meals, and snacks in light of changes by the Tax Cuts and Jobs Act (TCJA) and proposed regulations issued in February 2020. These changes make the long-standing exceptions under Internal Revenue Code Sec. 274 more relevant, change the documentation requirements, and help explain how the new rules interact with long-standing rules that remain after the TCJA. This chapter also addresses how the changes affect substantiation, recordkeeping, and tax planning.

¶ 102 LEARNING OBJECTIVES

Upon completion of this chapter, you will be able to:

- Identify and explain the tax rules applicable to a company's expenditures on entertainment, snacks, and meals for customers and employees
- Recognize and apply the rules of the proposed regulations under Code Sec. 274 released in February 2020
- Recognize and apply the Tax Cuts and Jobs Act (TCJA) changes and the IRS guidance addressing these changes

¶ 103 INTRODUCTION

The goal of this chapter is to identify the rules that are relevant to a company's expenditures on entertainment, meals, and snacks in light of the TCJA changes to Code Sec. 274. In addition, it will explain how to navigate the proposed regulations on meals and entertainment that were released in February 2020. Finally, it will discuss current issues in the meals and entertainment area and how to address them.

General Framework

The area of fringe benefits is a complicated one, but there is a general framework for determining the treatment of cash and noncash items given to employees. First, a company must identify what was given to the employee and its value. Then it should consider the following:

- Does any exclusion apply for the employee? Look at the Code, regulations, IRS rulings, and court cases. Generally, special detailed rules apply.
- Was it reimbursement for an expense incurred by an employee? Under an accountable plan?
- Is there any restriction on the employer deducting the amount, such as under Code Sec. 274? If yes, note that the disallowed amount may be different than the taxable value (if any) to the employee. If the amount is deductible, the employer is limited to the cost even if the taxable value to the employee is greater.
- If the amount is taxable, generally reporting (W-2) and withholding are required.

Examples: Treatment of Cash and Non-Cash Items Given to Employees

Item	Treatment
Cash salary, hourly wages, or bonus	Taxable; withholding generally required
Amazon gift card or season tickets to the San Jose Sharks	Taxable; withholding generally required
Holiday party primarily for employees other than highly compensated ones	Excluded (*de minimis* fringe per Code Sec. 132(e) and Reg Sec. 1.132-6)
Meals furnished for the convenience of the employer, furnished on business premises	Excluded per Code Sec. 119. Employer may only deduct 50 percent of cost; no deduction after 2025.
Hand sanitizer, tools for working at home, software, and materials for employee's children provided due to federally declared disaster	Excluded per Code Sec.139

Relevant Code Provisions

The following Code sections are important in determining the tax rules for a company's expenditures on entertainment, snacks, and meals for customers and employees:

- Code Sec. 61, Gross income defined
- Code Sec. 62, Adjusted gross income defined
- Code Sec. 119, Meals or lodging furnished for the convenience of the employer
- Code Sec. 132, Certain fringe benefits
- Code Sec. 274, Disallowance of certain entertainment, etc., expenses

Code Secs. 61 and 62 define *gross income* and *adjusted gross income*, respectively. Code Sec. 119 addresses meals or lodging furnished for the convenience of the employer, which is also a specially defined term. Code Sec. 132 comes into play because certain food and entertainment benefits may have been given to employees. Code Sec. 274 discusses when entertainment and other expenses are not deductible. An entity must first decide if an expense is an ordinary or a business expense. If it is an expense that falls under Code Sec. 274, such as entertainment and certain meals, then the entity has to determine that even though it is ordinary or necessary, all or part of the expense may not be deductible because of the special rules under Code Sec. 274. These relevant Code sections are explained in more detail in the following sections.

Code Sec. 61

Under Code Sec. 61, *gross income* is defined as follows: "all income from whatever source derived, including (but not limited to) the following items: compensation for services, including fees, commissions, *fringe benefits*, and similar items."

The general rule in this section is that everything an employee receives is taxable *unless* the employee (or employer) can point to a specific rule that applies and that the rule was properly followed. Several special exceptions are scattered throughout Chapter 1 of Subtitle A of the Internal Revenue Code. Code Sec. 61 includes many detailed regulations on valuation and related special rules.

Reg. Sec. 1.61-2 discusses compensation for services, including fees, commissions, and similar items. Under its general rules, compensation is interpreted broadly. Compensation that is received in a form other than cash should be valued at fair market value. Reg. Sec. 1.61-21 contains valuation rules, which are supplemented by IRS revenue rulings and revenue procedures. The regulation's subsections cover the following topics:

- Fringe benefits
- Valuation of fringe benefits
- Special valuation rules

- Automobile lease valuation rule
- Vehicle cents-per-mile valuation rule
- Commuting valuation rule
- Non-commercial flight valuation rule
- Commercial flight valuation rule
- Valuation of meals provided at an employer-operated eating facility for employees
- Commuting valuation rule for certain employees

Code Sec. 119

This section states that an employee can exclude 100 percent of the value of meals and lodging furnished to the employee for the convenience of the employer.

However, under the TCJA, these meals furnished for the convenience of the employer are only 50 percent deductible by the employer through 2025 and then 0 percent deductible after that. The IRS has issued a variety of rulings including private letter rulings and technical advice memoranda on the meaning of key terms used in Code Sec. 119.

> **COMMENT:** According to Code Sec. 132(e), ***de minimis fringe*** describes any property or service whose value is so small as to make accounting for it unreasonable or administratively impracticable.

Code Sec. 132

Code Sec. 132 lists certain fringe benefits that are excluded from gross income, including working condition fringe benefits and *de minimis* fringe benefits. Per Code Sec. 132(d), ***working condition fringe benefit*** means property or services provided by an employer to an employee that the employee could deduct under Code Sec. 162 if the employee had paid for them on their own.

Under the TCJA, from 2018 through 2025, employees cannot deduct these unreimbursed employee business expenses. However, the IRS has clarified that this does not affect the definition of ***working condition fringe benefit***.

Code Sec. 162

The general rule under this section is that for employees who travel for work, their traveling expenses, including amounts expended for meals and lodging (other than amounts that are lavish or extravagant) while in the pursuit of a trade or business, are deductible. Regulations under Code Sec. 162 also includes special rules relevant to meals and lodging:

- Reg. Sec. 1.162-2, Traveling expenses
- Reg. Sec. 1.162-10, Certain employee benefits
- Reg. Sec. 1.162-17, Reporting and substantiation of certain business expenses of employees
- Reg. Sec. 1.162-25, Deductions with respect to noncash fringe benefits
- Reg. Sec. 1.162-25T, Deductions with respect to noncash fringe benefits
- Reg. Sec. 1.162-32, Expenses paid or incurred for lodging when not traveling away from home

Code Sec. 274

This Code section discusses the disallowance of certain entertainment and other expenses. It was added as part of the Revenue Act of 1962, which aimed to increase economic growth, address inequities, and make the tax law simpler. Per his message to Congress on April 20, 1961, President John F. Kennedy had expressed concerns that the tax law should not encourage charging luxury spending to the Treasury.

Much of pre-TCJA Code Sec. 274 is similar to the 1962 version. A few changes were made over the years, including by the Tax Reform Act of 1986, which noted that the 1962 Act, "by not focusing sufficiently on the personal-consumption element of deductible meal and entertainment expenses, unfairly permitted taxpayers who could arrange business settings for personal consumption to receive, in effect, a Federal tax subsidy for such consumption that was not available to other taxpayers."

Business meals and entertainment expenditures tend to be more expensive than for personal spending (e.g., a business is more likely to buy the better seats at a sporting event). The act created the 20 percent disallowance, later changed to a 50 percent disallowance, with some exceptions that still allow a 100 percent deduction.

Code Sec. 274 regulations include the following:

- Reg. Sec. 1.274-1, Disallowance of certain entertainment, gift, and travel expenses
- Reg. Sec. 1.274-2, Disallowance of deductions for certain expenses for entertainment, amusement, recreation, or travel
- Reg. Sec. 1.274-4, Disallowance of certain foreign travel expenses
- Reg. Sec. 1.274-5 and -5T, Substantiation requirements
- Reg. Sec. 1.274-6, Expenditures deductible without regard to trade or business or other income producing activity
- Reg. Sec. 1.274-7, Treatment of certain expenditures with respect to entertainment-type facilities
- Reg. Sec. 1.274-8, Disallowance of certain employee achievement award expenses
- Reg. Sec. 1.274-9, Entertainment provided to specified individuals
- Reg. Sec. 1.274-10, Special rules for aircraft used for entertainment
- New Prop. Reg. Sec. 1.274–11, Disallowance of deductions for certain entertainment, amusement, or recreation expenditures paid or incurred after December 31, 2017
- New Prop Reg. Sec. 1.274–12, Limitation on deductions for certain food or beverage expenses paid or incurred after December 31, 2017

The proposed regulations will be discussed in more detail later in this chapter.

Key Points

The general rules for the tax implications of entertainment, meals, and snacks are:

- If an employee receives something, it's taxable.
  - — Unless an exclusion applies. In many cases, detailed requirements must be met.
- Employers can deduct ordinary and necessary business expenses.
  - — See the various limitations at Code Sec. 162, such as no deduction for penalties.

— If an expense is covered by Code Sec. 274, additional requirements must be met and some ordinary and necessary expenses, such as entertainment, are disallowed.

- If employers provide cash or non-cash items to employees, they are generally subject to reporting and withholding rules.

— Unless an exclusion applies and is properly followed.

— Generally, if an item is nondeductible to the employer (such as entertainment) but was ordinary and necessary, it is likely not taxable to the employee. For example, if an employee takes a client to dinner and a basketball game, the expense is not taxable income to the employee.

Keep in mind that there are many detailed rules in the Code, regulations, IRS rulings, and court cases involving fringe benefits, and meal and entertainment expenditures.

¶ 104 ENTERTAINMENT AND FOOD CHANGES TO CODE SEC. 274 MADE BY THE TCJA

The TCJA, signed into law in 2017, eliminated the deduction for any expenses related to activities generally considered entertainment, amusement, or recreation. With this change, it became clear that there is some confusion as to exactly what is entertainment. Back in 1962, the legislative language and history, and even a few court cases, indicated that entertainment included client business meals, but that is not what Congress seems to have intended after the TCJA. The IRS, in the proposed regulations and even in Notice 2018-76, has stated that client business meals are not considered entertainment. The regulations and the Joint Committee on Taxation Bluebook indicated that client business meals would still be deductible, meaning they are not considered entertainment, and of course would be subject to the 50 percent disallowance as before.

Under Code Sec. 274, the general rule for entertainment, amusement, recreation, or qualified transportation fringes is that no deduction is allowed. However, this is a fairly complicated Code section with a variety of exceptions and special rules, perhaps made even more complicated after the TCJA.

Much of Code Sec. 274 is still similar to the 1962 version, but it has been tweaked over the years. One notable change was the decision to disallow a percentage of meals and entertainment expenses. At first the disallowance was 20 percent, but later it changed to a 50 percent disallowance. Some things, like a holiday party for employees, have always been a 100 percent deductible. There are a fair amount of regulations here, including Reg. Sec. 1.274-2, which includes a definition of *entertainment*.

Note that the Code Sec. 274 changes are for expenses paid or incurred after December 31, 2017. Therefore, fiscal year taxpayers had to change midyear to conform to the TCJA version of Code Sec. 274.

COMMENT: Code Sec. 274 does not *allow* anything; its purpose is to *disallow* expenditures that were already allowed under Code Secs. 162 or 212.

The Bluebook to the TCJA explains the elimination of the deduction under prior law with respect to entertainment, amusement, or recreation. There is also a limitation on the deduction permitted to an employer under prior law for items that would be expected to qualify, such as transportation fringe benefits and employer-provided commuting. In addition, the provision impacts the deduction for expenses of an employer associated with providing food or beverages to employees through an eating facility that meets the requirements for the *de minimis* fringes and for the convenience of the employer.

There is also no deduction for entertainment, amusement, or recreation; or for membership dues to clubs organized for business, pleasure, recreation, or other social purposes. (The IRS should provide a clearer definition of those types of clubs.) The Bluebook does include a footnote about some of the exceptions. Taxpayers can still deduct 50 percent of certain business-related food and beverage expenses. They may still generally deduct 50 percent of the food or beverage expense associated with operating their business, such as meals consumed while employees are on work travel. Taxpayers may also continue to deduct 50 percent of the properly substantiated food or beverage expenses associated with a meal that is considered a business meal with a client, provided that meal is not lavish or extravagant. The exception for "lavish or extravagant" has been in the law for some time.

The TJCA Bluebook states that a meal included in an activity or event that primarily constitutes entertainment results in disallowance of a deduction for the entire activity, including the meal (page 189). This is important, because when the IRS issued Notice 2018-76, it took a different view. The IRS said, for example, a hotdog you bought for your client or prospective client at a ball game, is 50 percent deductible if it's separately charged or billed from the game tickets. Obviously, the Joint Committee said just the opposite. Notice 2018-76 was transitional guidance until proposed regulations were issued. The proposed regulations issued in February 2020 follow the IRS interpretation rather than that of the Joint Committee on Taxation.

For 2018 through 2025, employers can only deduct 50 percent of *de minimis* fringe meals that are for the convenience of the employer; afterward, they cannot deduct any of that expense.

No changes were made by the TCJA to the nine exceptions at Code Sec. 274(e), which are listed below:

1. Food and beverages for employees
2. Expenses treated as compensation
3. Reimbursed expenses
4. Employee recreational, social, or similar activities
5. Employees, stockholder, etc., business meetings
6. Meetings of business leagues, etc.
7. Items available to the public
8. Entertainment sold to customers
9. Expenses includible in the income of persons who are not employees

This is why some entertainment expenses are still deductible at 50 percent or 100 percent, such as holiday parties for employees (Code Sec. 274(a)(4)). Note that exceptions 2, 3, 4, 7, 8, and 9 are addressed in the proposed regulations, which will be discussed in the next section of this chapter. Once comments are received, there might be even more clarification on these exceptions in the final regulations. Also, final regulations may include changes from the proposed regulations.

Code Sec. 274(k) states that deductions are not allowed for meals that are lavish or extravagant and that the taxpayer (or the taxpayer's employee) must be present at such meals. Note that if the expense falls under exceptions 2, 3, 4, 7, 8, and 9 of Code Sec. 274(e), it is not subject to this limitation. Code Sec. 274(n), added by the Tax Reform Act of 1982, states that only 50 percent of meal expenses are allowed as a deduction. There have always been exceptions to this rule. One such exception though was removed by the TCJA. That is the exception for de minimus fringe benefit food and beverages. It is the repeal of this exception that makes this de minimis fringe only 50 percent deductible by employers (rather than 100 percent deductible prior to the TCJA). This and most other changes to Code Sec. 274 are effective for amounts paid or incurred or paid after December 31, 2017. New Code Sec. 274(o) disallows a deduction for meals for the convenience of the employer and *de minimis* food and beverage. This new subsection is effective for amounts incurred or paid after December 31, 2025. Thus such expenses will be completely disallowed after that date.

The following excerpt highlights the changes to Code Sec. 274(n):

> **(n) ONLY 50 PERCENT OF MEAL ~~AND ENTERTAINMENT~~ EXPENSES ALLOWED AS DEDUCTION**
>
> **(1) IN GENERAL** The amount allowable as a deduction under this chapter for—
>
> ~~**(A)**~~ any expense for food or beverages~~, and~~
>
> ~~**(B)** any item with respect to an activity which is of a type generally considered to constitute entertainment, amusement, or recreation, or with respect to a facility used in connection with such activity,~~
>
> shall not exceed 50 percent of the amount of such expense ~~or item~~ which would (but for this paragraph) be allowable as a deduction under this chapter.
>
> **(2) EXCEPTIONS** Paragraph (1) shall not apply to any expense if—
>
> **(A)** such expense is described in paragraph (2), (3), (4), (7), (8), or (9) of subsection (e),
>
> ~~**(B)** in the case of an expense for food or beverages, such expense is excludable from the gross income of the recipient under section 132 by reason of subsection (e) thereof (relating to de minimis fringes),~~
>
> ~~**(C)** such expense is covered by a package involving a ticket described in subsection (*l*)(1)(B),~~
>
> **(B~~D~~)** in the case of an employer who pays or reimburses moving expenses of an employee, such expenses are includible in the income of the employee under section 82, or
>
> **(C~~E~~)** such expense is for food or beverages—

The removal of "entertainment" from the heading of Code Sec. 274(n) and the fact that Code Sec. 274(e)(5) and (6) are not listed at Code Sec. 274(n)(2)(A) results in *entertainment* excepted at Code Sec. 274(e)(5) business meetings and (e)(6) business league meetings went from 50 percent allowed prior to the TCJA to 100 percent allowed after the TCJA. A technical correction would change this so that such entertainment is 0 percent deductible. The deleted subsections (B) is what makes Code Sec. 132(e) *de minimis* fringe benefit food or beverage expenses only 50 percent deductible after the TCJA; see the Code Sec. 274(o) addition for a 100 percent disallowance after 2025.

STUDY QUESTIONS

1. Which of the following identifies the first consideration with respect to determining if an expenditure is deductible by a business?

- **a.** Is it ordinary and necessary?
- **b.** Is it related to entertainment?
- **c.** Is it a charitable expense?
- **d.** Is there an exception under Code Sec. 274(e)?

2. Which of the following is normally excluded from an employee's gross income?

- **a.** Compensation for services
- **b.** Commissions
- **c.** *De minimis* fringe benefits
- **d.** Season tickets to the local sports team.

3. With respect to the deduction for food that is a *de minimis* fringe, the amounts paid or incurred after December 31, 2017, and before January 1, 2026, are reduced by:

- **a.** 25 percent
- **b.** 50 percent
- **c.** 75 percent
- **d.** 100 percent

¶ 105 PROPOSED REGULATIONS ON MEALS AND ENTERTAINMENT RELEASED IN FEBRUARY 2020

Proposed Reg. Secs. 1.274-11 and 1.274-12 (www.govinfo.gov/content/pkg/FR-2020-02-26/pdf/2020-03723.pdf), released in February 2020, are "reliance" regulations. They are not effective until the final regulations are published in the *Federal Register*, but they can be relied on now for expenditures paid or incurred after December 31, 2017. Taxpayers can continue to rely on IRS Notice 2018-76 until final regulations are published. The regulations address:

- The elimination of the Code Sec. 274 deduction related to entertainment, amusement, or recreation activities
- The definition of *entertainment*
- Limitations at Code Sec. 274(k) on business meals
- Limitations at Code Sec. 274(n) on the 50 percent meal disallowance (and its exceptions)
- Exceptions to the general disallowance and additional rules of Code Sec. 274(a), (k), and (n) at Code Sec. 274(e):
  - — (2) Expenses treated as compensation
  - — (3) Reimbursed expenses
  - — (4) Employee recreational, social, or similar activities
  - — (7) Items available to the public
  - — (8) Entertainment sold to customers
  - — (9) Expenses includible in the income of persons who are not employees

Prop. Reg. Sec. 1.274-11(a) follows Code Sec. 274(a):

> No deduction otherwise allowable under chapter 1 of the Code is allowed for any expenditure with respect to an activity that is of a type generally considered to be entertainment, or with respect to a facility used in connection with an entertainment activity. For purposes of this paragraph (a), dues or fees to any social, athletic, or sporting club or organization are treated as items with respect to facilities and, thus, are not deductible. In addition, no deduction otherwise allowable under chapter 1 is allowed for amounts paid or incurred for membership in any club organized for business, pleasure, recreation, or other social purpose.

It notes that there are exceptions to paragraph (a): the general disallowance of entertainment does not apply to the expenditures described in Code Sec. 274(e). The general rule under Prop. Reg. Sec. 1.274-11(a) is that no deduction is allowed for entertainment. For purposes of this paragraph, dues or fees to any social, athletic, or sporting club or organization are treated as items with respect to facilities and thus are not deductible. An additional deduction otherwise allowed is for amounts paid or incurred for membership at any club organized for business, pleasure, recreation, or other social purpose, but the regulation does not address that part in more detail.

Generally, the proposed regulation follows Notice 2018-76 guidance, so it excludes food and beverages from definition of *entertainment* unless provided at or during an entertainment activity and the costs are not separately stated from the entertainment costs.

According to the preamble: "Taxpayers may continue to rely upon existing rules in § 1.274–2, to extent applicable and not superseded by TCJA, for entertainment expenditures paid or incurred after December 31, 2017."

Following is a comparison of the definition of entertainment in existing Reg. Sec. 1.274-2(b), with changes from Prop. Reg. Sec. 1.274-11(b) and a portion of 1.274-12 noted in strikethrough and boldface:

> (i) *In general*. For **section 274** purposes ~~of this section~~, the term *entertainment* means any activity which is of a type generally considered to constitute entertainment, amusement, or recreation, such as entertaining at ~~**night clubs, cocktail lounges**~~ **bars**, theaters, country clubs, golf and athletic clubs, sporting events, and on hunting, fishing, vacation and similar trips, including such activity relating solely to the taxpayer or the taxpayer's family. **These activities are treated as entertainment under this section, subject to the objective test, regardless of whether the expenditure for the activity is related to or associated with the active conduct of the taxpayer's trade or business.** The term *entertainment* may include an activity, the cost of which **otherwise** is ~~**claimed as**~~ a business expense by the taxpayer, which satisfies the personal, living, or family needs of any individual, such as ~~**providing food and beverages,**~~ a hotel suite~~;~~ or an automobile to a business customer or ~~**his**~~ **the customer's** family. The term *entertainment* does not include activities which, although satisfying personal, living, or family needs of an individual, are clearly not regarded as constituting entertainment, such as ~~**(a) supper money provided by an employer to his employee working overtime, (b)**~~ a hotel room maintained by an employer for lodging of his employees while in business travel status, or ~~**(c)**~~ an automobile used in the active conduct of trade or business even though used for routine personal purposes such as commuting to and from work. On the other hand, the providing of a hotel room or an automobile by an employer to ~~**his**~~ **an** employee who is on vacation would constitute entertainment of the employee.
>
> **(ii) Food or beverages. Under this section, the term entertainment does not include food or beverages unless the food or beverages are provided during or at an entertainment activity. Food or beverages provided during or at an entertainment activity generally are treated as part of the entertainment activity. However, in the case of food or beverages provided during or at an entertainment activity, the food or beverages are not considered entertainment if the food or beverages**

are purchased separately from the entertainment, or the cost of the food or beverages is stated separately from the cost of the entertainment on one or more bills, invoices, or receipts. The amount charged for food or beverages on a bill, invoice, or receipt must reflect the venue's usual selling cost for those items if they were to be purchased separately from the entertainment, or must approximate the reasonable value of those items. Unless the food or beverages are purchased separately from the entertainment, or the cost of the food or beverages is stated separately from the cost of the entertainment on one or more bills, invoices, or receipts, no allocation can be made and the entire amount is a nondeductible entertainment expenditure.

The main purpose of this definition of food and beverages under the broad definition of entertainment is to state generally that food or a beverage is not considered entertainment unless that food or beverage is served at an entertainment activity and not separately billed using the usual selling costs for these separate items. An objective test is used to determine whether the activity is a type generally considered to be entertainment.

OBSERVATION: Missing from the new definition of *entertainment* in existing Reg. Sec. 1.274-2(b)(1)(iii) are rules to distinguish entertainment from gifts or travel. For example, if a business just gives baseball game tickets to a client so the client can attend the game on their own, it is considered a gift, not entertainment. This is not in the new definition, but the proposed regulations do not repeal the old regulation.

The examples in Prop. Reg. Sec. 1.274-11(d) use the term *business associate*, but that term is defined in Prop. Reg. Sec. 1.274-12, not Prop. Reg. Sec. 1.274-11.

In the following examples, assume the taxpayer (T) and the business associate are not engaged in a business that relates to the entertainment activity. Also assume that the expenditures are not lavish or extravagant.

EXAMPLE 1: T invites a business associate to a baseball game to discuss a proposed business deal. The cost of the tickets is disallowed entertainment.

EXAMPLE 2: Assume the same facts as in Example 1, but T also buys food at the game. Since the food was purchased separately, it is not entertainment, and T may deduct 50 percent of the expense if allowed under Code Sec. 162 and Reg. Sec. 1.274-12.

EXAMPLE 3: T invites a business associate to a basketball game in a suite with food provided, all for a single price. The game and the food are disallowed entertainment.

EXAMPLE 4: Assume the same facts as in Example 3, but the invoice breaks out the ticket and food prices using the venue's usual selling price as if they had been purchased separately. The ticket price is disallowed entertainment, but T may deduct 50 percent of the food expense if allowed under Code Sec. 162 and Reg. Sec. 1.274-12. The "venue's usual selling cost" is used in the regulations to clarify the statement in Notice 2018-76 that a taxpayer cannot inflate the amount charged for food to increase the deduction where the invoice covers entertainment and food/beverages (Prop. Reg. Sec. 1.274-11(b)(1)(ii)).

Prop. Reg. Sec. 1.274–12 addresses the limitation on deductions for certain food or beverage expenses paid or incurred after December 31, 2017. The proposed regulation follows the transitional guidance of IRS Notice 2018-76 (released on October 3, 2018). See the following table for a comparison:

Prop. Reg. Sec. 1.274-12	Notice 2018-76
(a) Food or beverage expenses—(1) In general. Except as provided in this section, no deduction is allowed for the expense of any food or beverages provided by the taxpayer (or an employee of the taxpayer) to another person or persons unless— • The expense is not lavish or extravagant under the circumstances; [Code Sec. 274(k)] • The taxpayer, or an employee of the taxpayer, is present at the furnishing of such food or beverages; [Code Sec. 274(k)] and • The food or beverages are provided to a business associate. [Code Sec. 162 and 274 regulations]	Meals are 50 percent deductible if five requirements are met: 1. Ordinary and necessary under Code Sec. 162; 2. Not lavish or extravagant; 3. Taxpayer or employee is present; 4. Provided to current or potential business customer, client, consultant, or similar business contact; and 5. If provided during or at entertainment activity, must be purchased separately or separately stated on the invoice; can't inflate the cost of the food/drink to try to deduct entertainment. This is intended to be transitional guidance until IRS issues final regulations.

Why did the number of factors change from five in Notice 2018-76 to three in Prop. Reg. Sec. 1.274-12(a)? The first item in Notice 2018-76 ("ordinary and necessary under Code Sec. 162") is not needed because the deduction must first meet Code Sec. 162 requirements before getting to Code Sec. 274. The fifth item in Notice 2018-76 ("If provided during or at entertainment activity, must be purchased separately or separately stated on the invoice") is missing from the proposed regulation because it was added to the definition of entertainment at Prop. Reg. Sec. 1.274-11(b)(1)(ii) defining *food and beverages* in relation to *entertainment*.

Assume in the following examples that the expenditures meet the Code Sec. 162 "ordinary and necessary" requirement and are not lavish or extravagant under Code Sec. 274(k).

EXAMPLE: *Scenario 1:* The taxpayer (T) takes a client to lunch to discuss the client's business activities.

Scenario 2: The taxpayer (T) takes an employee to lunch to discuss the employee's annual performance review.

Result: Per Code Sec. 274(k) and (n), and Prop. Reg. Sec. 1.274-12(a), 50 percent of these expenses are deductible by T.

Prop. Reg. Sec. 1.274-12(a)(4) states that to deduct travel meals, a taxpayer must follow the general rules plus the substantiation rule of Code Sec. 274(d). Generally, no deduction is allowed for the travel meal of a spouse, dependent, or others unless:

- It pertains to moving under Code Sec. 217 (but only for military employees for 2018 through 2025); or
- These three requirements are met:
  - — The person is an employee of the taxpayer,
  - — The travel is for a bona fide business purpose of T, *and*
  - — The expenses are otherwise deductible by the spouse, dependent, or other individual.

EXAMPLE: Jane works for ABC Co. Jane and her spouse George, who doesn't work for ABC, travel from New York to Boston for Jane's work. George is not traveling for a bona fide business purpose of ABC and the expenses are not otherwise deductible. The food and beverage expenses of George are not deductible by ABC. If the requirements of Code Secs. 162 and 274 are met (including (k) and (d)), ABC may deduct 50 percent of the food and beverage expenses of Jane.

Food and Beverages Defined

Prop. Reg. Sec. 1.274-12(b)(1) and (2) clarifies that the terms *food and beverages, meals, snacks,* or other types of food or beverage items all mean the same thing. The costs include any delivery fees, tips, and sales tax, whether or not treated as *de minimis* fringe benefits under Code Sec. 132(e).

For employer-provided meals at an eating facility, food or beverage expenses do *not* include expenses for operation of the eating facility, such as salaries of employees preparing and serving meals, and other overhead costs.

Entertainment: *Business Associate* and Other Definitions

The definition of *business associate* in Prop. Reg. Sec. 1.274–12 is fairly broad. *Business associate* "means a person who the taxpayer could reasonably expect to engage or deal in the active conduct of a trade or business such as the taxpayer's customer, client, supplier, employee, agent, partner, or professional advisor, whether established or perspective."

Prop. Reg. Sec. 1.274–12 also includes additional definitions:

1. Food or beverages
2. Food or beverage expenses
3. Business associate
4. Independent contractor
5. Client or customer
6. Payor
7. Reimbursement or other expense allowance arrangement
8. Primarily consumed
9. General public

Items 4 through 9 seem to be included mainly to explain the exceptions under Code Sec. 274(e) that are also addressed in the regulations under Prop. Reg. Sec. 1.274–12.

Exceptions Important to Understanding Code Sec. 274

The exceptions to the Code Sec. 274(a) disallowance, the Code Sec. 274(k) limitations, and the Code Sec. 274(n) 50 percent disallowance at Code Sec. 274(e)(2), (3), (4), (7), (8), and (9) are important to understanding how much food and entertainment is deductible. See the following chart for more detail:

Code Sec. 274(e) Exception:	Also Excepted From:		Guidance
	(k) employee/ taxpayer presence and can't be lavish or extravagant?	(n) 50 percent disallowance?	
(1) Food and beverages for employees	No	No	1.274-2(f)(2)(ii)
(2) Expenses treated as compensation	Yes	Yes	1.274-2(f)(2)(iii) Prop. 1.274-12(c)(2)(i)
(3) Reimbursed expenses	Yes	Yes	1.274-2(f)(2)(iv) Prop. 1.274-12(c)(2)(ii)
(4) Recreational, etc., expenses for employees	Yes	Yes	1.274-2(f)(2)(v) Prop. 1.274-12(c)(2)(iii)
(5) Employees, stockholder, etc., business meetings	No	No*	1.274-2(f)(2)(vi)

Code Sec. 274(e) Exception:	Also Excepted From:		Guidance
	(k) employee/ taxpayer presence and can't be lavish or extravagant?	(n) 50 percent disallowance?	
(6) Meetings of business leagues, etc.	No	No*	1.274-2(f) (2) (vii)
(7) Items available to public	Yes	Yes	1.274-2(f) (2) (viii) Prop. 1.274-12(c) (2) (iv)
(8) Entertainment sold to customers	Yes	Yes	1.274-2(f) (2) (ix) Prop. 1.274-12(c) (2) (v)
(9) Expenses includible in income of persons who are not employees	Yes	Yes	Prop. 1.274-12(c) (2) (i)

Notes:
"Yes" means 100 percent deductible if all requirements are met, including Code Sec. 162.
* Due to a TCJA drafting error, entertainment under (4) and (5) is 100 percent deductible rather than pre-TCJA 50 percent deductible amount; a technical correction would change it to 0 percent deductible. There is no effect on food/beverages under (4) and (5); they are still 50 percent deductible.

Exceptions for Expenses Treated as Compensation and Expenses Includible in Income of Non-Employees

According to Prop. Reg. Sec. 1.274-12 (c) (2) (i), if an entertainment expense is treated as compensation, it must be treated as compensation on the originally filed return and for employee withholding purposes. It must be taxable gross income for services rendered or as a prize or award by the recipient who is not the taxpayer's employee. The previous statement "does not apply to any amount paid or incurred by taxpayer if the amount is required to be included, or would be so required except that the amount is less than $600, in any information return filed by such taxpayer under part III of subchapter A of chapter 61 of the Code and is not so included."

If the taxpayer deducts the expense while also taking a position that it has zero value to the recipient or a value less than required under the Reg. Sec. 1.61-21 valuation rules, it will not fall under either the Code Sec. 274(e) (2) or (9) exception. Therefore, such entertainment expenses would be disallowed under Code Sec. 274(a) and food/beverages would be subject to the Code Secs. 274(k) lavish and extravagant provision and the 274(n) 50 percent disallowance rule.

The following are examples of exceptions for expenses treated as compensation that meet the Code Sec. 162 requirements and are not lavish or extravagant.

EXAMPLE 1: Employer A provides food and beverages to employees at no charge at the company cafeteria. The food and beverages are not a *de minimis* fringe under Code Sec. 132(e). Employer A treats the expenses as employee compensation, measuring their value per Reg. Sec. 1.61-21. The expenditure is fully deductible to Employer A. It meets the exception to the Code Sec. 274(a) disallowance per Code Sec. 274(e) (2) and the proposed regulations.

EXAMPLE 2: Employer B provides meals to employees at no charge, for the convenience of the employer under Code Sec. 119. Under Reg. Sec. 1.61-21(b) (1), nothing is included in employee compensation, so the exception at Code Sec. 274(e) (2) does not apply, and therefore Employer B may only deduct 50 percent of the expenses for the food and beverages provided to its employees.

Exception for Reimbursed Food or Beverage Expenses

Prop. Reg. Sec. 1.274-12(c)(2)(ii) states that when food/beverage expenses are paid or incurred by one person in connection with the performance of services for another person under a reimbursement or other expense allowance arrangement, the Code Sec. 274(a) limitations on deductions apply to the person making the expenditure or to the person who actually bears the expense, but not to both.

The regulations explain that another rule might disallow the expense, such as when the expense is really a dividend paid to a shareholder, unreasonable compensation paid to employees, or a personal expense.

Prop. Reg. Sec. 1.274-12(c)(2)(ii) provides rules for reimbursement arrangements involving employees and persons that are not employees (such as independent contractors). The Code Sec. 274(d) documentation rule likely applies if an independent contractor is involved.

Reimbursement Arrangements Involving Employees

In this type of arrangement, the employee is subject to the Code Sec. 274(a) limitations on deductions if the employer treats the reimbursement or other payment of the expense as wages to the employee with withholding, or the payor is subject to the limitations to the extent that reimbursement or other payment of the expense is not treated as wages to the employee.

Reimbursement Arrangements Involving Persons That Are Not Employees

In the case of expenses for food/beverages paid or incurred by an independent contractor in connection with the performance of services for a client or customer under a reimbursement or other expense allowance arrangement with the contractor, the Code Sec. 274(a) limitations apply to the party expressly identified in an agreement between the parties as subject to the limitations. If the agreement does not expressly identify the party subject to the limitations, then they apply to:

- The contractor to the extent he or she does not account to the client or customer per the Code Sec. 274(d) documentation requirement, or
- The client or customer if the contractor accounts to that party per the Code Sec. 274(d) documentation requirement.

If the reimbursement or other expense allowance arrangement involves persons who are not employees and the agreement between the parties does not expressly identify the party subject to the limitations on deductions in Code Sec. 274(a), such limitations apply to the independent contractor unless the contractor accounts to the client or customer with substantiation that satisfies the requirements of Code Sec. 274(d).

The following examples are for reimbursed food/beverage expenses that meet the Code Sec. 162 requirements and are not lavish or extravagant.

> **EXAMPLE 1:** Employee EE performs services under an arrangement in which Employer ER, an employee leasing company, pays EE a per diem allowance of $10/day for services performed for ER's client C. The per diem covers travel and food/beverages. Client C and ER have a written agreement under which C agrees to reimburse ER for any substantiated reimbursements for travel expenses, including meals, that ER pays to EE.
>
> EE provides ER with substantiation per Code Sec. 274(d) for meals while traveling away from home, and ER pays the $100 reimbursement to EE.

ER provides a copy of this to Client C. Client C pays the expenses plus the rest of the contract amount. Neither ER nor Client C treats the $100 as compensation or wages.

EE and ER have a reimbursement or other expense allowance arrangement (per the definition at Reg. Sec. 1.274-12(b)(7)(i)). Because the reimbursement is not treated as compensation paid to EE, EE is not subject to the Code Sec. 274(a) limitations. However, ER is subject to the limitations, unless ER meets the requirements of Code Sec. 274(e)(3)(B) and Reg. Sec. 1.274-12(c)(2)(ii)(C).

Since the agreement between ER and C says C will reimburse ER for substantiated reimbursements for travel that ER pays to EE, they have a reimbursement arrangement. ER provides Code Sec. 274(d) documentation to C. Therefore, C—rather than ER—is subject to the Code Sec. 274(a) limitations.

EXAMPLE 2: Assume the same facts as in Example 1, except the arrangement is that ER provides substantiation directly to Client C, and Client C pays the per diem directly to EE. C, the payor, is subject to the Code Sec. 274(a) limitations.

EXAMPLE 3: Again assume the same facts as in Example 1, except that the written agreement between ER and Client C provides that the Code Sec. 274(a) limitations will apply to Client C. In this case, Client C is subject to the limitations.

EXAMPLE 4: The facts are the same as in Example 1, but the agreement between ER and C does not provide that Client C will reimburse ER for travel expenses. Therefore, ER is subject to the Code Sec. 274(a) limitations.

Exception for Recreational Expenses for Employees

The exception at Prop. Reg. Sec. 1.274-12(c)(2)(iii) applies to any food or beverage expenses paid or incurred for a recreational, social or similar activity provided primarily for the benefit of employees other than highly compensated employees, officers, shareholders, or others who own a 10 percent or greater interest in the business. The related party rule at Code Sec. 267(c)(4) applies in measuring ownership.

Thus, holiday parties, annual picnics, summer outings, and similar events for employees are still 100 percent deductible. The exception does not apply to the following (which are instead 50 percent disallowed):

- Free food and beverages in an employee breakroom that do not constitute a recreational, social, or similar activity (and that qualify as a de minimis fringe benefit).
- Meals provided for the convenience of the employer under Code Sec. 119 because "by definition . . . they cannot also be primarily for the benefit of the employees, even if some social activity occurs during the provision of food or beverages."

The following examples are for recreational expenses for employees that meet the Code Sec. 162 requirements and are not lavish or extravagant.

EXAMPLE 1: Employer A invites all employees to a hotel for a buffet dinner and open bar in the hotel ballroom. Under the exception at Code Sec. 274(e)(4), Employer A may deduct 100 percent of the cost of the party.

EXAMPLE 2: The facts are the same as in Example 1, but Employer A only invites highly compensated employees to the buffet dinner with the open bar, and the invoice breaks out the cost of the food/beverages from the cost of the ballroom rental at the hotel's usual selling price for the food/beverages. In this case, the exception at Code Sec. 274(e)(4) is not applicable, so no entertainment costs are deductible. However, because they are separately billed, the food/beverages are not considered entertainment and are 50 percent deductible.

EXAMPLE 3: Employer A provides free coffee, soda, bottled water, chips, donuts, and other snacks in the breakroom open to all employees. The breakroom "is not a recreational, social, or similar activity primarily for the benefit of the employees." The exception at Code Sec. 274(e)(4) does not apply. The food and beverages are subject to the Code Sec. 274(n) limitation, so only 50 percent of the expenses are deductible.

Exception for Items Available to the Public

The exception at Prop. Reg. Sec. 1.274-12(c)(2)(iv) applies to expenses for food or beverages provided to employees if similar food or beverages are provided by the employer to, and are primarily consumed by, the general public. *Primarily consumed* means more than 50 percent of the actual or reasonably estimated consumption. The *general public* includes customers, clients, and visitors, but not employees, partners, contractors, or the taxpayer. It also does not include an "exclusive list of guests" (***Churchill Downs, Inc.,*** 307 F.3d 423 (6th Cir. 2002)).

The following are examples of the exception for items available to the public that meet the Code Sec. 162 requirements and are not lavish or extravagant.

EXAMPLE: *Scenario 1:* A real estate agent provides refreshments at open houses that are consumed by employees, potential buyers, and other real estate agents.

Scenario 2: An auto service center provides refreshments for employees and customers in the waiting area.

The Code Sec. 274(e)(7) exception applies if over 50 percent of the refreshments are consumed by the real estate agent's potential buyers and other real estate agents (and by the auto service center's customers). If 50 percent or less is consumed by that group, only the costs attributable to those food and beverages are excepted from the 50 percent disallowance.

OBSERVATIONS: If 50 percent or more of the food costs are attributable to employee consumption then such costs are only 50 percent deductible (unless a different Code Sec. 274(e) exception is met).

Recordkeeping is needed to show whether the public consumed over 50 percent of the food/beverages provided.

Depending on the situation, it might be better to put the employee food/ beverages in the employee breakroom (50 percent deductible) and let employees know not to eat the food for the public (100 percent deductible).

Exception for Entertainment Sold to Customers

Prop. Reg. Sec. 1.274-12(c)(2)(v) follows the TCJA Bluebook. The TCJA changes "to limit deduction for expenses of the employer associated with providing food or beverages to employees through an employer-operated eating facility that meets the requirements of § 132(e)(2) do not affect other exceptions to the 50 percent limitation on deductions for food or beverage expenses. For example, a restaurant or catering business may continue to deduct 100 percent of its costs for food or beverage items, purchased in connection with preparing and providing meals to its paying customers, which are also consumed at the worksite by employees who work in the employer's restaurant or catering business."

OBSERVATION: Code Sec. 274(e)(8) uses the term *entertainment* sold to customers, whereas Prop. Reg. Sec. 1.274-12(c)(2)(v) uses the term *goods or services* sold to customers.

The word *customer* "includes anyone who is sold food or beverages in a bona fide transaction for an adequate and full consideration in *money or money's worth*. For example, employees of the taxpayer are customers when they purchase food or beverages from the taxpayer in a bona fide transaction for arm's length, fair market value prices." Note that *money or money's worth* does not include payment through services provided.

EXAMPLE: Employer D operates a restaurant and provides food/beverages to its food service employees before, during, and after their shifts at no charge. The Code Sec. 274(e)(8) exception is met, so Employer D can deduct 100 percent of the costs of that food.

Documentation Reminders

Note that travel expenses (including meals and lodging while away from home) are still subject to the Code Sec. 274(d) substantiation requirements. Food and beverage expenses are subject to the general substantiation requirements of Code Sec. 162 plus the requirement under Code Sec. 6001 to maintain books and records. Thus, the *Cohan* rule (see ***Cohan v. Commissioner***, 39 F.2d 540 (2d Cir. 1930), modifying 11 B.T.A. 743 (1928)) could apply, but it is best not to plan for that.

The Code Sec. 274(d) documentation requirements are still relevant for the Code Sec. 274(e)(3) and Prop. Reg. Sec. 1.274-12(c)(2)(ii) exception for reimbursement or other expense allowance arrangement involving non-employees and if the agreement does not expressly identify the party subject to the Code Sec. 274(a) limitations.

Note that state tax law might still require Code Sec. 274(d)-type documentation (such as in California, which does not conform to the Code Sec. 274 changes).

¶ 106 CURRENT ISSUES IN THE FOOD AND FUN AREA AND HOW TO ADDRESS THEM

Schedule M-1 Cautions

The 2019 Schedule M-1 is the same as for 2017 despite new book–tax differences starting in 2018. Practitioners should consider highlighting these differences for their clients. These items include 100 percent disallowance for most entertainment expenses as well as qualified transportation fringe benefit costs.

The following excerpts from IRS Publication 535, *Business Expenses*, explain the "nondeductible club dues" noted in Line 5c of the Schedule M-1 instructions:

> **Club dues and membership fees.** Generally, you can't deduct amounts paid or incurred for membership in any club organized for business, pleasure, recreation, or any other social purpose. This includes country clubs, golf and athletic clubs, hotel clubs, sporting clubs, airline clubs, and clubs operated to provide meals under circumstances generally considered to be conducive to business discussions.
>
> ***Exception.*** The following organizations aren't treated as clubs organized for business, pleasure, recreation, or other social purpose unless one of the main purposes is to conduct entertainment activities for members or their guests or to provide members or their guests with access to entertainment facilities:

- Boards of trade.
- Business leagues.
- Chambers of commerce.
- Civic or public service organizations.
- Professional organizations such as bar associations and medical associations.
- Real estate boards.
- Trade associations.

Also see Reg. Sec. 1.274-2(a)(2) and be alert for more IRS guidance on this topic.

Despite the Definition of *Entertainment*, There Will Still Be Some Tight Calls

Whether something is entertainment versus a meal is a bigger question post-TCJA because before, both meals and entertainment were usually 50 percent disallowed, but now generally, entertainment is 100 percent disallowed and meals 50 percent disallowed.

OBSERVATION: Consider the following scenario: A sole proprietor takes a client to a wine tasting event.

- Is the wine deductible if its price is separately stated?
- Is this just a food/meal event, or is the wine inherently part of the entertainment (assuming it is entertainment)?
- What if the wine is very expensive? What is "lavish" under Code Sec. 274(k)?

Meals for the Convenience of the Employer and *de Minimis* Fringe Food

The definitions of meals for the convenience of the employer and *de minimis* fringe food continue to be a challenging interpretive area as well as an IRS audit area. Practitioners should be aware of the cautions and planning considerations from recent rulings and read the summary of Code Sec. 132(e) *de minimis* meals from IRS Publication 15-B, *Employer's Tax Guide to Fringe Benefits* (in addition to the Code and regulations on this provision).

In ***Jacobs v. Commissioner*** (148 TC 24, June 26, 2017), the court ruled that the Boston Bruins hockey team's away game meals were a *de minimis* fringe benefit. For their away games:

- The hockey team arrives the day before a game,
- The hotel provides meals under the Boston Bruins' supervision, and
- The employees are required to attend breakfast and lunch; a late afternoon snack is optional.

The IRS stated that because the meals fall under Code Sec. 274 as associated with the active conduct of a trade or business, the Bruins can only deduct 50 percent of the cost per Code Sec. 274(n). (Code Sec. 274(n)(2)(B) is not applicable.) However, the court ruled that the meals fall under Code Sec. 274(n)(2)(B) and therefore the 50 percent limit does not apply and the meals are 100 percent deductible. (As explained earlier, this exception was removed by the TCJA.)

In its Action on Decision (AOD) 2019-01, the IRS noted that it "will follow *Jacobs* only with respect to cases involving sports teams in which the material facts are substantially identical to those present in *Jacobs*."

> **NOTE:** After the TCJA changes to Code Sec. 274, meals for the convenience of the employer and *de minimis* fringe food are only 50 percent deductible through 2025 and 0 percent deductible after that.

IRS Technical Advice Memorandum (TAM) 201903017

In TAM 201903017, the IRS addressed the topic of meals provided for the convenience of the employer. Although the IRS cannot substitute its judgment for employers', it can determine if employees actually follow stated business policies and practices. The IRS stated:

> Employers who provide specific business policies as substantial noncompensatory business reasons for furnishing meals to employees must be able to substantiate that such policies exist in substance not just in form by showing they are enforced on the specific employees for whom the employer claims these policies apply and must demonstrate how these policies relate to the furnishing of meals to employees.

The IRS found that the employer in question had "little factual support related to its claim that its employees could not safely obtain meals off business premises under usual circumstances." The IRS considered the availability of a mobile meal delivery service. It also found that the employer had no policies related to employee health for the meals, or protection of intellectual property or safety. However, it did find that a few employees needed meals to be available for emergencies.

In the end, the IRS stated the employer was unable to show that at least half of all employees were furnished meals for the convenience of the employer. According to the IRS, the employer did not meet the reasonable belief test that meals were excludable, and so the benefit was treated as wages to the employees subject to withholding, FICA, and FUTA.

Snacks in the Breakroom All the Time

In response to whether snacks that are always available in the breakroom meet the definition of a *de minimis* fringe benefit, the IRS stated the following in Chief Counsel Advice (CCA) 200219005:

- "The smaller in value and less frequently a particular benefit is provided, the more likely that such a benefit is properly characterized as a *de minimis* fringe benefit."
- "Section 1.132-6(b)(2) provides that, where it would be administratively difficult to determine frequency with respect to individual employees, the frequency with which the employer provides similar fringe benefits is determined by reference to frequency with which the employer provides the fringe benefits to the workforce as a whole ('employer-measured frequency'). Therefore, under this rule, the frequency with which any individual employee receives such a fringe benefit is not relevant and in some circumstances, the *de minimis* fringe exclusion may apply with respect to a benefit even though a particular employee receives the benefit frequently."
- "The method chosen by the employer of accounting for benefits provided to employees is not determinative of whether accounting for the value of the benefits is administratively impracticable."

¶ 107 REMINDERS FOR PRACTITIONERS

Practitioners should remember to do the following:

- Ensure adequate recordkeeping to prove the employer qualifies for a particular deduction or to treat something as an employee non-taxable fringe benefit.
- Realize that some states might not follow the TCJA changes. For example, California does not conform to the Code Sec. 274 changes. Adequate recordkeeping can help ensure that taxpayers do not overlook the California deductions or improperly claim disallowed items on federal returns.
- Consider whether books and accounts should be modified to help in tracking disallowed items for federal and state tax purposes.
- Ensure that clients understand what has changed in this area.
- Watch for final regulations and missing guidance for the Code Sec. 274 changes by the TCJA.
- Read not only the relevant IRS publications (listed below), but also review the Code and regulations for all the details, as these rules are complex.

These IRS Publications include important information on meals and entertainment:

- Publication 463, *Travel, Entertainment, Gift, and Car Expenses*, www.irs.gov/forms-pubs/about-publication-463
- Publication 535, *Business Expenses*, www.irs.gov/pub/irs-pdf/p535.pdf
- Publication 15-B, *Employer's Tax Guide to Fringe Benefits*, www.irs.gov/pub/irs-pdf/p15b.pdf
- Publication 5137, *Fringe Benefit Guide*, www.irs.gov/pub/irs-pdf/p5137.pdf
- *IRS Training Materials for Employee Meals in the Hospitality Industry*, www.irs.gov/pub/irs-drop/eemeals.pdf

STUDY QUESTIONS

4. Regarding changes to Code Sec. 274, meals provided for the convenience of the employer are ***not*** deductible for amounts incurred or paid after what date?

a. December 31, 2022
b. December 31, 2023
c. December 31, 2024
d. December 31, 2025

5. Which of the following Code Sec. 274(e) exceptions is also excepted from both the employee/taxpayer lavish or extravagant provision and the 50 percent disallowance?

a. Food and beverages for employees
b. Meetings of business leagues
c. Expenses treated as compensation
d. Employee business meetings

6. Which of the following IRS Publications should you refer to for information with respect to travel, gift, and car expenses?

a. Publication 463
b. Publication 535
c. Publication 15-B
d. Publication 5137

MODULE 1 : BUSINESS—Chapter 2: Section 199A Qualified Business Income

¶ 201 WELCOME

This chapter covers the final rules that govern the qualified business income deduction. Topics discussed include the definition of *trade or business* and *service business*, a rental as a business, aggregation options, segregation rules, and more.

¶ 202 LEARNING OBJECTIVES

Upon completion of this chapter, you will be able to:

- Compute the Section 199A deduction for taxpayers above the threshold income level and for other taxpayers
- Identify planning opportunities to maximize the deduction
- Define a service business as that term is used in Section 199A
- Describe the basic structure of Section 199A
- Recognize how qualified business income (QBI) applies to clients
- Define a trade or business as the term applies to Section 199A
- Identify aggregation factors
- Recognize what is included as a service business
- Identify unadjusted basis immediately after acquisition (UBIA)
- Recognize when a special allocation of UBIA or W-2 wages may be made by a partnership

¶ 203 INTRODUCTION

The mechanics of the qualified business income deduction (QBID) are not that difficult, but the deduction either phases out or may be limited if taxable income exceeds a threshold amount. For non-service businesses, the deduction may be limited based on the W-2 wages paid from the business or a combination of W-2 wages and unadjusted basis of property used in the business. For service businesses, the deduction can be lost when income reaches the end of the phaseout range. There is a two-step limitation applied to service businesses: first, an applicable percentage is applied to parameters in computing the deduction, then the "regular" threshold income limitation is applied.

A specified service trade or business (SSTB) is generally any trade or business in the fields of accounting, health, law, consulting, athletics, financial services, brokerage services, or any business where the principal asset of the business is the reputation or skill of one or more of its employees. However, in some cases, it may not be clear whether a business is a SSTB. The regulations provide clarification and largely protect taxpayers under the "reputation or skill" definition of a SSTB, but many questions remain (e.g., what is consulting?). It may also be possible to plan to maximize the deduction when the taxpayer is otherwise in the phaseout range or is subject to a general taxable income limitation. Increasing taxable income, deductions, W-2 wages, or capital can have unexpected consequences when the QBID interaction is considered.

How is a business defined? For high-income taxpayers this can be important because it determines how much W-2 wages and capital are included in the deduction computations. What special issues will arise when the business is operated through a pass-through entity? Can changing an S corporation shareholder's wages allow for a larger deduction? How do partnership allocation provisions interact with the threshold income limitations? Can wages be paid by a professional employer organization (PEO)? Can partnerships report preferred distributions rather than guaranteed payments to maximize the deduction? These and other topics will be addressed in this chapter.

¶ 204 GENERAL PROVISIONS

Section 199A Authority

The primary source for this chapter is Section 199A of the Internal Revenue Code, effective for tax years after December 31, 2017. On August 8, 2018, the U.S. Department of the Treasury released the proposed regulations under Section 199A. The proposed regulations were finalized on January 18, 2019. The final regulations were tweaked on February 1, 2019, primarily to correct minor drafting errors.

Section 199A Basic Structure

Section 199A allows a 20 percent deduction for qualified business income (QBI), limited to 20 percent of taxable income determined without regard to net capital gain income. The deduction is available to taxpayers other than C corporations and may be reported on Schedule C, or on Schedule E if the taxpayer is an individual operating the business. The QBID may be phased out if taxable income exceeds a threshold amount.

STUDY QUESTION

1. Which of the following is true regarding the basic structure of Section 199A?

a. A 30 percent deduction for qualified business income is available to certain taxpayers.

b. The deduction is available to C corporations.

c. The deduction is limited to 20 percent of taxable income.

d. There is no phaseout for the deduction.

Capital Gain Income

The deduction limitation is taxable income before any net capital gain. The term *net capital gain* is defined in Section 1222(11) as the excess of net long-term capital gain over net short-term capital loss. Note that Section 1231 gains treated as part of net capital gain are not QBI eligible (Reg. Sec. 1.199A-3(b)(2)(ii)(A)).

QBI Adjustments

Qualified dividend income is not part of taxable income for limitation purposes. Certain deductions attributable to the trade or business reduce QBI:

- Self-employed health insurance deduction
- One-half the self-employed tax deduction

The preamble to the final regulations indicates that the Treasury and IRS may consider other adjustments. The instructions to IRS Form 8995, *Qualified Business Income Deduction: Simplified Computation*, also state that charitable contributions reduce QBI, although this is illogical and is not an item mentioned in the regulations.

Loss from a Qualified Business

The general 20 percent QBID applies to the taxpayer's "combined" QBI. Therefore, a loss from one business offsets income from another. If there is a net loss from qualified businesses, that loss carries to the next tax year and will reduce an otherwise allowed QBID.

Offset Rules with Income and Loss

If the taxpayer has an overall QBI profit, but one or more loss activities:

- The loss(es) are apportioned among the profitable operations.
- The apportionment is done by relative business income of the profitable operations.

The allocation is needed because each separate business must compute W-2 wages and unadjusted basis immediately after acquisition (UBIA; discussed later in this chapter). See Reg. Sec. 1.199A-1(d).

STUDY QUESTION

---

2. Marty has an overall QBI profit of $60,000 from the following sources: Company A, $70,000; Company B, $30,000; Company C, ($40,000). None of the loss of Company C is limited on Marty's tax return. Which of the following statements regarding Marty's QBI is true?

a. Marty's QBID is based on $100,000 of QBI.

b. Company A will be allocated $28,000 of Company C's loss.

c. Company C's loss will be carried forward to the next tax year.

d. Company A will be apportioned 100 percent of the loss of Company C.

Income Limitations

For the 2019 tax year, the "threshold income" is $321,400 for taxpayers married filing jointly and $160,700 for other filers. The phaseout ends at income of $421,400 for married filing jointly and at $210,700 for other filers. These figures are adjusted annually for inflation. The deduction is reported on Form 8995. The limit applies to:

- SSTBs—Deduction goes to zero.
- Other businesses—A separate limitation applies based on wages or wage/capital.

Wage/Wage-UBIA Limits

W-2 wages are those paid to the employees of the business. Wages paid by a professional employer organization (PEO) or similar third-party payor count for the business in which the employee works. Wages are allocated (in proportion to the deduction) if a worker performs services in more than one business. If a business is sold or acquired, the wages are allocated by the time of the services.

The regulations introduced the term UBIA, which stands for unadjusted basis immediately after acquisition. UBIA must be depreciable—it cannot be land or amortizable intangibles. UBIA is before any claimed depreciation or expense election, and survives for the full recovery period of the property. This means that generous bonus depreciation or Section 179 expensing may result in no tax basis, but the UBIA continues unchanged.

The ability to claim rapid (including immediate) expensing for tangible property while continuing to report UBIA may impact purchase price allocation incentives. Allocations to depreciable assets may be more valued than to amortizable assets, particularly when those assets are short-lived or subject to expense elections or bonus depreciation. It also makes it more important for taxpayers to have detailed fixed asset schedules beyond the time when continued depreciation deductions may be available.

Non-Service Business

If a taxpayer is a non-service business (non-SSTB) and its taxable income exceeds the threshold, the deduction may be limited to the greater of:

- 50 percent of W-2 wages for the business, or
- 25 percent of W-2 wages plus 2.5 percent of the unadjusted basis of depreciable business assets.

If the business has W-2 wages or capital, there will be some deduction allowed without regard to the taxpayer's taxable income.

STUDY QUESTION

---

3. A taxpayer with a non-service business who exceeds the taxable income threshold will have a QBI deduction (QBID) limited to:

a. The taxpayer's overall QBI

b. 20 percent of the taxpayer's AGI

c. The taxpayer's total wages

d. 50 percent of W-2 wages for the business

Service Business

As mentioned earlier, a service business, or SSTB, includes specified businesses such as consulting, law, accounting, and so on. It also includes any business where the principal asset is the skill or reputation of one or more of the employees (Section 1202(e)(3)(A) definition). The regulations took a friendly approach to "skill and reputation" as well as "brokers." Because the deduction for high-income taxpayers may go to zero, such taxpayers will be expected to contend that the business is not a SSTB.

Threshold Income Limitation

If a taxpayer's taxable income exceeds the threshold income limit, the otherwise allowed deduction is reduced. The reduction is proportionate throughout the phaseout range. The reduction computation depends on whether the business is a SSTB. The SSTB deduction can go to zero. For non-SSTBs, it is limited to changes to wage or wage/UBIA.

EXAMPLE 1: BASE POINT: Taxpayer A's QBI is $200,000. The taxpayer is married filing jointly and reports taxable income of $250,000. Because the taxable income does not exceed the threshold of $321,400, the QBID is then $40,000 (20 percent of $200,000). This is so for all business types.

EXAMPLE 2: Taxpayer B is married filing jointly and reports taxable income of $450,000. His QBI from a non-service business is $100,000. The normal QBID is $20,000 (20 percent of $100,000). Taxpayer B's W-2 wages are $60,000, and his UBIA is $400,000.

The taxpayer's wage limit is $30,000 (50 percent of $60,000), and his wage/capital limit is $25,000 (25 percent of $60,000 plus 2.5 percent of $400,000).

The taxable income limit is not applicable to Taxpayer B because the 20 percent of QBI limit ($20,000) is less than the wage or wage/capital limit ($30,000). Therefore, the deduction is $20,000.

COMMENT: For a non-service business, "too much" taxable income causes the otherwise allowed deduction based on QBI to drop to the wage or wage/UBIA limit (whichever is greater).

If the 20 percent of QBI figure is already below the wage or wage/UBIA limit, no amount of taxable income can cause the deduction to become lower (because the 20 percent of QBI is already below the floor for high-income taxpayers). This is true only for a non-service business; a SSTB will have a separate reduction for the "applicable percentage."

EXAMPLE 3: Taxpayer C is married filing jointly and has taxable income of $450,000. Her QBI from a non-service business is $200,000. The normal QBID is $40,000 (20 percent of $200,000). Taxpayer C's W-2 wages are $60,000, and her UBIA is $400,000. The wage limit is $30,000 (50 percent of $60,000), and the wage/UBIA limit is $25,000 (25 percent of $60,000 plus 2.5 percent of $400,000).

The taxable income limit applies because the 20 percent of QBI limit ($40,000) is more than the wage or wage/UBIA limit ($30,000).

Because Taxpayer C's taxable income is greater than or equal to $421,400, the deduction is limited to $30,000 (the full reduction to wage limit).

STUDY QUESTIONS

---

4. A taxpayer is married filing jointly and reports taxable income of $600,000. His QBI from a non-service business is $350,000. Wages from the business are $200,000, and UBIA is $400,000 What is the taxpayer's QBID?

a. $0

b. $60,000

c. $70,000

d. $100,000

5. A taxpayer is married filing jointly and reports taxable income of $600,000. Her QBI from a non-service business is $350,000. Wages from the business are $100,000, and UBIA is $400,000. What is the taxpayer's QBID?

a. $35,000

b. $50,000

c. $70,000

d. $120,000

EXAMPLE 4: Taxpayer D is married filing jointly and reports taxable income of $391,400. The taxpayer's QBI from a non-service business is $200,000. The normal QBID is $40,000 (20 percent of $200,000). Taxpayer D's W-2 wages are $60,000, and his UBIA is $400,000. Her wage limit is $30,000 (50 percent of $60,000), and her wage/UBIA limit is $25,000 (25 percent of $60,000 plus 2.5 percent of $400,000).

The taxable income limit applies because the 20 percent of QBI limit ($40,000) is more than the wage or wage/UBIA limit ($30,000). The $40,000 deduction is reduced by 70 percent ($391,400 – $321,400/$100,000) of the excess of the $40,000 over the $30,000, so the deduction is reduced by $7,000 (70% of $40,000 – $30,000) from $40,000 to $33,000.

In Example 3, Taxpayer C had a 100 percent reduction (from $40,000 to $30,000) because it was all of the way through the phaseout. In Example 4, Taxpayer D has too much taxable income. Adding deductions to reduce taxable income within the phaseout range can lead to a benefit (measured by taxable income) in excess of 120 percent of the additional deductions. This is not intuitive, but it is easy to demonstrate. See the following explanation.

Added Deductions

The chart below illustrates added deductions for two spouses. Taxpayer Husband (who has a non-service business) can reduce taxable income by 140 percent for each dollar of added deductions. His QBID is reduced from $40,000 to $0 based on taxable income throughout the full phaseout range. Starting at $371,400 taxable income, the QBID is $20,000. Notice that if the couple adds a deduction of $20,000 (perhaps through a retirement plan contribution), the effect of the phase out and the additional deduction reduces overall taxable income by $28,000. Thus each dollar of deduction produces a 140% ($28,000/$20,000) reduction in taxable income.

Husband's Schedule C (no wage or capital)	Wife's W-2 Job	Taxable Income, Revised	Add a Deduction of	QBID at this Taxable Income
$200,000	$195,800	$371,400	None—Base	$20,000
$200,000	$195,800	$351,400	$20,000	$28,000
$200,000	$195,800	$321,400	$50,000	$40,000

Now assume the same taxable income, but the income all comes from a business eligible for the QBID. The same $20,000 deduction will interact with the phase out to reduce taxable income by $35,832 (the QBID increases from $39,580 to $55,412, an increase of $15,832, and the taxpayer also gets the benefit of the $20,000 deduction). The QBID benefit is then 179.16% of the added deduction ($35,832/$20,000). At some point this illustration runs into the overall limit of 20% of taxable income. So, for example, the benefit is less than 179.16% when income drops to $321,400.

The actual benefit in threshold income situations would also need to consider interactions with other deductions that are affected by adjusted gross income or taxable income. Tax software can easily generate the actual benefit. But it is important to be aware that when a taxpayer is in the threshold range, the benefit of added deductions can be magnified.

Husband's Schedule C	Revised Taxable Income	Added Deductions	QBID Post-Adjustment
$395,800	$371,400	Base	$39,580
$395,800	$351,400	$20,000	$55,412
$395,800	$321,400	$50,000	$64,280 (taxable income limit)

EXAMPLE 5: Taxpayer E is married filing jointly and reports taxable income of $4 million. His QBI from a non-service business is $2 million. The normal QBID is $400,000 (20 percent of $2 million). The taxpayer has no W-2 wages, and his UBIA is $40 million.

Taxpayer E's wage limit is zero, and his wage/UBIA limit is $1 million (25 percent of zero plus 2.5 percent of $40 million).

The taxable income limit does not apply because the 20 percent of QBI limit ($400,000) is less than the wage or wage/UBIA limit ($1 million). The deduction is $400,000 (20 percent of QBI).

STUDY QUESTION

---

6. A taxpayer is married filing jointly and reports taxable income of $6,000,000. His QBI from a non-service business is $3,000,000. There are no W-2 wages, and his UBIA is $40,000,000. What is the taxpayer's QBID?

a. $0

b. $600,000

c. $1,000,000

d. $1,200,000

EXAMPLE 6: Taxpayer F is married filing jointly and reports taxable income of $4 million. Her QBI from a non-service business is $2 million. The normal QBID is $400,000 (20 percent of $2 million). The taxpayer has no W-2 wages, and her UBIA is $8 million.

Taxpayer E's wage limit is zero, and her wage/UBIA limit is $200,000 (25 percent of zero plus 2.5 percent of $8 million).

The taxable income limit applies because the 20 percent of QBI limit ($400,000) is more than the wage or wage/UBIA limit ($200,000). Because the taxpayer's taxable income is greater than or equal to $421,400, the deduction is limited to $200,000 (100 percent reduction from $400,000 to $200,000).

Limitation for Service Business

When taxable income exceeds the threshold amount, the deduction limitation can go to zero. This occurs because there is a separate (beyond the wage or wage/UBIA) limit to first determine the pre-taxable income deduction. The otherwise allowed deduction is reduced to the "applicable percentage" found by 100 percent minus the percentage in the quotient (taxable income – threshold income)/$100,000.

Therefore, if the taxable income of a married filing jointly taxpayer is greater than or equal to $421,400, the service deduction becomes zero (i.e., the applicable percentage is zero, 100 percent – 100 percent).

EXAMPLE 7: Taxpayer G, whose business is a law firm (SSTB), is married filing jointly and reports taxable income of $450,000. Its QBI is $200,000. The normal QBID is $40,000 (20 percent of $200,000). Taxpayer G's W-2 wages are $60,000, and its UBIA is $400,000. The taxable income limit applies.

The taxpayer's W-2 limit is $30,000 (50 percent of W-2 exceeds wage/capital). Because the taxable income is greater than or equal to $421,400, the $30,000 deduction is reduced to zero.

The percentage allowed is 100 percent – 100 percent using the formula.

Because Taxpayer G's taxable income equals or exceeds the "full" threshold level of $421,400, the applicable percentage is reduced to zero. This means that in determining the QBID, each relevant figure must first be multiplied by the applicable percentage so that QBI is zero, W-2 wages are zero, and UBIA is zero. Therefore, it is easy to see why the QBID is reduced to zero.

EXAMPLE 8: Taxpayer H, whose business is a law firm (SSTB), is married filing jointly and reports taxable income of $391,400. The taxpayer's QBI is $200,000. The normal QBID is $40,000 (20 percent of $200,000). The taxpayer's W-2 wages are $60,000 and unadjusted basis of capital is $400,000. The taxable income limit applies.

The percentage allowed is 100% – 70% = 30% using the formula:

100% – [($391,400 – $321,400) / $100,000] = 30%

Each component of the QBID is reduced by the applicable percentage (30 percent). Taxpayer H's QBI is $200,000 (.3) = $60,000, and 20 percent of the QBI is $12,000 (ceiling).

Taxpayer H's W-2 wages are $60,000 (.3) = $18,000; therefore, 50 percent of the taxpayer's W-2 wages is $9,000 (floor).

The allowed deduction is reduced from $12,000 to $9,900 (70 percent reduction); this is 70 percent of the way from the ceiling to the floor. This is 30 percent of the $33,000 allowed for the taxpayer in Example 4, which had the same figures but was a non-service business.

STUDY QUESTION

7. A taxpayer is married filing jointly and in 2019 reports taxable income of $391,400. Her QBI from a service business is $300,000. Wages from the business are $60,000, and UBIA is $400,000 What is the taxpayer's QBID?

a. $0

b. $9,000

c. $18,000

d. $30,000

¶ 205 ANCILLARY ISSUES

The law is not clear in many areas related to the QBID. To reduce "game playing," the statute includes a few countermeasures. It allows for legislative regulations to clarify items after the game starts—the regulations are the law, whether taxpayers like them or not. The Section 6662 substantial understatement penalty applies for understatements of 5 percent of proper liability (it is 10 percent in general) if caused by the Section 199A deduction.

Possible Penalty Exposure

Code Section 6662 includes a 10 percent substantial understatement penalty for the amount of an understatement attributable to a position. Practitioners must be aware of this because they need to advise clients that they might be subject to this penalty. Practitioners also must understand that with regard to the QBID, there is a lower threshold of 5 percent. The Section 6662 penalties apply not only to taxpayers, but also to practitioners because they affect their professional obligations to make taxpayers aware of the potential for a penalty.

Issues of Concern: Legislative Regulations and Expanded Penalty

Some items that were not clear in the statute were clarified in the regulations, but others remain open questions. For example:

- What is the definition of a trade or business from the standpoint of real estate rentals?
- Can (or should) separate businesses be aggregated?
- Can a non-SSTB be segregated from a (related) SSTB?
- What is the definition of an SSTB?
- Are special allocations allowed of W-2 wages and UBIA to threshold income partners?
- Can we substitute preferred distributions for Section 707(c) "guaranteed" payments?

The rental or licensing of property to a related trade or business is itself a trade or business if the businesses are commonly controlled. This would "allow" aggregation of the non-rental business with the rental business, but can serve as an anti-abuse rule. See the following regulations:

- Reg. 1.199A-4 provides definitions of common control for purposes of aggregation.
- Reg. 1.199A-5(c)(2) mandates aggregation of SSTB and non-SSTB based on source of gross receipts.
- Reg. 1.199A-5(c)(1) mandates aggregation of SSTB and non-SSTB based on shared expenses and de minimis gross receipts in non-SSTB.

The preamble to the Section 1411 regulations stated that the Section 162 test would be adopted because it is clear, but anyone who has researched this issue would see that is not the case. The Fifth Circuit has defined a trade or business, using the Section 162 test, as requiring "a sufficient quantum of focused activity." Gambling has been held to basically be a trade or business if a taxpayer is addicted to gambling and requires an intervention. However, the courts have applied a different standard.

¶ 206 RENTAL AS A TRADE OR BUSINESS

Historically, this issue has arisen primarily (although not exclusively) in connection with Section 1231 status. This was to allow the taxpayer an ordinary Section 1231 loss (with gains one ordinarily can live with capital gain classification). Section 1221(a)(2) excludes as a capital asset, and Section 1231(b) includes as a Section 1231 asset:

- Depreciable property used in a trade or business
- Any real property used in a trade or business

Trade or Business Definitions

The definitions turn on the level of taxpayer activity. Courts have defined a trade or business as one in which:

- The taxpayer is "involved in the activity with continuity and regularity." (***Commissioner v. Groetzinger***, 480 US 23 (1987))
- The taxpayer is "engaged in a sufficient quantum of focused activity." (***Suburban Realty v. United States***, 615 F.2d 171 (5th Cir. 1980))
- The "scope of the taxpayer's activities . . . are so extensive." (IRS Ltr. Rul. 9840026 (June 30,1998))

The activity may be the taxpayer's or the agent's activity; that is, an agent's work can make the activity a trade or business. The QBID does not require any participation by the taxpayer.

Single Rental as a Trade or Business

Section 162 does not clearly define a trade or business, so case law is often looked upon for guidance. The level of taxpayer activity may determine whether an activity is a trade or business. For example, in ***Fegan v. Commissioner***, 71 TC 791 (1979), a single motel property met the "longstanding definition . . . as . . . the rental of one property." In ***Curphey v. Commissioner***, 73 TC 766 (1980), a well-known office-in-home case, the court ruled that a single rental can be a trade or business, but it is a factual test and not a matter of law.

Hazard v. Commissioner (7 TC 372 (1946)) involved a taxpayer who lived in his Kansas City home for nine years and then accepted a new job in Pittsburgh. The taxpayer listed the Kanas City home for rent/sale in January 1940 and purchased the Pittsburgh home in February of the same year. The taxpayer rented the Kansas City home from early 1940 to November 1943, and then it sold at a loss. The Tax Court said this rental constituted a trade or business.

The facts do not state how much time the taxpayer spent on the activity; however, during the entire rental period, the taxpayer was in Pittsburgh, which is about 850 miles from Kansas City. Thus, the taxpayer likely did little more than approve tenants and make the management decisions of an agent.

In the following cases and ruling, the rental property did not constitute a trade or business:

- ***Grier v. United States,*** 218 F.2d 603 (2nd Cir. 1955): The taxpayer inherited rental property, waited for the lease to expire, and then sold it at a loss. The court ruled that this did not constitute a trade or business but rather a rental only to allow the existing lease to lapse before the sale. *Balsamo*, TC Memo 1987-477, had similar facts and result.
- ***Foehl v. Commissioner,*** TC Memo 1961-93: The taxpayer had a short-term rental for minimal consideration. The court ruled the taxpayer had no profit-making intent because he was renting the property at below fair market value
- ***Vandeyacht v. Commissioner,*** TC Memo 1994-148: This case involved an investment property/vacation home that was occasionally rented to children or friends, never for more than 12 weeks/year, and not to the general public. This is not considered a trade or business activity.
- Rev. Rul. 73-522, 1973-2 CB 226: A nonresident alien owner of net leased property came to the United States once a year to supervise lease negotiations. The IRS stated his actions did not constitute a trade or business.

STUDY QUESTION

8. Which of the following statements is true regarding the definition of a trade or business?

a. Rental activity is included as trade or business under Section 162.

b. Trade or business is defined in Section 1231.

c. A single rental may be a trade or business.

d. The term *trade or business* is clearly defined under Section 162.

¶ 207 AGGREGATION OPTIONS

The taxpayer must decide what is a business, and this may involve the aggregation/segregation of operations. Reg. Sec. 1.199A-4 allows aggregation and requires certain segregation. (Note that *segregation* is the author's term to describe when a SSTB and a non-SSTB cannot be combined.) In both cases, the regulation spells out rules to follow. Aggregation *may* be done, but it is not required (as is true for Sections 469 and 1411). The Section 469 activity tests are *not* applicable.

Why would a taxpayer want to aggregate? It allows for single business reporting, and the W-2 wages and UBIA of the two operations are combined. Aggregation is not required (there must be at least two distinct businesses), so a taxpayer should first decide whether it wants to aggregate and then decide if the following factors allow for aggregation:

- The businesses have greater than or equal to 50 percent common ownership (direct or indirect).
- The same product or service is offered together, or the nature of the service and the product is such that they are commonly offered together.
- The businesses share facilities or business elements.
- The businesses are operated in coordination or with reliance on one another.
- There is no aggregation of a service business with a non-service business.

Aggregating Service Businesses with Non-Service Businesses

Service and non-service operations can be aggregated if the SSTB is incidental to the non-service business. There is a *de minimis* test based on gross receipts. If the aggregate gross receipts are less than or equal to $25 million for the year, service income must be less than 10 percent of the total. If the aggregate gross receipts are greater than or equal to $25 million for the year, the service income must be less than 5 percent of the total. Some clarification may be needed on this rule (the rule creates a cliff).

STUDY QUESTION

9. Which of the following is true regarding the aggregation factors?

a. Businesses that share facilities may be allowed to aggregate.

b. Businesses with different year ends may be aggregated.

c. SSTBs may be aggregated with non-SSTBs.

d. The businesses must have 20 percent or more common ownership.

¶ 208 SEGREGATION RULES

A taxpayer has an incentive to carve out a non-service business from a service operation if the taxpayer would be subject to the high-income reduction or elimination of QBID. Examples include an optician who also sells eyeglass lenses and frames, or a veterinarian who also has boarding facilities and sells pet supplies. The question is whether a taxpayer *can* segregate its non-service businesses (in our examples, the sales of eyeglasses and pet supplies) from its service businesses (e.g., eye exams and pet vaccinations).

According to Reg. Sec. 1.199A-5(c)(1), a taxpayer cannot segregate the non-service portion of its business if it has greater than or equal to 50 percent common ownership. Non-SSTB income is earned from providing services or products to the SSTB. The proportionate share of income based on sales to the controlled entity are a separate SSTB. This prohibits the typical veterinarian/optician scenario mentioned earlier.

Can a separate entity that rents to the service business segregate? Before the final regulations under Section 199A were issued, some major law firms segregated their building from the firm itself for the sole purpose of generating a QBID, because the partners in these large law firms are threshold income taxpayers. The deduction passed through from the law firm. This is not allowed under the final regulations. Commonly controlled businesses are not allowed to segregate the rental operation from the service business; both must be treated together.

Reg. Sec. 1.199A-5(c)(3) states that segregation is allowed if there are shared expenses of a commonly owned service and non-service business and less than or equal to 5 percent of the total gross receipts comes from the non-service operation; that is, the non-SSTB is incidental to the SSTB. The regulation provides an example of a dermatologist who earns less than or equal to 5 percent from sale of skincare products. The optician and veterinarian mentioned earlier may run into the same issue.

STUDY QUESTION

10. Jan and Jim each own 50 percent of a law practice and each are over the taxable income threshold. To create QBI, they purchased a building to rent to the law practice. Which of the following statements regarding this situation is true?

- **a.** The rental will be considered a non-SSTB because it is not a service business.
- **b.** The rental will be considered non-SSTB income if they rent an office to an unrelated party.
- **c.** The law firm and the rental cannot be segregated.
- **d.** The rental is considered non-SSTB income because it is renting to a non-SSTB business.

Relevant Pass-Through Entity Aggregation

Because aggregation is not required, a relevant pass-through entity (RPE) need not aggregate, but similar to the passive loss and net investment income tax (NIIT) provisions, a RPE may choose to aggregate. If the RPE aggregates, the partner or shareholder cannot disaggregate. However, the partner or shareholder may choose to further aggregate.

Passive activity loss and NIIT aggregation may be required based on the factors in the regulations. This aggregation is not harmful because the partner or shareholder would otherwise be required to do the same. For the QBID, the RPE need not aggregate. Accounting records may dictate some of these aggregation decisions. The decisions made for PAL and NIIT purposes do not affect the QBID aggregation (or lack of aggregation).

Compensation for Services/Capital

An S corporation shareholder's QBI does not include reasonable compensation as "defined" for other purposes—that is, it will lead to disputes as it has for payroll tax purposes.

- QBI is reduced for the deduction for the compensation.
- QBI does not include Section 707(c) guaranteed payments, both for services and for capital.
- QBI does not include Section 707(a) non-partner type payments if made for services.
- The partner's QBI is reduced by the deduction for Section 707(a) or Section 707(c) payments.

Service Business

Remember that a SSTB includes specified businesses such as consulting, law, accounting, and so on. It also includes any business where the principal asset is the skill or reputation of one or more of the employees (Section 1202(e)(3)(A) definition). Because the deduction for high-income taxpayers may go to zero, such taxpayers will be expected to contend that the business is not a service business.

Architects and engineers are excluded from the definition of a service business. Older IRS rulings offered some guidance (e.g., veterinarians and physical therapists are in a service business), but the "skill and reputation" issue was expected to create gray areas. The IRS was much more explicit in the regulations, but there remain some uncertain scenarios

The debate as to whether a business is a SSTB will occur only for taxpayers with income above the threshold amount. A non-service business has the wage or wage/UBIA limit as a floor on the allowed deduction; a SSTB deduction can go to a zero deduction.

Even a non-service business needs W-2 wages or capital to get a deduction for high-income taxpayers. Reg. Section 1.199A-6 provides guidance. Following are some factoids regarding whether a business is considered a service business:

- State licensing is not relevant. What is done matters, not whether a license is required.
- "Skill and reputation" is limited to income from endorsing products or services, licensing an image/name/signature/voice, or appearance fees. This is an extremely limited interpretation.
- "Accounting" includes bookkeeping.
- "Law" includes paralegals/arbitration/mediation.
- "Health care" is generally providing services to patients although the final regulations also included other service situations.
- "Actuarial science" is the analysis and assessment of risk and uncertainty.
- "Performing arts" includes actors, musicians, directors, athletes, and coaches.
- "Financial services" is broad and includes financial advisers, underwriters, wealth management, retirement planning, valuations, and merger and acquisition advice.
- "Brokerage" is surprisingly limited to a fee for arranging a buyer–seller transaction for securities, not real estate or insurance. Therefore, brokerage services do not include insurance agents/brokers or real estate agents/brokers.

Consulting may be the wild card. The regulations define consulting as the "provision of professional advice and counsel to assist the client in achieving goals and solving problems." The "goals" and "problems" are not limited, in the regulatory definition, to financial issues or some other specific area of concern. Note that the services must be advice and counsel—training and education are not considered consulting services.

STUDY QUESTION

11. A service business includes:

a. Architects

b. Insurance agents

c. Lighting technicians

d. Bookkeepers

Pass-through Entities

Supplemental information such as the following must be reported to the owner of a pass-through business:

- QBI
- Share of W-2 wages for the partner
- Share of unadjusted basis of business assets for the partner
- Classification of the business as specified service activity or otherwise
- Income or loss by the business

Section 751 ordinary income is QBI. Pass through entities do not generally aggregate/segregate to allow the owners greater flexibility but the pass through entity does classify a service business; the owner cannot then change that classification. Also, the deduction is not available for reasonable compensation, a guaranteed payment for services, or a non-partner payment for services. This may affect how the entity wants to classify payments.

In pass-through entities, the W-2 wages are allocated among owners based on how the wage deduction is allocated. Shares of capital are allocated among the entity owners based on how book (Section 704(b)) depreciation shares are allocated. The use of book depreciation eliminates the need to consider Section 704(c) shares. Section 734 adjustments are *not* part of UBIA, but Section 743 "excess" is. UBIA is based on the shares on the last day of the tax year; the taxpayer must have an interest on that last day to receive a UBIA share.

STUDY QUESTION

12. Supplemental information required to be reported to an owner of a pass-through entity includes:

a. The amount of the owner's QBID

b. The owner's wages reported on his or her own W-2

c. Whether the entity is a specified service activity or otherwise

d. A recommendation for the owner to aggregate

Special Allocations

It may be tempting to use special allocations of wage and depreciation deductions to shift W-2 wages and UBIA to threshold income partners. This is possible; however, a current year shift of deductions that does not change the overall deductions allocated to each partner, but just the type of deduction, would fail substantiality as a shifting allocation. Excess wage deductions or depreciation shares offset by future period operating income would fail substantiality as a transitory allocation if they are within five years. It may be possible with an income chargeback funded by sale of partnership property, protected from transitory classification by the value-equals-basis presumption.

Is Special Allocation 1 below acceptable?

Special Allocation 1		
Original	**Partner A**	**Partner B**
W-2 Wages	500,000	500,000
Other Deductions	1,000,000	1,000,000

Proposed Revision	**Partner A**	**Partner B**
W-2 Wages	1,000,000	-0-
Other Deductions	500,000	1,500,000

No, it is not. This is a "shifting" allocation. It includes a shift of deductions within the same period (intraperiod). There is no effect on the partners' Section 704(b) capital, and therefore no effect on the dollar amounts to be received from the partnership. The shifting allocation is insubstantial; this is not a debatable point. Now review Special Allocation 2 below.

Special Allocation 2		
Original	**Partner A**	**Partner B**
W2 Wages	500,000	500,000
Other Deductions	1,000,000	1,000,000

Proposed Revision	**Partner A**	**Partner B**
W2 Wages	1,000,000	-0-
Other Deductions	1,000,000	1,000,000

This special allocation might be okay. It is likely that Partner A will want a gain chargeback to Partner A in the amount of the prior excess deduction of $1,000,000. The intent would be to bring his Section 704(b) capital, and therefore his right to assets, back in line with what it would have been absent the wage allocation. The issue then becomes how the chargeback is funded. Operating income is a transitory (insubstantial) allocation if it actually occurs within five years. Gain from sale of property would be okay since it is protected by the "value-equals-basis" presumption and will be assumed to be unavailable when testing for insubstantiality under the transitory test (interperiod).

¶ 209 SECTION 707 PAYMENTS

Both Section 707(a) and 707(c) payments are not part of QBI. Many such payments are not really "guaranteed," and it may be advisable to consider a change to preferred distributions. The same income allocations may be achieved by use of target allocations with the preferred distributions (the income will follow the distributions).

The distinction between a preferred distribution and a Section 707 payment is unclear in many fact patterns, but a change in classification can boost the QBID of the payee by 20 percent. Section 707(c) payments stem from the partner–partnership relationship. There is some authority that partners should be able to define such relationships. Cash flow–based payments have a strong, although not definitive, argument.

Three-Step Analysis of Partnership-to-Partner Payments

IRS Technical Advice Memorandum (TAM) 8642003 offers this step-by-step method:

- First, was this a payment made in a non-partner capacity?
  - If so, it is a Section 707(a) payment, treated as made to a non-partner for all purposes of the tax laws.
  - It most likely occurs when the service provider provides similar services to parties other than the partnership (***Wegener***, 119 F.2d 49 (5th Cir. 1941)).
- Second, was this a partnership–partner payment?
  - Was it called for in the agreement?
  - If yes, was it based on income? If no, it can receive Section 707(c) treatment but only for purposes of Sections 61 and 162.
- Third, the default is a Section 731 distribution.

Preferred Distribution Versus Section 707(c) Payment

Suppose there is a two-person partnership, with member A and member B. Its prepayment income is $400,000. Member A gets $60,000. The beginning of year Section 704(b) capital is zero for each member, and the partnership agreement calls for target allocations. The income allocations target Section 704(b) capital based on hypothetical distributions upon liquidation. The liquidating distributions if there is no Section 707(c) payment are as follows: (1) return investment, (2) $60,000 cumulative preference to member A, and (3) 50 percent to each member. To determine the liquidating distributions if there is a Section 707(c) payment, simply skip step (2) above.

Use of Section 707(c) payment to member A for $60,000: Partnership income is reduced from $400,000 to $340,000. This income is split 50 percent to each member ($170,000 each). Section 704(b) capital then becomes:

- Member A: $0 plus $170,000 = $170,000 at year end
- Member B: $0 plus $170,000 = $170,000 at year end

This would result in liquidating distributions of $170,000 to each member. Because member A already received $60,000, member A gets $230,000 and member B gets $170,000.

Use of preferred distribution with target allocations of income: There is no Section 707(c) payment, and partnership income is $400,000. A hypothetical sale and liquidation results in the following:

	Member A	Member B
Return investment	-0-	-0-
Preference return	60,000	-0-
50 percent split of balance	170,000	170,000
Target capital (asset share)	230,000	170,000
income allocation	230,000	170,000

CPE NOTE: When you have completed your study and review of chapters 1 and 2, which comprise Module 1, you may wish to take the Final Exam for this Module. Go to **cchcpelink.com/printcpe** to take this Final Exam online.

MODULE 2: TAX UPDATE—Chapter 3: Federally Declared Disaster Areas: Tax Provisions Including COVID-19

¶ 301 WELCOME

This chapter discusses the federal tax consequences of presidentially declared disasters under the Stafford Act, with detailed coverage of the coronavirus (COVID-19) disaster declaration and IRS Notice 2020-18.

¶ 302 LEARNING OBJECTIVES

Upon completion of this chapter, you will be able to:

- Calculate interest and penalties if tax is not paid by the Notice 2020-18 due date
- Identify which clients are best served by filing early
- Recognize the amount of taxes clients must pay by April 15

¶ 303 BACKGROUND

There is a formal process for declaring a disaster in the United States. First, the president declares a disaster area under the Robert T. Stafford Disaster Relief and Emergency Assistance Act (known as the Stafford Act). Next, the president sends a letter to certain cabinet members, including the Secretary of the Treasury, who chooses the particular disaster relief to provide. For the coronavirus (COVID-19) disaster, President Trump made the declaration on March 13, 2020.

With regard to the COVID-19 disaster, the relief has been trickling out piecemeal. The first round of COVID-19 relief, Notice 2020-17, *Relief for Taxpayers Affected by Ongoing Coronavirus Disease 2019 Pandemic*, was released March 17, 2020. At that time, the relief was strictly intended to provide liquidity to the economy. It was not really about taxpayer relief at that point; it had a larger macroeconomic purpose. It did not provide taxpayers with an extension of time to file their tax returns.

Notice 2020-18 was released soon after and did provide taxpayers with additional time to file tax returns. It was designed to defer as much as $300 billion in tax payments. The due date for filing federal income tax returns and making federal income tax payments otherwise due April 15, 2020, was delayed to July 15, 2020. Disaster relief that started out as a liquidity infusion began to change to taxpayer relief.

The problem with this deferral is that if your clients did not pay their taxes on April 15, they may not have had enough money saved to pay them by July 15. The Treasury Department, by trying to preserve the economy, may be putting some taxpayers into an awkward situation. Some clients are not good at saving, especially in light of the difficult financial circumstances resulting from the COVID-19 pandemic. Practitioners should discuss the deferral for filing and payments with their clients, and make plans to set money aside to pay the taxes when due. See the following example.

EXAMPLE: In *Godwin v. Commissioner*, TC Memo 2003-289, Mr. Godwin, a former IRS attorney, was practicing in Alabama. He received a large legal fee (in excess of $1 million) in 1997 and used the money to construct a new house and purchase timberland. Then a federal disaster was declared. Godwin could not pay his federal taxes because he had spent so much on the house and land. The Tax Court waived the resulting penalties and interest during the disaster period, but not after it. Consequently, Godwin owed a large amount of penalties.

¶ 304 NOTICE 2020-18: NARROW RELIEF

Disaster relief applies to *affected taxpayers*, which generally include the following:

- A taxpayer with a principal residence located in a covered disaster area
- A taxpayer with a principal place of business located in a disaster area
- Certain relief workers assisting in a disaster area
- Spouses of an affected taxpayer, solely for a joint return
- Individuals, business entities, and sole proprietorships, not located in a covered disaster area, but whose records necessary to meet a deadline for a postponed act are located or maintained in a disaster area
- Estates or trusts, if their tax records are maintained in a disaster area
- Any individual visiting a disaster area who is killed or injured as a result of a disaster; or
- Any other person determined by the IRS to be affected by a disaster (Reg. Sec. 301.7508A-1(d))

However, an affected taxpayer for purposes of COVID-19 relief under Notice 2020-18 means any person with a federal income tax return or with a federal income tax payment due on April 15, 2020, including:

- Individuals
- Trusts and estates
- Partnerships (although the postponement is unlikely to apply to them)
- Corporations
- Other non-corporate tax filers

The relief provided is narrow; it automatically postpones the April 15 deadlines to July 15, 2020.

EXAMPLE: Michelle has a tax payment due on April 15. Neither she nor anyone she knows has been quarantined for coronavirus or contracted the virus. She has not been affected by coronavirus in any way. Michelle *is* an "affected taxpayer" who qualifies for relief under Notice 2020-18. Since she has a tax payment due on April 15, 2020, she is *not* required to pay the tax or file her return until July 15, 2020.

Extended payments and extended filings are detailed in the following charts:

Extended Payment Acts		
Act	**Postponed**	**Not Postponed**
Income tax (including self-employment tax) payments due April 15, 2020	X	
Estimated tax payments due April 15, 2020	X	
Early distributions (10 percent) excise tax on IRA/retirement withdrawals	X	
Estimated tax payments due June 15, 2020		X

Extended Payment Acts		
Estimated tax payments for 2019 tax year		X
Depositing employment and excise taxes		X
Estate and gift tax payments		X

Extended Filing Acts		
Act	**Postponed**	**Not Postponed**
Income tax returns due April 15 (including Forms 1040, 1120, and 1041)	X	
Estate and gift tax returns		X
Filing employment and excise taxes (Form 941, etc.)		X
Filing information returns		X
Withdrawing excess elective deferrals		X
Filing refund claim for 2016 tax year		X
Returns due May 15 or June 15 (includes calendar year Form 990s)		X*

According to Notice 2020-18, section III, "There is no limitation on the amount of payment that may be postponed."

EXAMPLE: Joe is a professional basketball player. His employer is under withholding. Joe will owe $12 million on his 2019 Form 1040. He may defer the entire $12 million payment until July 15, 2020; there will be no penalties or interest due if he pays by July 15. However, if Joe does not pay what he owes by July 15, interest and penalties begin to accrue on July 16 (Treas. Reg. Sec. 301.7508A-1(f), example 4).

Additional Relief

The IRS has the discretion to choose to postpone some acts, but not others. According to the Joint Committee on Taxation, in P.L. 107-134: "The suspension of time *may* apply to the following acts." Similarly, Rev. Proc. 2018-58 states: "[G]uidance may provide relief of only certain acts." However, unless the guidance indicates relief is limited, the guidance will "generally postpone all of the acts listed in the regulations and this revenue procedure" (Rev. Proc. 2018-58, section 4). As mentioned previously, the relief provided in Notice 2020-18 is limited.

Relief Possibilities: Authority

There are three basic sources of the IRS's authority to extend time for performing acts:

- Treas. Reg. Sec. 301.7508A-1(c)
- Rev. Proc. 2018-58
- Rev. Proc. 2016-53

Treas. Reg. Sec. 301.7508A-1(c) states that the IRS can provide postponement of the following:

- Filing and/or paying
- Income tax, estate/gift/generation-skipping transfer tax, most excise taxes, harbor maintenance tax, alcohol/tobacco taxes, or employment tax

- Making contributions to qualified retirement plans: individual retirement accounts (IRAs), pensions, Simplified Employee Pension (SEP) plans, SIMPLE plans
- Making distributions of current IRA contributions before the extended due date
- Recharacterizing IRA contributions before the extended due date
- Making a rollover under Code Secs. 402(c), 403(a)(4), 403(b)(8), or 408(d)(3)
- Filing a petition with the Tax Court, or for review of a decision rendered by the Tax Court
- Filing a claim for credit or refund of any tax
- Bringing suit upon a claim for credit or refund of any tax
- Any other act specified in a revenue ruling, revenue procedure, notice, announcement, news release, or other guidance published in the *Internal Revenue Bulletin* (see Rev. Proc. 2018-58)

Although it has not happened yet, the IRS can also give itself extra time to collect and assess tax. For example, under normal statute of limitations rules, assessment of tax for 2016 Forms 1040 filed on or before April 15, 2016, must occur by April 15, 2020. Therefore, many 2016 tax returns will no longer be subject to assessment, unless the IRS used the Stafford Act to extend its own deadline. This is also true for collections statutes. Once the IRS determines that a taxpayer owes more tax, it has only 10 years from the assessment to collect that tax.

There are a staggering number of acts (39 pages' worth) that may be postponed under Rev. Proc. 2018-58, including:

- An extension of the 75-day retroactive period for S corporation elections
- Required minimum distributions
- IRA recharacterization
- Elections for trust distributions made within 65 days of the year end as from the prior year
- An extension of Code Sec. 1031 time periods: 45-day identification and 180-day closing periods

Even though the coronavirus-related tax relief provided so far is quite limited, it is quite possible the IRS will expand this relief in the future. Practitioners should stay tuned for developments. The following charts detail the relief provided so far in response to the coronavirus and other recently declared disasters.

Narrow Relief			
Acts Postponed	**Coronavirus**	**Tennessee Tornados**	**Hurricane Florence**
Filing income tax returns due	Returns due April 15, 2020 (1 day)	Returns due from March 3 to July 15, 2020 (147 days)	Returns due between September 7, 2018, to January 31, 2019 (135 days)
Estimated tax payments	April 15	April 15 and June 15	September 17 and January 15
Employment/excise tax late deposit penalty waived?	No	Yes: Payroll/excise tax deposits due from March 3 to March 18, 2020 (if deposited by March 18, 2020)	Yes: Payroll/excise tax deposits due from September 7, 2017, to March 24, 2018 (if deposited by March 24, 2018)

Comparison: Taxpayer Acts			
Possible Relief	**Coronavirus**	**Tennessee Tornados**	**Hurricane Florence**
IRA deposits	No	Yes	Yes
Other time-sensitive acts (Treas. Reg. Sec. 301.7805A-1(c)): • Filing gift tax, estate tax, employment tax forms • Payments except "deposits" of P/R and most excise tax • Installment agreement payments • Filing a Tax Court petition • Filing a refund claim, or filing suit upon same • Other time-sensitive acts by published guidance (below)	No	Yes	Yes
Other time-sensitive acts (Rev. Proc. 2018-58 or 2007-56)	No	Yes	Yes

STUDY QUESTION

1. The COVID-19 postponements are unlikely to apply to which of the following taxpayers?

a. Partnerships
b. Individuals
c. Trusts
d. Estates

¶ 305 DO TAXPAYERS NEED TO FILE AN EXTENSION?

It appears that taxpayers who cannot meet the new July 15, 2020, deadline will be able to file for an additional extension before July 15. Frequently asked question number 12 in Notice 2020-18 states: "You must request an automatic extension by July 15, 2020. If you properly estimate your 2019 tax liability using information available to you and file an extension form by July 15, 2020, your return will be due October 15, 2020."

¶ 306 REFUNDS

Due to the COVID-19 pandemic, many businesses and individuals will face financial difficulties. Clients who might have refunds coming will want to move ahead, and that's one way practitioners can do their part in this crisis. The IRS is urging taxpayers expecting refunds to file early and to use e-file to speed up refunds. The IRS will continue to process returns (both e-file and paper). Most refunds will be paid within 21 days (IR-2020-58). Taxpayers who have not filed their 2017 and 2018 returns are encouraged to file them right away.

¶ 307 HOW DO TAXPAYERS GET RELIEF?

Typically, the IRS puts a special code on the returns of taxpayers who live in an affected disaster area. As discussed earlier, all taxpayers are affected by the COVID-19 disaster. If a taxpayer receives a notice, they should call the disaster hotline number included in the notice.

The IRS distributes an internal disaster relief memo to all its employees so they are aware of the disaster relief provisions. It also issues a public news release (or other guidance) with disaster details (see Rev. Proc. 2018-58, section 4).

¶ 308 PAYMENTS AFTER JULY 15

For taxpayers who do not pay their federal taxes due by July 15, 2020, interest and penalties apply beginning July 16.

- **Failure-to-pay penalty.** Being one day late results in full month's .5 percent penalty. There is a reasonable cause exception for estimated tax penalties.
- **Failure-to-file penalty.** This penalty applies if the taxpayer fails to seek a filing extension by July 15, unless there is reasonable cause. Again, being one day late results in full month's 5 percent penalty.
- **Estimated tax penalty.** This penalty will apply if the taxpayer neglects to pay the estimated tax installment by June 15. However, an exception is provided in Code Sec. 6654(e), which specifically mentions disasters. To avoid the estimated tax penalty, the taxpayer should check the box on Form 2210, Part III, and attach a statement to the tax return explaining why the taxpayer cannot make the estimated tax payment by the due date.

Interest cannot be abated after July 15, 2020. It can be suspended under Code Sec. 6404(i), but only for the duration of the disaster period (which ends July 15). See the Preamble to TD 8911 and Treas. Reg. Sec. 301.7508A-1(f), example 7.

Also according to the TD 8911 Preamble, if an employer misses a payroll tax deposit, the IRS will consider waiving the penalty for reasonable cause.

¶ 309 PLANNING IDEAS

These planning ideas mainly spring from the recent stock market decline. Taxpayers should consider taking the following actions:

- Fund IRAs now. This is a good idea even though the time for making IRA contributions has been extended. Taxpayers can fund 2019 tax year and 2020 tax year IRAs now. They should also fund their pensions now.
- Harvest losses. For example, a taxpayer could sell her stock, stay out of it for 30 days and take a tax loss, and then buy it back 31 days later (to avoid the wash sale rules).
- Convert a traditional IRA to a Roth IRA.
- Consider gifting. Keep in mind the potential for a step-up on assets included in the estate.

EXAMPLE: Dmitri, a young taxpayer, has been contributing to his traditional IRA for five years., but the value has plummeted. It may be a good time to consider converting to a Roth IRA. However, Dmitri should be aware that he will need cash to pay the tax on the conversion.

EXAMPLE: Feliciano is planning to make a contribution to his Roth IRA. He's been told that he has until July 15 to do so. You, as his tax practitioner, might suggest that now is a good time for him to make the contribution. However, suggest that Feliciano discuss this with an investment advisor, as it is difficult to predict future market movements.

¶ 310 DEVELOPMENTS

Because guidance can change, practitioners must stay on top of the latest developments related to the COVID-19 and other declared disasters. The IRS has already altered the coronavirus tax relief provisions twice. The first change was Notice 2020-18 superseding Notice 2020-17. Then, the IRS issued new frequently asked questions that granted somewhat wider relief. Check the following for new developments:

- IRS Coronavirus Tax Relief and Economic Impact webpage: https://www.irs.gov/coronavirus
- IRS Newsroom: https://www.irs.gov/newsroom
- Other recent disasters:
  - ☐ By state: https://www.irs.gov/newsroom/around-the-nation
  - ☐ By year: https://www.irs.gov/newsroom/tax-relief-in-disaster-situations

¶ 311 STATE-BY-STATE RULES

Most states, and even some cities (e.g., Chicago and New York) have extended coronavirus relief. It's important to check the state tax relief provisions for a particular state to best advise clients. The Federation of Tax Administrators provides links to all state tax websites at https://www.taxadmin.org/state-tax-agencies. Note that you might have to do some searching once you get to a particular state's page.

¶ 312 OTHER MATTERS

Here are some other issues to keep in mind when dealing with coronavirus (COVID-19) disaster relief:

- The IRS has made sweeping changes to the collections area (see IR-2020-59). It is suspending payments on installment agreements due between April 1 and July 15, 2020. Clients might wish to keep making these payments to reduce the interest and penalties.
- Taxpayers with pending offer in compromise (OIC) applications have until July 15, 2020, to provide information. They also have the option to defer OIC payments until July 15.
- The time for providing earned income (for the earned income tax credit, or EITC) has been extended until July 15, 2020.
- The following have been suspended through July 15, 2020: liens and levy actions, and passport certifications.
- The IRS will continue to issue statutory notices of deficiency to avoid the statute of limitations running.

Practical advice for tax professionals includes:

- It might be a good idea to create a new "July 15" due date list.
- Consider expediting clients' Forms 941 because of the new tax credits under the Families First Coronavirus Response Act.
- If you run into problems, do not hesitate to contact the taxpayer advocate (by filing Form 911, *Request for Taxpayer Advocate Service Assistance*), the IRS disaster hotline, or IRS appeals.

STUDY QUESTIONS

2. Which of the following acts was postponed due to COVID-19 legislation?

- **a.** Filing estate and gift tax returns
- **b.** Filing employment and excise taxes
- **c.** Filing income tax returns due April 15
- **d.** Withdrawing excess elective deferrals

3. Each of the following identifies a planning idea from the stock market decline, ***except:***

- **a.** Fund IRAs now
- **b.** Convert Roth IRA to a traditional IRA
- **c.** Harvest losses
- **d.** Fund pensions now

MODULE 2: TAX UPDATE—Chapter 4: Families First Coronavirus Response Act and CARES Act: Strategic Tax and Business Planning

¶ 401 WELCOME

The Families First Coronavirus Response Act (FFCRA) and the Coronavirus Aid, Relief, and Economic Security (CARES) Act are momentous stimulus bills intended to provide assistance to individuals and businesses impacted by coronavirus. This course describes the grants, loans, expanded employee and unemployment benefits, and tax provisions designed to provide relief to impacted taxpayers, and considers how the provisions in the legislation apply in a variety of scenarios to help clients determine what they are eligible for and how to apply for or claim the benefits.

¶ 402 LEARNING OBJECTIVES

Upon completion of this chapter, you will be able to:

- Describe the key features of the Families First Coronavirus Response Act and the CARES Act that apply to businesses and individual taxpayers
- Recognize how provisions of these acts apply in common factual scenarios
- Identify how to determine whether taxpayers are eligible for provided benefits under the acts
- Recognize how Pandemic Emergency Unemployment Compensation applies
- Describe what happens to an EIDL loan received before April 3, 2020, for COVID-19 related purposes

¶ 403 EXPANDED UNEMPLOYMENT BENEFITS: CARES ACT

Each state administers its own unemployment insurance program, although generally the states follow federal guidelines. Each state determines the following for its unemployment program:

- Eligibility levels
- Benefit amounts
- Duration of benefits
- Whether benefits are charged to employer accounts
- Whether unemployment insurance (UI) is available for individuals who are self-employed, unable to work, quit, were fired for misconduct, or refused to accept a job without a good reason.

Federal Pandemic Unemployment Compensation

Section 2104 of the CARES Act provides guidance to states for Federal Pandemic Unemployment Compensation (FPUC). Under FPUC, states will administer a supplemental unemployment amount funded by the federal government. The benefit is available to individuals who, as determined by the applicable state unemployment agency, meet that state's usual criteria to receive UI benefits.

The FPUC provides an increase of a flat payment of $600 per week to the amount regularly available for unemployment under state law. It applies to weeks of unemployment beginning after the state agrees to participate in the program through July 31, 2020 (approximately four months).

STUDY QUESTION

1. Which of the following is true regarding Federal Pandemic Unemployment Compensation?

- **a.** It is available to every U.S. resident.
- **b.** It requires states to pay a minimum amount of unemployment compensation under state law.
- **c.** It provides an increase of a flat payment of $600 per week.
- **d.** It applies to state unemployment programs through September 30, 2020.

Pandemic Unemployment Assistance

Pandemic Unemployment Assistance (PUA), detailed in Section 2102 of the CARES Act, is available to individuals who are not usually eligible for unemployment benefits, including those who are furloughed or out of work as a direct result of the COVID-19 pandemic, self-employed and independent contractors, and those who have exhausted all rights to regular or extended UI benefits under state or federal law.

> **NOTE:** PUA is not available to individuals who have the ability to telework with pay and those who are receiving paid sick leave or other paid benefits (even if they otherwise satisfy the criteria described below to receive assistance under the new law).

The PUA benefit is equal to the minimum weekly benefit amount described in the Stafford Act Disaster Unemployment Assistance (DUA) program, plus the $600 per week federally funded supplement (generally designed to equal what is provided to UI recipients under the FPUC). Applicants for PUA must provide self-certification that they are (1) partially or fully unemployed or (2) unable and unavailable to work for specified reasons. The PUA benefit covers the period from January 27, 2020, through December 31, 2020. Qualified reasons for unemployment under PUA include the following:

- The individual has been diagnosed with COVID-19 or is experiencing symptoms of COVID-19 and seeking a medical diagnosis;
- A member of the individual's household has been diagnosed with COVID-19;
- The individual is providing care for a family member or a member of the individual's household who has been diagnosed with COVID-19;
- A child or other person in the household for which the individual has primary caregiving responsibility is unable to attend school or another facility that is closed as a direct result of the COVID-19 public health emergency and such school or facility care is required for the individual to work;
- The individual is unable to reach the place of employment because of a quarantine imposed as a direct result of the COVID-19 public health emergency;

- The individual is unable to reach the place of employment because the individual has been advised by a healthcare provider to self-quarantine due to concerns related to COVID-19;
- The individual was scheduled to commence employment and does not have a job or is unable to reach the job as a direct result of the COVID-19 public health emergency;
- The individual has become the breadwinner or major support for a household because the head of the household has died as a direct result of COVID-19;
- The individual has to quit his or her job as a direct result of COVID-19;
- The individual's place of employment is closed as a direct result of the COVID-19 public health emergency; or
- The individual meets other criteria established by the Secretary of Labor.

Pandemic Emergency Unemployment Compensation

Under Section 2107 of the CARES Act, Pandemic Emergency Unemployment Compensation (PEUC) is available to UI recipients who exhaust all of their regular state UI benefits, which range from as few as 12 weeks to a maximum of 26 weeks depending on the state. PEUC provides an additional 13 weeks of state UI benefits. Individuals must have exhausted their regular state UI benefits and be actively engaged in searching for work. PEUC is available through December 31, 2020, unless otherwise extended.

CARES Act Unemployment Benefits: Troubles with Implementation

As of April 17, 2020, approximately two-thirds of states were providing the $600 supplemental benefit. Many states were just getting prepared for PUC (independent contractors and self-employed). In addition, a number of states have reportedly had trouble meeting demand for unemployment filings with their existing systems and resources (both administratively and financially). As of June 30, 2020, more than 19 million U.S. workers are still receiving unemployment benefits.

¶ 404 BUSINESS TAX PROVISIONS

This section discusses several key business tax provisions of the CARES Act, including:

- Bonus depreciation for qualified improvement property
- Net operating loss (NOL) carrybacks
- Alternative minimum tax (AMT) credit carryforwards
- Increased business interest expense limitations

Bonus Depreciation for Qualified Improvement Property

The CARES Act accelerates the depreciation deduction for qualified improvement property (QIP). QIP refers to any improvement made by a taxpayer to an interior portion of an existing building that is nonresidential real property; residential rental property is excluded. Examples of such qualifying improvements include installation or replacement of drywall, ceilings, interior doors, fire protection, mechanical systems, electrical systems, and plumbing.

The act provides QIP with a 15-year depreciable life, reduced from 39 years under the Tax Cuts and Jobs Act (TCJA). QIP is now eligible for bonus depreciation. The changes are retroactive to January 1, 2018 (which corrects a TCJA drafting error). This provides for several planning opportunities, such as amending returns and pushing depreciation to "good years" prior to the COVID-19 recession.

STUDY QUESTION

2. Qualified improvement property includes:

a. Exterior portions of a building

b. Replacement of drywall

c. Construction of a new building

d. Residential rental property

NOL Carrybacks for Corporate Taxpayers

Prior to the CARES Act, NOLs could only be carried forward, and NOL carryforwards could only offset 80 percent of taxable income in a given year. Under the CARES Act, NOLs arising in tax years beginning after December 31, 2017, and before January 1, 2021, can now be carried back five years. NOL carrybacks and carryforwards can be used to offset 100 percent of taxable income in a given year, and NOLs can still be carried forward indefinitely.

Corporations with 2018 or 2019 NOLs can immediately file amended returns seeking refunds. Carrying back NOLs to the 2017 tax year or earlier will maximize refunds by offsetting tax at the 35 percent corporate income tax rate in effect prior to the 2017 tax reform (rather than the post-reform rate of 21 percent).

Corporations anticipating a 2020 NOL should review their year-to-date estimated tax payments. The NOL carryback may affect the calculation of tax credits in prior years.

NOL Carrybacks for Noncorporate Taxpayers

Before the CARES Act, the amount of business losses from a flow-through entity (sole proprietorship, partnership, or S corporation) that an individual could use to offset nonbusiness income (wages, investment income) was limited to $250,000 ($500,000 for joint filers), and excess losses were carried forward as an NOL. CARES eliminates the $250,000/$500,000 limitation for tax years beginning in 2018, 2019, and 2020. Impacted taxpayers can immediately file returns seeking refunds.

STUDY QUESTIONS

3. Which of the following statements is true regarding corporate NOLs under the CARES Act?

a. The changes apply to all NOLs from 2020 forward.

b. The NOL carryforwards can offset up to 80 percent of taxable income.

c. The NOLs can offset up to $250,000 of taxable income in a given year.

d. Certain NOLs may now be carried back.

4. Under the CARES Act, noncorporate taxpayers with business losses from a flow-through entity:

a. Are not limited to the amounts provided in the TCJA.

b. Can only offset those losses with other flow-through business income.

c. Must carry forward any excess losses as an NOL.

d. Can deduct business losses incurred between 2020 and 2025 without limitation.

Alternative Minimum Tax Credit Carryforwards

Prior to 2017 tax reform, corporations were subject to a corporate AMT. The 2017 tax reform eliminated the AMT, and corporations with remaining AMT credit carryforwards were generally required to spread those carryforwards over a four-year period ending in 2021. Under the CARES Act, a corporation with remaining AMT credit carryforwards may claim a refund for any remaining AMT credit carryforward on its 2018 or 2019 tax return.

Interest Expense Limitations: Corporations

Generally, a corporation's interest expense deductions for a taxable year cannot exceed the sum of:

- The corporation's business interest income for the year,
- The corporation's floor plan financing interest expense for the year, and
- Thirty percent of the corporation's adjusted taxable income (ATI) for the year.

The CARES Act increases the limitation from 30 percent of ATI to 50 percent of ATI for 2019 and 2020. CARES allows taxpayers to elect to use 2019 ATI to compute their 2020 ATI limitation. Corporate taxpayers seeking refunds for 2019 can file their returns now.

Interest Expense Limitations: Partnerships

Generally, a partnership's interest expense deductions for a taxable year cannot exceed the sum of:

- The partnership's business interest income for the year,
- The partnership's floor plan financing interest expense for the year, and
- Thirty percent of the partnership's ATI for the year.

For partnerships, the CARES Act increases the ATI limitation from 30 percent to 50 percent only for the 2019 tax year. Partnerships that want refunds can immediately file their tax returns.

Corporate AMT Relief

The CARES Act gives corporations the ability to accelerate their utilization of any of their remaining minimum tax credits under the pre-TCJA corporate AMT regime. The corporate AMT was repealed by the TCJA, effective for tax years beginning after December 31, 2017; transition rules were adopted to allow taxpayers to utilize their remaining minimum tax credits before 2022.

The TCJA allowed corporations to fully utilize minimum tax credits against regular tax liability (reduced by certain credits). In addition, for tax years beginning in 2018, 2019, or 2020, corporations could receive a refundable credit equal to 50 percent of the excess of the minimum tax credit for the tax year over the amount of the credit allowable for the year against regular tax liability. For a tax year beginning in 2021, corporations could receive a refundable credit equal to 100 percent of the excess of the minimum tax credit for the tax year over the amount of the credit allowable for the year against regular tax liability.

The CARES Act accelerates corporations' ability to utilize any remaining minimum tax credits they may have. Instead of allowing a 50 percent credit for tax years beginning in 2018 through 2020, with a 100 percent credit allowed in 2021, the legislation now allows a 50 percent credit for 2018 and a 100 percent credit for 2019. Alternatively, a corporation may elect to claim the entire refundable credit amount for 2018.

¶ 405 INDIVIDUAL TAX ISSUES: CARES ACT

The CARES Act contains several important tax provisions for individuals as well.

Penalty Relief for Early Retirement Account Withdrawal

The general rule is that an early withdrawal from a qualified retirement plan is subject to a 10 percent additional tax unless the distribution meets a laundry list of exceptions. Under the new law, an early withdrawal from a retirement plan is allowed without penalty (up to $100,000) if made by a "qualified individual." The distribution is still included in the taxpayer's gross income.

A qualified individual is one who needs the early withdrawal due to coronavirus. The definition of *qualified individual* in the CARES Act is fairly broad and includes individuals who:

- Are diagnosed with coronavirus
- Have a spouse or dependent who has coronavirus
- Are unable to work due to coronavirus or whose reduced work hours are causing financial hardship
- Have had a job offer rescinded or a job start date delayed due to coronavirus

Other factors are included in the definition as well. Loans against retirement plan accounts are still an option; the act includes an increased borrowing ceiling ($100,000).

STUDY QUESTION

5. Under the CARES Act, early retirement account withdrawals may be made without penalty:

a. Up to any amount

b. Only for those that have contracted the coronavirus

c. To those who need the early withdrawal due to the coronavirus

d. And are not included in gross income

Employer Payment of Student Loans

The general rule is that an employee's gross income does not include up to $5,250 per year of employer payments, in cash or kind, made under an educational assistance program for the employee's education. The exclusion does not include payments made for the education of the employee's spouse or dependents.

The new law adds eligible student loan repayments to the types of educational payments excluded from employee gross income. However, there is a deadline—loan repayments must be made before January 1, 2021.

Supercharged Charitable Contributions

Generally, adjusted gross income (AGI) is gross income less certain deductions (above-the-line deductions). Charitable deductions are itemized deductions that further reduce AGI, and are known as below-the-line deductions.

The new law adds new charitable deductions to the calculation of gross income for tax years beginning in 2020, making them above-the-line deductions. Although the deduction limit is $300, it is still meaningful. The CARES Act helps charitable organizations that depend on modest gifts from a large number of donors, even those that do not elect to itemize deductions.

Generally, individuals are allowed a deduction for cash contributions to certain charitable organizations. The limitation was increased under the TCJA to 60 percent of AGI in a tax year. The excess could be carried forward for five years. Under the CARES Act, for 2020 only, "qualified contributions" are disregarded in applying the 60 percent AGI limitation on cash contributions to qualifying charitable organizations. However, there are many limitations. For example, the charity must be a qualifying charity; donor-advised funds and supporting organizations are excluded.

Individual Retirement Plan Charitable Rollover

Under the CARES Act, taxpayers who are 70½ years old or older can donate up to $100,000 in individual retirement account (IRA) assets outright to a qualified charity each year. This satisfies the required minimum distribution (RMD) requirement (the RMD is suspended for 2020). The rollover is not included in taxable income. Note that the IRA charitable rollovers are limited to public charities.

Estate Planning

The COVID-19 pandemic presents a good opportunity for taxpayers to get their estate plans in order. Taxpayers should check their beneficiary designations, because in most instances, those designations overrule instructions in wills and trusts. They are also advised to review their life insurance policies; IRAs; 401(k), 403(b), and 457 plans; and retirement annuities. Practitioners can help their clients review deferral opportunities for retirement assets after the owner's death.

Medical Planning Documents

Taxpayers should review their health and medical directives as well. These include:

- Living will/end-of-life decisions
  - Instructions about end-of-life decisions can be included in a patient advocate designation.
- "Do not resuscitate" order
  - In a hospital situation
  - Outside of a hospital situation
  - Must be signed by a physician
- Court-ordered guardianship
  - If no decision maker is appointed
  - No informal decision makers
  - Disagreement among informal decision makers
  - Decisions beyond emergency care

STUDY QUESTION

---

6. Under the CARES Act, charitable contributions made by individuals:

a. Will result in dips in charitable giving.

b. May disregard the 60 percent AGI limitation for 2020.

c. Are no longer limited to qualifying charities.

d. Include an above-the-line deduction, but can only be claimed if the taxpayer itemizes deductions.

¶ 406 EMPLOYEE BENEFIT AND RETIREMENT PLAN PROVISIONS

Several provisions related to employee benefits and retirement plans are contained in the CARES Act and the FFCRA.

Employee Paid Leave

The FFCRA requires certain employers to provide employees with paid sick leave or expanded family and medical leave for specified reasons related to COVID-19. The U.S. Department of Labor administers and enforces the new law's paid leave requirements. These provisions will apply from the effective date through December 31, 2020:

- Two weeks (up to 80 hours) of paid sick leave at the employee's regular rate of pay where the employee is unable to work because the employee is quarantined (pursuant to federal, state, or local government order or the advice of a healthcare provider) and/or experiencing COVID-19 symptoms and seeking a medical diagnosis; or
- Two weeks (up to 80 hours) of paid sick leave at two-thirds the employee's regular rate of pay because the employee is unable to work due to a bona fide need to care for an individual subject to quarantine (pursuant to federal, state, or local government order or the advice of a healthcare provider), or to care for a child (under 18 years of age) whose school or child-care provider is closed or unavailable for reasons related to COVID-19, and/or the employee is experiencing a substantially similar condition as specified by the Secretary of Health and Human Services, in consultation with the Secretaries of the Treasury and Labor; and
- Up to an additional 10 weeks of paid expanded family and medical leave at two-thirds the employee's regular rate of pay where an employee, who has been employed for at least 30 calendar days, is unable to work due to a bona fide need for leave to care for a child whose school or child-care provider is closed or unavailable for reasons related to COVID-19.

Covered employers. The paid sick leave and expanded family and medical leave provisions of the FFCRA apply to certain public employers and to private employers with fewer than 500 employees. Most employees of the federal government are not covered by the expanded family and medical leave provisions of the FFCRA. Small businesses with fewer than 50 employees may qualify for exemption from the requirement to provide leave due to school closings or child-care unavailability if the leave requirements would jeopardize the viability of the business as a going concern.

Eligible employees. All employees of covered employers are eligible for two weeks of paid sick time for specified reasons related to COVID-19. Employees employed for at least 30 days are eligible for up to an additional 10 weeks of paid family leave to care for a child under certain circumstances related to COVID-19.

STUDY QUESTION

7. Which of the following statements is true regarding the paid sick and expanded family and medical leave provisions of the FFCRA?

a. It applies to employers with more than 500 employees.

b. Employers with less than 50 employees may qualify for exemption from the requirement.

c. Up to an additional 10 weeks of paid expanded family and medical leave may be available for employees that have been at the company for at least one year.

d. It covers employees who are able to telework.

Reasons for leave. Under the FFCRA, an employee qualifies for paid sick time if the employee is unable to work (or unable to telework) due to a need for leave because the employee:

- Is subject to a federal, state, or local quarantine or isolation order related to COVID-19;
- Has been advised by a healthcare provider to self-quarantine related to COVID-19;
- Is experiencing COVID-19 symptoms and is seeking a medical diagnosis;
- Is caring for an individual subject to an order described in the first bullet point or self-quarantine as described in the second bullet point above;
- Is caring for a child whose school or place of care is closed (or child-care provider is unavailable) for reasons related to COVID-19; or
- Is experiencing any other substantially similar condition specified by the Secretary of Health and Human Services, in consultation with the Secretaries of Labor and Treasury.

Under the FFCRA, an employee qualifies for expanded family leave if the employee is caring for a child whose school or place of care is closed (or child-care provider is unavailable) for reasons related to COVID-19.

Retirement Plans

Distributions. The new law allows distributions of up to $100,000 to be made until December 31, 2020, from most defined contribution retirement plans (401(k), IRA, etc.) as a result of COVID-19, even if the participant does not satisfy the usual hardship distribution rules. No penalty applies. The participant must certify that he, his spouse, or one of his dependents tested positive for COVID-19 or suffered adverse financial consequences as a result of COVID-19.

The distribution is not subject to mandatory income tax withholding or the 10 percent penalty tax even if the participant is younger than age 59½. The taxpayer may repay the distribution to the plan (or an IRA) within three years without being taxed on it. If not repaid, the distribution is treated as regular income spread equally over the three-year period from the date of the distribution for federal income tax purposes.

Loans. Participants may receive loans of up to $100,000 (or 100 percent of their account balance in the retirement plan, if less) until September 28, 2020. Payments due in 2020 on loans currently outstanding and new loans taken out during the remainder of 2020 may be put on hold for one year. The five-year repayment period is also extended to six years under the new law. Interest continues to accrue on the loan during the one-year grace period on repayment. The 10-year penalty tax is not generally waived if a participant later defaults, so a distribution may be a better option.

Planning opportunities. Taxpayers should continue contributing to their retirement plans in 2020 if possible. If they have the financial means to do so, they may want to frontload contributions before the market goes back up (though it is impossible to time the market and to know what is the "bottom"). Some taxpayers might consider a Roth conversion. The taxes due on the conversion will be significantly less as a result of the decline in the value of the participant's account, and the future growth in the assets will be income tax free.

Other retirement plan provisions. Minimum required distribution requirements that apply to defined contribution retirement plans (but not defined benefit plans) and IRAs are waived for the 2020 plan year. Also, sponsors of defined benefit pension plans receive some relief from the minimum funding requirements for 2020. If an employer wants to reduce employer contributions to its retirement plans, a 30-day advance written notice is generally required if the plan is a safe harbor plan.

Health Savings Accounts and Flexible Spending Accounts

The CARES Act allows high-deductible health plans paired with health savings accounts (HSAs) to cover telehealth services before a patient has met the plan deductible. Normal cost-sharing can still be imposed for telehealth visits, such as through co-pays that the plan may require after the deductible is paid. This provision is temporary and will sunset on December 31, 2020, unless Congress extends it or makes it permanent.

Individuals may use their HSAs, health reimbursement arrangements (HRAs), or flexible spending accounts (FSAs) to buy over-the-counter medical products, such as drugs and surgical masks, without a prescription. HSAs, HRAs, and FSAs can be used to pay for certain menstrual care products, such as tampons and pads, as eligible medical expenses (not COVID-19 related). These are permanent changes and apply retroactively to purchases beginning January 1, 2020.

Health Plans Required to Cover COVID-19 Testing and Care

The CARES Act and FFCRA require fully insured and self-insured plans to cover coronavirus testing without cost-sharing or a deductible. This includes any services or items provided during a medical visit that result in coronavirus testing, including an in-person or telehealth visit to a doctor's office, an urgent care center, or an emergency room. This coverage requirement remains in effect only while there is a declared public health emergency as defined under federal law.

¶ 407 EXTENSION OF TAX FILING DEADLINES

IRS Notice 2020-18 postponed the April 15 due date for filing an income tax return or making an income tax payment and filing an extension to July 15, 2020. Notice 2020-20 extended to July 15, 2020, the due date for federal gift tax or generation-skipping tax payments due April 15, 2020 or a requirement to file or extend Form 709 on April 15, 2020. These Notices only apply to federal income and gift tax returns.

State Tax Filing Deadlines Extended

All states that have a personal income tax have extended their April 15 due dates. The following 40 states have extended their deadline for filing individual income tax returns and making payments from April 15 to July 15: Alabama, Alaska, Arkansas, Arizona, California, Colorado, Connecticut, District of Columbia, Delaware, Georgia, Illinois, Indiana, Kansas, Kentucky, Louisiana, Massachusetts, Maine, Maryland, Michigan, Minnesota, Missouri, Montana, North Carolina, North Dakota, Nebraska, New Jersey, New Mexico, New York, Ohio, Oklahoma, Oregon, Pennsylvania, Rhode Island, South

Carolina, Tennessee, Texas, Utah, Vermont, Wisconsin, West Virginia. The same extension applies to the U.S. Virgin Islands.

The following five states extended their due dates for individual income tax returns and payments to other dates in light of the coronavirus pandemic:

- Iowa: July 31
- Hawaii: July 20
- Idaho: June 15
- Mississippi: May 15
- Virginia: May 15 for filings; June 1 for payments

The new deadline for individual income tax returns and payments in Puerto Rico was June 15. In New Hampshire, the deadline for business tax, interest, and dividends tax was June 15. The due date is the same in Washington for annual business and occupation tax.

Payroll Tax Deferral

Employers are generally required to withhold Social Security tax at 6.2 percent from their employees' wages, up to the annual wage limit ($137,700 for 2020). In addition, they must pay their own share of Social Security tax at the same rate as employees. Usually, employers must submit their share of Social Security tax plus their employees' portion to the IRS either monthly or semiweekly.

Under the CARES Act, employers can defer paying their share of Social Security tax; 50 percent of the deferred amount must be paid by December 31, 2021, and the remaining 50 percent is due by December 31, 2022. Social Security tax for employees and self-employed individuals must be paid as normal. Note that this deferral does not pertain to Medicare tax.

STUDY QUESTION

8. Which of the following statements is true regarding the payroll tax deferral under the CARES Act?

a. It applies to Social Security and Medicare taxes.

b. Fifty percent of the deferred amount must be paid by December 31, 2021.

c. The Social Security wage limit was reduced.

d. It applies to the employee and employer portions of Social Security tax.

¶ 408 CHANGES TO BANKRUPTCY LAW

The Small Business Reorganization Act (SBRA), which became effective in February 2020, allows businesses with debts under a certain amount to more quickly, and less expensively, reorganize. Under the SBRA, a business's debts must be $2,725,625 in order to file for Subchapter 5 bankruptcy. (A Subchapter 5 bankruptcy is easier and quicker than a Chapter 11 bankruptcy.) The debt limit increases to $7.5 million under Section 1113 of the CARES Act. This change applies only to bankruptcy cases filed after the CARES Act became effective and will only be applicable for one year. The debt limit will revert to $2,725,625 after one year passes.

The CARES Act allows a debtor to request modification of a plan under Section 1329(d)(1)(A) if the debtor is experiencing or has experienced a material financial hardship due, directly or indirectly, to the COVID-19 pandemic. Further, debtors may extend plan payments under the plan for up to seven years after the initial plan payment was due. These changes apply to any case for which a plan has been confirmed before the enactment of the CARES Act.

Bankrupt debtors are allowed to request a post-confirmation modification of their plans if the debtors are experiencing or have experienced a material financial hardship due, directly or indirectly, to the coronavirus pandemic, including extending their payments for up to seven years after the initial plan payment was due.

The definition of *income* in the Bankruptcy Code for Chapters 7 and 13 has been amended to exclude coronavirus-related economic stimulus payments from being treated as "income" for purposes of filing bankruptcy. The act also clarifies that the calculation of disposable income for purposes of confirming a Chapter 13 plan shall not include coronavirus-related payments. All of these provisions will expire after one year from the date of the CARES Act, unless extended.

¶ 409 FEDERAL STUDENT LOAN PAYMENTS DEFERRED

The CARES Act requires the Secretary of Education to defer all federally held student loan payments, principal, and interest for six months, through September 30, 2020, without penalty to student loan borrowers, and to suspend involuntary collection for all federally owned loans. These changes will affect more than 95 percent of student loan borrowers.

¶ 410 LOANS AVAILABLE FOR BUSINESSES

Businesses that have been hit hard by the coronavirus pandemic have an increasing number of options for loans.

Economic Injury Disaster Loans

Economic Injury Disaster Loans (EIDLs) are specifically available to the following organizations directly affected by the disaster:

- Small businesses within the Small Business Administration (SBA) size standards (see https://www.sba.gov/size)
- Small agricultural cooperatives and aquaculture businesses
- Private non-profit organizations (regardless of size)

NOTE: Religious organizations, charitable organizations, and gambling concerns are not eligible for an EIDL.

EIDL provisions include the following.

- Eligible entities may qualify for loan amounts of up to $2 million.
- Interest rates on an EIDL are 3.75 percent for small businesses and 2.75 percent for non-profit organizations.
- Terms of up to 30 years are available, with the first payment due 12 months after funds are issued.

Working capital loans may be used to pay fixed debts, payroll, accounts payable, and other bills that could have been paid had the disaster not occurred. EIDLs help entities stay afloat during the declared disaster, so they will be ready to "restart" their operations once circumstances allow. EIDLs are not meant for business expansions.

To be approved for an EIDL, an applicant must have a credit history acceptable to the SBA; the SBA must determine that the applicant's business has the ability to repay the loan; and the applicant's business must be physically located in a disaster-designated area and have suffered working capital losses due to the declared disaster.

Paycheck Protection Loans

The Paycheck Protection Program (PPP) provides $349 billion of loan funds to support small businesses and other eligible entities impacted by COVID-19. Eligible expenses include funds to pay workers, interest on mortgage obligations, rent, insurance, paid sick or medical leave, utilities, and payroll-related costs incurred from February 15, 2020, to June 30, 2020. Up to eight weeks of eligible expenses during the covered period can be forgiven from the loan principal as long as the employer maintains previous payroll counts during this emergency.

The PPP provides small businesses with loans that may be partially or fully forgiven and are 100 percent federally guaranteed. The program leverages the existing SBA 7(a) lenders and program, while increasing the available amount of funds, improving loan terms, streamlining borrower requirements, and providing for the expansion of eligible lenders of SBA PPP loans. Other provisions include the following:

- There are no collateral requirements or personal guarantees for the loan.
- There are no fees for the borrower to apply for the loan.
- The SBA "credit elsewhere" test does not apply to the loan.

Applicants can apply for a loan up to a maximum of $10 million, from participating lenders. Loan amounts are based on the applicant's previous payroll and covered cost amounts (2.5 times the average total monthly "payroll costs" up to $10 million). The interest rate is 1 percent per year with a term of two years. There are no fees for borrowers to apply for a PPP loan, and no prepayment fees. Loan repayments will be deferred for six months.

To qualify for a PPP loan, an entity must have been operational by February 15, 2020, and had payroll and paid taxes. The covered loan period is either (1) the 24-week (168-day) period beginning on the PPP Loan Disbursement Date, or (2) if the Borrower received its PPP loan before June 5, 2020, the Borrower may elect to use an eight-week (56-day) Covered Period.

If the business has already received an SBA EIDL and chooses to refinance that loan with a PPP loan, the outstanding EIDL loan amount can be added to the loan amount, subject to the $10 million cap. Applicants are eligible to apply for a PPP loan until August 8, 2020.

Uses for PPP loans. Borrowers will be required to make a good faith certification that the loan proceeds will be used for:

- Payroll costs
- Costs related to the continuation of group healthcare benefits during periods of paid sick, medical, or family leave, and insurance premiums
- Employee compensation
- Business-related mortgage interest payments (not principal), lease payments, or utility payments
- Interest on any other business debt obligations that were incurred prior to February 15, 2020

Eligibility. The following businesses are eligible for a PPP loan:

- A small business with fewer than 500 employees (or a business in an industry that has an employee-based size standard through the SBA that is more than 500 employees)

- Section 501(c)(3) nonprofits with fewer than 500 employees
- Tribal businesses defined under Section 31(b)(2)(C) with fewer than 500 employees
- Section 501(c)(19) veteran organizations with fewer than 500 employees
- A restaurant, hotel, or a business that falls within the North American Industry Classification System (NAICS) code 72, "Accommodation and Food Services," and has fewer than 500 employees at each location
- Businesses in the hospitality and restaurant industries, and franchises that are approved on the SBA's Franchise Directory
- Businesses that receive financial assistance from the Small Business Investment Company (SBIC) program
- Sole proprietors, independent contractors, gig economy workers, and self-employed individuals

STUDY QUESTIONS

9. Which of the following statements is true regarding the EIDL?

a. The EIDL is available to religious organizations.

b. Interest rates are based on the prime rate.

c. Terms of up to 30 years are available.

d. Eligible entities may qualify for loans up to $5 million.

10. The PPP loan:

a. Is up to a maximum of $10 million.

b. Has an interest rate of 3.75 percent.

c. Requires applicant entities to have been operational by January 1, 2020.

d. Is based on average revenue.

Payroll cost calculations. Payroll costs for businesses include salaries; wages; cash tips; payments for vacation, parental, family, medical, or sick leave; payments for group healthcare benefits; and certain other employment-related expenses. Payroll costs for sole proprietors and independent contractors include wages and net earnings from self-employment. Compensation for an individual employee, sole proprietor, or independent contractor above $100,000 annually (prorated for the period) is excluded.

The average payroll will be calculated over (1) 12 months prior to the loan origination; (2) for seasonal employers, the period between February 15, 2019, through June 30, 2019, or, at the election of the borrower, March 1, 2019 through June 30, 2019; or (3) the period between January 1, 2020, and February 29, 2020, for businesses not in operation during the period between February 15, 2019, and June 30, 2019.

Loan forgiveness. A borrower is eligible for loan forgiveness equal to the amount spent by the borrower during either a twenty four-week period or an eight-week period after the origination date of the PPP loan, for qualified expenditures. The eight-week period applies for loans disbursed prior to June 8, 2020. The following can be included in the PPP loan forgiveness amount:

- Payroll costs
- Interest payment on a mortgage or debt that originated prior to February 15, 2020

- Payment of rent on a lease that began prior to February 15, 2020
- Payment on any utility for which service began before February 15, 2020

Amounts forgiven may not exceed the principal amount of the loan and accrued interest. Loan proceeds used for any other purposes will *not* be forgiven. Any cancelled indebtedness will not be included in the borrower's taxable income. Also, no more than 40 percent of non-payroll costs can be forgiven. Other loan forgiveness provisions include the following:

- If a business keeps all of its employees, the entirety of the loan will be forgiven.
- If the employees are laid off employees, the forgiveness will be reduced by the percent decrease in the number of employees.
- If total payroll expenses on workers making less than $100,000 annually decreases by more than 25 percent, loan forgiveness will be reduced by the same amount.
- If employees are already laid off, the loan can still be forgiven for the full amount of payroll costs if those employees are rehired by December 31, 2020.
- If the full principal of the PPP loan is forgiven, the borrower is not responsible for the interest accrued in the eight-week covered period. Any remainder of the loan that is not forgiven will convert into a two-year loan at 1 percent interest.
- If a borrower uses less than 60 percent of the loan amount for payroll costs during the forgiveness covered period, the borrower will continue to be eligible for partial loan forgiveness, subject to at least 60 percent of the loan forgiveness amount having been used for payroll costs.

The SBA and U.S. Department of the Treasury will be providing more guidance on loan forgiveness in the future.

Refinancing an EIDL into a PPP Loan

If a business received an EIDL loan related to COVID-19 between January 31, 2020, and April 3, 2020, it can refinance the EIDL into a PPP loan for loan forgiveness purposes. Note that a borrower cannot take out an EIDL and a PPP loan for the same purposes. The remaining portions of the EIDL, for purposes other than those laid out in loan forgiveness terms for a PPP loan, would remain a loan. If the borrower took advantage of an emergency EIDL grant award of up to $10,000, that amount would be subtracted from the amount forgiven under the PPP.

Recordkeeping and Verification

Businesses must be prepared to provide documentation of all payroll (including benefits), rent, mortgage, and other eligible expenses. Such businesses are advised to open a separate bank account for loan proceeds to keep track of expenditures, for purposes of obtaining loan forgiveness. This is easier to do if funds are not commingled.

STUDY QUESTION

---

11. Which of the following statements is true regarding PPP loan forgiveness?

a. If a business keeps at least half of its employees, the entire loan amount will be forgiven.

b. If any employees have been laid off, no portion of the loan will be forgiven.

c. If employees are already laid off, the loan can still be forgiven.

d. Payroll costs are not included in the PPP loan forgiveness amount.

¶ 411 EMPLOYEE RETENTION CREDIT

The employee retention credit is a refundable tax credit against certain employment taxes equal to 50 percent of the qualified wages an eligible employer pays to employees after March 12, 2020, and before January 1, 2021. Eligible employers can get immediate access to the credit by reducing the employment tax deposits they are otherwise required to make. Also, if the employer's employment tax deposits are not sufficient to cover the credit, the employer may get an advance payment from the IRS.

For each employee, wages (including certain health plan costs) up to $10,000 can be counted to determine the amount of the 50 percent credit. Because this credit can apply to wages already paid after March 12, 2020, many struggling employers can get access to this credit by reducing upcoming deposits or requesting an advance credit on Form 7200, *Advance Payment of Employer Credits Due to COVID-19*.

Employers, including tax-exempt organizations, are eligible for the credit if they operate a trade or business during calendar year 2020 and experience either:

- The full or partial suspension of the operation of their trade or business during any calendar quarter because of governmental orders limiting commerce, travel, or group meetings due to COVID-19, or
- A significant decline in gross receipts.

A significant decline in gross receipts begins on the first day of the first calendar quarter of 2020 for which an employer's gross receipts are less than 50 percent of its gross receipts for the same calendar quarter in 2019. The significant decline in gross receipts ends on the first day of the first calendar quarter following the calendar quarter in which gross receipts are more than 80 percent of its gross receipts for the same calendar quarter in 2019.

STUDY QUESTION

12. The employee retention credit:

a. Is a nonrefundable tax credit.

b. Is equal to 25 percent of qualified wages.

c. Applies to wages paid after January 1, 2020.

d. Applies to wages up to $10,000 per employee.

Qualified Wages

The credit applies to qualified wages (including certain health plan expenses) paid during this period or any calendar quarter in which operations were suspended. The definition of *qualified wages* depends on how many employees an eligible employer has. If an employer averaged more than 100 full-time employees during 2019, qualified wages are generally those wages, including certain healthcare costs (up to $10,000 per employee), paid to employees who are not providing services because operations were suspended or due to the decline in gross receipts. These employers can only count wages up to the amount that the employee would have been paid for working an equivalent duration during the 30 days immediately preceding the period of economic hardship.

If an employer averaged 100 or fewer full-time employees during 2019, qualified wages are those wages, including healthcare costs (up to $10,000 per employee), paid to any employee during the period operations were suspended or the period of the decline in gross receipts, regardless of whether or not its employees are providing services.

Intersection with Other Loans and Credits

An eligible employer's ability to claim the employee retention credit is impacted by other credit and relief provisions as follows:

- If an employer receives a Small Business Interruption Loan under the PPP, authorized under the CARES Act, then the employer is not eligible for the employee retention credit.
- Wages for this credit do not include wages for which the employer received a tax credit for paid sick and family leave under the FFCRA.
- Wages counted for this credit cannot be counted for the credit for paid family and medical leave under Section 45S of the Internal Revenue Code.
- Employees are not counted for this credit if the employer is allowed a Work Opportunity Tax Credit under Section 51 of the Internal Revenue Code for the employee.

How to Claim the Credit

To claim the new employee retention credit, eligible employers will report their total qualified wages and the related health insurance costs for each quarter on their quarterly employment tax returns (Form 941 for most employers), beginning with the second quarter. The credit is taken against the employer's share of Social Security tax, but the excess is refundable under normal procedures.

In anticipation of claiming the credit, employers can retain a corresponding amount of the employment taxes that otherwise would have been deposited, including federal income tax withholding, the employees' share of Social Security and Medicare taxes, and the employer's share of Social Security and Medicare taxes for all employees, up to the amount of the credit, without penalty, taking into account any reduction for deposits in anticipation of the paid sick and family leave credit provided in the FFCRA. Eligible employers can also request an advance of the employee retention credit by submitting Form 7200.

¶ 412 FFCRA TAX CREDITS FOR PAID LEAVE

The FFCRA gives businesses with fewer than 500 employees funds to provide employees with paid sick and family and medical leave for reasons related to COVID-19, either for the employee's own health needs or to care for family members.

Workers may receive up to 80 hours of paid sick leave for their own health needs or to care for others and up to an additional 10 weeks of paid family leave to care for a child whose school or place of care is closed or child-care provider is closed or unavailable due to COVID-19 precautions. The FFCRA covers the costs of this paid leave by providing small businesses with refundable tax credits. Certain self-employed individuals in similar circumstances are entitled to similar credits.

Tax Credits for Providing Leave

The FFCRA requires employers to provide paid leave through two separate provisions: the Emergency Paid Sick Leave Act and the Emergency Family and Medical Leave Expansion Act, which entitles workers to certain paid family and medical leave. The FFCRA provides that employers subject to paid leave requirements under the two acts are entitled to fully refundable tax credits to cover the cost of the leave required to be paid for these periods of time during which employees are unable to work. Certain self-employed persons in similar circumstances are entitled to similar credits.

Tax Credits for Sick Leave

Eligible employers are entitled to a fully refundable tax credit equal to the required paid sick leave. This tax credit also includes the eligible employer's share of Medicare tax imposed on those wages and its allocable cost of maintaining health insurance coverage for the employee during the sick leave period. The eligible employer is not subject to the employer portion of Social Security tax imposed on those wages.

Tax Credits for Leave Under the Family and Medical Leave Act (FMLA)

An eligible employer is entitled to a fully refundable tax credit equal to the required paid family and medical leave. This tax credit also includes the eligible employer's share of Medicare tax imposed on those wages and its cost of maintaining health insurance coverage for the employee during the family leave period. The eligible employer is not subject to the employer portion of Social Security tax imposed on those wages.

How to Get the Credits

According to the IRS, eligible employers that pay qualifying sick and/or child-care leave will be able to retain an amount of federal payroll taxes equal to the amount of qualifying sick and child-care leave payments rather than depositing the federal payroll taxes with their quarterly payroll tax returns to the IRS. Per the IRS release, the payroll taxes available for retention are withheld federal income taxes, the employee share of Social Security and Medicare taxes, and the employer share of Social Security and Medicare taxes "with respect to all employees."

In the event that the amount of payroll taxes retained is insufficient to cover qualifying sick and child-care leave payments made by an employer, the employer will be able to file a request for an accelerated payment from the IRS, which the IRS expects to process within two weeks or less. Under the examples provided by the IRS, the amount of qualifying leave credit is deducted from the amount of payroll taxes withheld and payable to the IRS.

¶ 413 PLANNING OPPORTUNITIES

The CARES Act and FFCRA have introduced several key planning opportunities for tax practitioners and their clients, including the following:

- Practitioners can create a strategy to get the maximum benefits for their clients through the PPP loan program or employee retention credit.
- Clients might benefit from converting their IRA or 401(k) plan to a Roth IRA with no required minimum distributions.
- Charitable contributions have been enhanced.
- There are opportunities for net operating loss (NOL) planning and corporate AMT credits.
- As of this writing, there is discussion about reinstating the state and local tax (SALT) deduction with no cap, perhaps retroactive to 2018 and 2019.
- Accelerating income to match up with expected losses in 2020 might be an option for some clients.

Tax professionals should stay abreast of updates on these significant pieces of legislation to identify how they can best advise their clients.

MODULE 2: TAX UPDATE—Chapter 5: COVID-19 Employment Tax Changes for Employers and the Self-Employed

¶ 501 WELCOME

Among several tax changes in the Families First Coronavirus Response Act (FFCRA) and the Coronavirus Aid, Relief, and Economic Security (CARES) Act are a few providing employment tax relief for many employers and self-employed individuals. This chapter explains the paid leave credits of the FFCRA and the employee retention payroll tax credit and the delay for depositing payroll and self-employment taxes. These rules interact with other credits and tax rules as well. Examples, documentation, and planning considerations are also covered.

¶ 502 LEARNING OBJECTIVES

Upon completion of this chapter, you will be able to:

- Identify employment tax relief for employers and self-employed individuals in the FFCRA and CARES Acts
- Compute the employee retention credit with and without the employer OASDI tax deferral provision
- Recognize how the payroll/self-employment tax relief interacts with other COVID-19 and general tax provisions

¶ 503 COVID-19 LEGISLATION AND ADMINISTRATIVE OVERVIEW

The legislative actions related to the COVID-19 pandemic have been released in several phases.

- Phase 1: Coronavirus Preparedness and Response Supplemental Appropriations Act, P.L. 116-123 (H.R. 6074, March 6, 2020)
  - — This act provides $8.3 billion in emergency funding for federal agencies to respond to the coronavirus outbreak. No tax changes were included.
- Phase 2: Families First Coronavirus Response Act (FFCRA), P.L. 116-127 (H.R. 6201, March 18, 2020)
  - — The FFCRA includes new refundable paid leave payroll and self-employment tax credits tied to labor law changes for required sick and family/medical leave.
  - — The credits are generally effective April 1, 2020.
- Phase 3: Coronavirus Aid, Relief, and Economic Security (CARES) Act, P.L. 116-136 (H.R. 748, March 27, 2020)
  - — The CARES Act includes many tax changes, including changes to the Tax Cuts and Jobs Act (TCJA) requiring amended returns and new calculations and planning. Sec. 2301 of the CARES Act outlines the employee retention credit for employers subject to closure due to COVID-19. Sec. 2302 discusses the delay of payment of employer payroll taxes.

— The act provides for a new/expanded Small Business Administration (SBA) loan program (the Paycheck Protection Program (PPP)) that includes loan forgiveness, with an application period opening on April 3, 2020 (April 10 for the self-employed and independent contractors).

- Phase 3.1: Paycheck Protection Program and Health Care Enhancement Act, P.L. 116-139 (H.R. 266, April 24, 2020)

  — This act increases the CARES Act PPP loan authorization from $349 billion to $659 billion and provides for additional Department of Health and Human Services (HHS) funding.

- Phase 3.2: Paycheck Protection Program Flexibility Act, P.L. 116-142 (H.R. 7010; 6/5/20)

  — Extends the covered period time frame and a few other PPP changes.

- Phase 3.3: P.L. 116-147 (S. 4116, 7/7/20)

  — Provides additional time to request a PPP loan (to August 8) and other changes.

IRS Actions and Payroll Tax Relevance

The IRS offered administrative relief for certain filings and payments in Notice 2020-23 (April 9, 2020). Basically, if a due date (normal or already extended) fell on or after April 1, 2020, through July 15, 2020, it was extended to July 15, 2020. This also applies to actions listed in Rev. Proc. 2018-53.

There is no filing extension for payroll returns; they are not included as specified forms in Notice 2020-23. According to the IRS FAQs (www.irs.gov/newsroom/filing-and-payment-deadlines-questions-and-answer): "Notice 2020-23 does not address payroll tax deposits, but it does provide postponement relief for filing a claim for credit or refund and bringing suit upon a claim for credit or refund for any tax, including payroll taxes."

Notice 2020-35 (May 28, 2020) modifies Notice 2020-23 by postponing the deadlines for specified time-sensitive actions with respect to certain employment taxes, employee benefit plans, exempt organizations, and Coverdell education savings accounts on account of the ongoing COVID-19 pandemic. The notice also provides a temporary waiver of the requirement for a certified professional employer organization (CPEO) to file certain employment tax returns and their accompanying schedules electronically. Notice 2020-35 also includes the correction of employment tax reporting errors using the interest-free adjustment process under Code Secs. 6205 and 6413.

IRS Reminder on Code Sec. 139 Exclusion and Payroll

Code Sec. 139 provides that gross income does not include amounts received by an individual if such payments meet the definition of "qualified disaster relief payment." IRS FAQs on COVID-19 issues includes one noting that qualified wages are not excludible "qualified disaster relief payments" under Code Sec. 139. Although there are no regulations on the Code Sec. 139 exclusion, the following provide some guidance:

- Joint Committee on Taxation explanation of enacting legislation (P.L. 107-134) at www.jct.gov/x-93-01.pdf
- Joint Committee on Taxation explanation of the change made by P.L. 109-7 at https://www.jct.gov/publications.html?func=startdown&id=2023
- Rev. Rul. 2003-12 at https://www.irs.gov/pub/irs-drop/rr-03-12.pdf

Possible items that may fall under this income exclusion rule include technology for home use (work or family needs), resources for school-age children of employees (technology and software for learning), and household supplies to help with the pandemic and shelter-in-place orders, but *not* wages.

According to Code Sec. 139(h): "Denial of double benefit: Notwithstanding any other provision of this subtitle, no deduction or credit shall be allowed (to the person for whose benefit a qualified disaster relief payment or qualified disaster mitigation payment is made) for, or by reason of, any expenditure to the extent of the amount excluded under this section with respect to such expenditure."

CAUTION: This seems to cover payments made to S corporation shareholders because the S corporation deducts the payment in the income passed through to its shareholders. For example, the S corporation cannot exclude the employer Code Sec. 139 payment for a computer ***and*** deduct it via the reduced net income passed through to shareholder/employee from the S corporation. However, IRS clarification on this subject would be helpful.

Subsection 139(h) was added in 2005 by P.L. 107-9. The Joint Committee on Taxation Bluebook states: "The provision provides that no additional deduction or credit is allowed with respect to amounts excluded from income under the provision. The provision also applies this denial of double benefit rule to amounts received as qualified disaster relief payments under present law Code Sec. 139 of the Code."

OBSERVATION: It is likely a good idea to determine how much money an employer has for this Code Sec. 139 benefit and how to be equitable and reasonable among employee needs. The employer should document its plan to show it is in line with Code Sec. 139 intent and is *not* regular (taxable) compensation.

STUDY QUESTIONS

1. Which piece of legislation introduced the Paycheck Protection Program (PPP)?

a. Families First Coronavirus Response Act (FFCRA)

b. CARES Act

c. Tax Cuts and Jobs Act (TCJA)

d. P.L. 116-123

2. Which of the following statements about IRS Notice 2020-23 is correct?

a. It waives the requirement for a certified professional employer organizations (CPEOs) to file employment tax returns electronically.

b. It includes a filing extension for payroll returns.

c. It provides credit for sick leave for self-employed individuals.

d. It offers administrative relief for certain filings and payments.

¶ 504 PAID LEAVE REFUNDABLE CREDITS FOR SMALL EMPLOYERS AND SELF-EMPLOYED INDIVIDUALS

The Families First Coronavirus Response Act (FFCRA) requires employers with fewer than 500 employees (per headcount) to provide up to two weeks of sick leave and up to 10 weeks of family/medical leave if the employee meets eligibility requirements. The maximum amount to pay matches new refundable credits available to the employer. The employer credits also include allocable qualified health plan expenses as defined in the FFCRA.

The FFCRA also provides comparable credits to self-employed individuals, but those are claimed only on the individual's 2020 Form 1040. In contrast, employers claim paid leave credits against Form 941 taxes starting in the second quarter of 2020 and can get the excess refunded by filing the new Form 7200, *Advance Payment of Employer Credits Due to COVID-19*. The act also added paid leave requirements that modify the existing labor law rules (such as the Family and Medical Leave Act of 1993 (FMLA)).

CAUTION: Practitioners should focus on providing tax advice to their clients rather than interpreting labor laws for them (which could be construed as the unauthorized practice of law).

The refundable credits and related rules are in the FFCRA; they have not been added to the Internal Revenue Code. The credits tie to required paid leave for sick leave (up to two weeks) and paid family and medical leave (up to 10 weeks), as specified in the FFCRA.

FFCRA Refundable Credits and Related Tax Rules

The credits and related rules as are follows:

- Payroll Credit for Required Paid Sick Leave (Act Sec. 7001)
- Credit for Sick Leave for Certain Self-Employed Individuals (Act Sec. 7002)
- Payroll Credit for Required Paid Family Leave (Act Sec. 7003)
- Credit for Family Leave for Certain Self-Employed Individuals (Act Sec. 7004)
- Special Rules Related to Tax on Employers (Act Sec. 7005)
  - — Wages paid under the paid leave rules of the FFCRA are not subject to the employer's 6.2 percent OASDI tax.
  - — Credits allowed under Secs. 7001 and 7003 are increased by Medicare tax (Code Sec. 3111(b)) on qualified sick and family leave wages for which the credit is allowed by Secs. 7001 and 7003.
  - — The employer's gross income is increased by the amount of the credit.
  - — The General Fund is used to make the OASDI trust funds whole.

An additional $15 million was provided to the IRS to carry out the FFCRA. The IRS can issue regulations to prevent abuse, minimize compliance and recordkeeping burdens, and more. Note that there are no new Code sections; these provisions are only in the FFCRA language.

Eligible (Covered) Employers

Employers with fewer than 500 employees must provide a specified amount of paid sick leave and emergency family and medical leave. Counted in the number of employees are U.S. full-time and part-time workers, employees on leave, temporary employees jointly employed, and day laborers employed by a temporary agency, but not independent contractors; see the U.S. Department of Labor temporary rules (preamble and Section 826.40) and FAQs for details. Some government employers are included. According to the DOL, "In general, two or more entities are separate employers unless they meet the integrated employer test under the Family and Medical Leave Act of 1993 (FMLA)" (www.dol.gov/agencies/whd/pandemic/ffcra-questions#2).

Eligible employers include businesses and non-profits (but not government entities) with under 500 employees. Governments may otherwise be subject to FMLA and sick leave laws—federal and state—but likely are not eligible for tax credits.

Secs. 3102 and 5111 give the Secretary of Labor the authority to issue regulations for good cause to exclude certain healthcare providers and emergency responders from the definition of *eligible employee* and to exempt small businesses with fewer than 50 employees when imposition of such requirements would jeopardize the viability of the business as a going concern. Sec. 3105 states: "An employer of an employee who is a health care provider or an emergency responder may elect to exclude such employee from the application of the provisions in the amendments made under section 3102 of this Act [dealing with the paid family/medical leave]." Sec. 5102 notes the following about paid sick leave: "an employer of an employee who is a health care provider or an emergency responder may elect to exclude such employee from the application of this subsection."

How Many Employers Are Subject to the FFCRA?

Per the April 6, 2020, DOL Interim Final Rule, 5,976,761 firms have fewer than 500 employees. There are 5,755,307 firms with fewer than 50 employees that are potentially exempt from the requirement to provide paid leave if the leave payments would jeopardize the business as a going concern.

Emergency Paid Sick Leave Act (EPSLA)

The Emergency Paid Sick Leave Act (EPSLA) requires eligible employers to provide a specified amount of paid sick leave (generally, two weeks) to the following:

- Full-time employees
- Part-time employees, based on the number of hours worked on average over a two-week period
- An employee who is *unable to work or telework* because of one of six reasons. The employee is:
  1. Subject to a federal, state, or local quarantine or isolation order related to COVID-19;
  2. Advised by a healthcare provider to self-quarantine due to concerns related to COVID-19;
  3. Experiencing symptoms of COVID-19 and seeking a medical diagnosis;
  4. Caring for an individual subject to an order described in (1) or has been advised as described in (2);
  5. Caring for his or her son or daughter if the school or place of care of the son or daughter has been closed, or the childcare provider of such son or daughter is unavailable, due to COVID-19 precautions; or
  6. Experiencing any other substantially similar condition specified by Secretary of Health and Human Services in consultation with Secretary of the Treasury and Secretary of Labor.

There is no requirement for the employee to have been employed for a minimum number of days for the sick leave (although there is such a requirement for the family/medical leave in the FFCRA). This provision expires on December 31, 2020.

Unable to work or telework means the employer must have work for the employee to do, the employer is not shut down and has not furloughed the employee, and the employee is unable to work due to one of the six specified reasons listed above. For the purposes of the EPSLA, a *quarantine or isolation order* includes:

> quarantine, isolation, containment, shelter-in-place, or stay-at-home orders issued by any Federal, State, or local government authority that cause the Employee to be unable to work even though his or her Employer has work that the Employee could perform but for the order. This also includes when a Federal, State, or local government authority has advised categories of

citizens (e.g., of certain age ranges or of certain medical conditions) to shelter in place, stay at home, isolate, or quarantine, causing those categories of Employees to be unable to work even though their Employers have work for them. [DOL Temporary rule (April 6, 2020) Sec. 826.10(a)]

The Department of Labor provides answers to questions on this topic at https://www.dol.gov/agencies/whd/pandemic/ffcra-questions.

Emergency Family and Medical Leave Expansion Act (EFMLEA)

The FFCRA also contains the Emergency Family and Medical Leave Expansion Act (EFMLEA), which generally allows leave for an employee who:

- Has been employed at least 30 calendar days by the employer with respect to whom leave is requested
- Is unable to work (or telework) due to a need for leave to care for his or her son or daughter under the age of 18 if the school or place of care has been closed, or the childcare provider of such son or daughter is unavailable, due to a public health emergency (reason No. 5 above).

According to the Department of Labor, there is only one qualifying reason for leave under the EFMLEA: the employee needs to care for his or her child whose school or childcare provider is closed or unavailable for reasons related to COVID-19. The initial two weeks of EFMLEA leave is "unpaid": employees can use paid sick leave under the EPSLA, or accrued paid time off under their employer's benefit package. Up to 10 weeks of paid leave is available.

Payroll Tax Credit for Required Paid Sick Leave

Under FFCRA Act Sec. 7001, a 100 percent credit is allowed by the employer against payroll taxes. This is generally limited to $200 per employee for 10 days (but may be higher if sick leave is due to reasons 1, 2 or 3 above). The credit is limited to payroll tax imposed under Code Secs. 3111(a) or 3221(a) but is refundable, so employers are allowed to reduce all payroll taxes owed. Employers should use Form 7200 to obtain a refund if the credits are greater than the payroll taxes owed.

Employers can also get a credit for "certain health plan expenses," generally for a group health plan excluded from an employee's income under Code Sec. 106 (Code Sec. 7001(d)). There is no double benefit:

- The employer increases gross income by the amount of the credit.
- Wages used to generate the credit may not be used to compute the Code Sec. 45S family and medical leave credit.

The credit is calculated "based on the employee's required compensation under subparagraph (B) and number of hours the employee would otherwise be normally scheduled to work (or the number of hours calculated under subparagraph (C)), except that in no event shall such paid sick time exceed—

- $511 per day and $5,110 in the aggregate for a use described in paragraph (1), (2), or (3) of Sec. 5102(a); and
- $200 per day and $2,000 in the aggregate for a use described in paragraph (4), (5), or (6) of Sec. 5102(a)." Sec. 5110(5) provides a special rule for care of family members whereby paid sick time provided for reasons 4, 5 or 6, the employee's required compensation shall be two-thirds of the required rate of pay.

The credit amount also ties to the $200 and $511 amounts (or less if normal wages are less). There are many rules regarding the coverage period, notice, prohibited acts, enforcement, definitions including "employee," public entities, and so on. For example, the "employer may not require employee to use other paid leave provided by the employer before the employee uses the paid sick time" provided by this new law. See the following examples.

EXAMPLE 1: Amber, a full-time employee, is unable to work because she has been advised by a healthcare provider to self-quarantine due to concerns related to COVID-19 (reason #2). Amber is unable to work starting the week of June 1, 2020. No health insurance costs are involved, and her employer has work for her to do. Amber's regular hourly pay is $24/hour. The minimum wage under the Fair Labor Standards Act (FLSA) is $7.25/hour, and the local minimum wage is $15.25/hour. Therefore, the greater amount is $24/hour: $24 × 8 hours = $192.

This is the sick leave daily amount, and it is below the maximum of $511 per day for leave taken for reasons 1, 2 or 3. Amber's maximum leave is two weeks (10 days). Her employer needs to get documentation from Amber for the leave.

EXAMPLE 2: Assume the same facts as in Example 1, except Amber is taking leave due to reason #4 (caring for her son because a doctor ordered him to self-quarantine). Again, she is unable to work starting the week of June 1, 2020. No health insurance costs are involved, and her employer has work for her to do. Amber's regular hourly pay is $24/hour. The minimum wage under the FLSA is $7.25/hour, and the local minimum wage is $15.25/hour. Therefore, the greater amount is $24/hour.

However, leave for reason #4 is calculated at two-thirds of the above amount ($16/hour), and $16 × 8 = $128. This amount is below the maximum of $200/day. Amber's maximum leave is two weeks (10 days). Her employer needs to get documentation from Amber regarding the leave.

Amber should see if she qualifies for any other leave from her employer or for other reasons. Note that the employer only gets a refundable tax credit for FFCRA leave.

EXAMPLE 3: Amber, a full-time employee, is claiming leave for reason #5 to care for her seven-year old son as school is closed and no childcare is available. Amber has worked for her employer for 30 days or more and is unable to work starting the week of April 6, 2020. No health insurance costs are involved, and her employer has work for Amber to do. Amber's regular hourly pay is $24/hour. The minimum wage under the FLSA is $7.25/hour, and the local minimum wage is $15.25/hour. Therefore, the greater amount is $24/hour.

Leave for reason #5 is calculated at two-thirds of the above amount ($16/hour), and $16 × 8 = $128. This amount is below the maximum of $200/day. Amber's maximum sick leave is two weeks (10 days).

Because reason #5 applies, Amber can get an additional 10 weeks of leave if she continues to qualify (discussed further below). Keep in mind that if school closes for summer break before then, reason #5 no longer applies, unless Amber is unable to obtain other child care. If Amber's reason for family leave after school closes for summer is unavailability of summer camp, the Department of Labor issued additional requirements for this reason to qualify. See DOL Field Assistance Bulletin No. 2020-4 (6/26/20); https://www.dol.gov/sites/dolgov/files/WHD/legacy/files/fab_2020_4.pdf.

As is the case in the other examples, Amber's employer must get documentation from her. If the reason for Amber's leave changes from school closure to lack of child care after school closes for summer break (but still within a 10 week leave period for Amber), new documentation is needed.

EXAMPLE OF CREDIT AMOUNT: Eligible Employer X pays $10,000 in qualified sick leave wages and qualified family leave wages in the second quarter of 2020. Assume the employer has no qualified health plan expenses. X does not owe the employer's share of Social Security tax on the $10,000 but owes $145 for its share of Medicare tax.

X's credits equal $10,145 ($10,000 in qualified leave wages + $145 for X's share of Medicare tax). X claims this credit against any federal employment taxes it is liable for on any wages paid in the second quarter 2020.

Any excess credit over this amount can be refunded using Form 7200. X must still withhold the employee's share of Social Security and Medicare taxes on the qualified leave wages it pays.

The payroll tax credit for required paid sick leave applies to leave taken starting April 1, 2020, and ending on December 31, 2010. Thus, it started for the second quarter of payroll for 2020.

Credit for Sick Leave for Certain Self-Employed Individuals

This credit is detailed in FFCRA Act Sec. 7002. It is a refundable credit against self-employment tax. The "qualified sick leave equivalent amount" equals the number of days the individual is unable to perform services for a reason that would entitle an employee to sick leave times the lesser of:

- $200 ($511 in the case of any day of paid sick time described in paragraph (1), (2), or (3) of Sec. 5102(a) of Emergency Paid Sick Leave Act), or
- 67 percent (100 percent in the case of any day of paid sick time described in paragraph (1), (2), or (3) of Sec. 5102(a) of the Emergency Paid Sick Leave Act) of the *average daily self-employment income* of the individual for the tax year.

The average daily self-employment income equals net earnings from self-employment for the year divided by 260. Information for 2020 is needed for the calculation, but a taxpayer can consider estimating it for estimated tax purposes. The maximum number of days allowed for sick leave is 10. If an individual is also receiving paid sick leave as an employee (for other work), an adjustment is required to avoid a double benefit.

Per Notice 2020-21, the credit for sick leave for self-employed individuals is effective starting April 1, 2020, through December 31, 2020. Specific IRS FAQs on paid leave credits for the self-employed are available at: https://www.irs.gov/newsroom/covid-19-related-tax-credits-special-issues-for-employees-and-additional-questions-faqs#specific.

Payroll Tax Credit for Required Paid Family Leave

Act Sec. 7003 of the FFCRA provides a 100 percent credit allowed by an employer against payroll taxes (Code Sec. 3111(a) or Code Sec. 3221(a)). The hours of leave are paid at two-thirds of the employee's regular rate of pay. The amount of qualified family leave wages taken into account for any individual shall not exceed:

- For any day (or portion thereof) for which the individual is paid qualified family leave wages, $200, and
- In the aggregate with respect to all calendar quarters, $10,000 ($200 per day times five days per week times ten weeks).

A credit is also allowed for "certain health plan expenses" (Act Sec. 7003(d)).

The payroll tax credit for required paid family leave is refundable against employment taxes. No double benefit is allowed:

- The employer increases gross income by the amount of the credit.
- Wages used to generate the credit may not be used to compute the Code Sec. 45S family and medical leave credit.

The IRS is to provide regulations needed to carry out the purpose of this credit. As of July 1, 2020, the IRS has provided answers to more than 60 FAQs about this credit at: https://www.irs.gov/newsroom/covid-19-related-tax-credits-for-required-paid-leave-provided-by-small-and-midsize-businesses-faqs.

Credit for Family Leave for Certain Self-Employed Individuals

FFCRA Act Sec. 7004 outlines a refundable credit against self-employment tax equal to 100 percent of the *qualified family leave equivalent amount*, which "means, with respect to any eligible self-employed individual, an amount equal to the product of:

- (A) the number of days (not to exceed 50) during the tax year that individual is unable to perform services in any trade or business for a reason with respect to which such individual would be entitled to receive paid leave, multiplied by
- (B) the lesser of—
- (i) 67 percent of *average daily self-employment income* of the individual for the tax year, or
- (ii) $200."

Average daily self-employment income is an amount equal to the net earnings from self-employment income of the individual for the taxable year, divided by 260.

If an individual is also receiving paid family leave as an employee (for other work), an adjustment is required to avoid a double benefit. Although self-employed individuals cannot claim the credit until they file their 2020 return, they can reduce their estimated taxes for the credit. The IRS will provide documentation requirements for this credit in the future.

Credit for Certain Health Plan Expenses

Certain health plan expenses can also generate a paid leave credit for employers. The general rule is that the employer credit is increased by so much of the employer's qualified health plan expenses as are properly allocable to qualified sick or family leave wages for which such credit is allowed. The amount of qualified health plan expenses taken into account in determining the credit generally includes both the portion of the cost paid by the eligible employer and the portion of the cost paid by the employee with pre-tax salary reduction contributions. Qualified health plan expenses do not include amounts that the employee paid for with after-tax contributions. For more details see FAQs 31–36 at https://www.irs.gov/newsroom/covid-19-related-tax-credits-determining-the-amount-of-allocable-qualified-health-plan-expenses-faqs.

Interaction of the Two Types of Paid Leave under the FFCRA

In its questions and answers related to FFCRA paid leave provisions (www.dol.gov/agencies/whd/pandemic/ffcra-questions), the DOL addresses how the two types of leave interact:

> **If I am home with my child because his or her school or place of care is closed, or child care provider is unavailable, do I get paid sick leave, expanded family and medical leave, or both—how do they interact?**
>
> You may be eligible for both types of leave, but only for a total of twelve weeks of paid leave. You may take both paid sick leave and expanded family and medical leave to care for your child whose school or place of care is

closed, or child care provider is unavailable, due to COVID-19 related reasons. The Emergency Paid Sick Leave Act provides for an initial two weeks of paid leave. This period thus covers the first ten workdays of expanded family and medical leave, which are otherwise unpaid under the Emergency and Family Medical Leave Expansion Act unless you elect to use existing vacation, personal, or medical or sick leave under your employer's policy. After the first ten workdays have elapsed, you will receive 2/3 of your regular rate of pay for the hours you would have been scheduled to work in the subsequent ten weeks under the Emergency and Family Medical Leave Expansion Act.

Please note that you can only receive the additional ten weeks of expanded family and medical leave under the Emergency Family and Medical Leave Expansion Act for leave to care for your child whose school or place of care is closed, or child care provider is unavailable, due to COVID-19 related reasons.

COMMENT: As of July 1, 2020, the DOL had published more than 90 FAQs to explain the FFCRA paid leave rules, and the IRS had published more than 60. Note that the FAQs are not binding guidance.

Guidance on Reporting Qualified Sick Leave Wages and Qualified Family Leave Wages Paid Pursuant to the Families First Coronavirus Response Act

In July 2020, the IRS issued Notice 2020-54 per its authority under the FFCRA Secs. 7002(g) and 7004€ to prescribe guidance as necessary to carry out the purposes of Secs. 7002 and 7004 of FFCRA on the sick and family leave for self-employed against self-employment tax. Also, the FFCRA provides that self-employed individuals are limited to $2,000 (or up to $5,110 sick leave credit for reasons 1, 2, 3) or $10,000 for family leave, so they must reduce any paid leave from an employer to be sure they do not exceed the maximums available to an employee.

To prevent self-employed individuals who are also employees from claiming too much sick and/or family leave (and related credits against self-employment tax) under the FFCRA, Notice 2020-54 requires the following of employers:

- Employers must separately state the total amount of qualified sick leave wages paid for reasons (1), (2), or (3) of Sec. 5102(a) of FFCRA, qualified sick leave wages paid pursuant to reasons (4), (5), and (6) of Sec. 5102(a), and qualified family leave wages paid per Sec. 3102(b) of FFCRA. Employers must separately state each of these wage amounts either on Form W-2, Box 14, or on a separate statement.
- Self-employed individuals claiming FFCRA credits against self-employment tax must attach new Form 7202, *Credits for Sick Leave and Family Leave for Certain Self-Employed Individuals*, and reduce (but not below zero) any qualified sick leave or qualified family leave equivalent credits by the amount of these qualified leave wages.

NOTE: At the time Notice 2020-54 was issued, there was no draft Form 7202 so it was not clear whether this form is needed only for self-employed individuals who are also employees or if it is also used to calculate the FFCRA leave credits for any self-employed individual.

The notice provides additional details on how to report the information on Form W-2 and that such information must be provided at the same time the employee is given the Form W-2.

Paid Leave Requirements and Tax Credits: Reminders

Taxpayers and practitioners should stay tuned for additional guidance from the IRS and DOL regarding the FFCRA paid leave requirements.

- Employers should watch for continued guidance (in any form) from the Treasury Department and the DOL, including any changes to the updated Form 941, *Employer's Quarterly Tax Return,* for the second quarter of 2020.
- Payroll processors should be providing information as well as asking clients for information on who gets paid leave under this law. Consider how to coordinate the documentation.
- Per Notice 2020-21, payroll and self-employment tax credits can first be claimed for qualified leave starting April 1, 2020, and through December 31, 2020.
- Notice 2020-22 provides relief from the penalty for failure to deposit employment taxes (both for FFCRA paid leave credits and the employee retention credit under the CARES Act).
- Self-employed: Unless the IRS provides another technique, self-employed taxpayers should adjust their 2020 estimated tax payments to reflect any credit for which they are eligible under the FFCRA and document why they are eligible.
- Although the question of whether an employee is entitled to paid leave under the FFCRA (or other laws) is a labor law determination/issue, the FFCRA leave ties closely to tax credits claimed.
- Practitioners must ensure their clients have reviewed the rules so they are properly paying sick or family leave per FFCRA reasons to get the credits. If they are paying for some other reason, the FFCRA paid leave credits are not available. Non-attorney tax practitioners will want to avoid answering client questions about the leave as whether or not an employee is entitled to paid leave under the FFCRA is not a tax matter.

COMMENT: Is it really okay not to deposit your payroll taxes? Yes. According to Notice 2020-22, there is no failure to deposit penalty under Code Sec. 6656. For example, the CARES Act Sec. 2301(k) states: "Secretary shall waive any penalty under Code Sec. 6656 for any failure to make a deposit of any applicable employment taxes if the Secretary determines that such failure was due to the reasonable anticipation of the credit allowed under this section."

Obtaining an Advance of Employer FFCRA Credits Due to COVID-19

The following example is adapted from IRS FAQ 40 (www.irs.gov/newsroom/covid-19-related-tax-credits-how-to-claim-the-credits-faqs#40).

EXAMPLE: ABC, an eligible employer, paid $10,000 in qualified leave wages (and allocable qualified health plan expenses and its share of Medicare tax on the qualified leave wages) and is otherwise required to deposit $8,000 in federal employment taxes, including taxes withheld from all of its employees, on wage payments made during the same quarter.

ABC can keep the $8,000 of taxes that it was otherwise required to deposit, without penalties, as a portion of the credits it is otherwise entitled to claim on its Form 941.

ABC may file a request for an advance credit for the remaining $2,000 by completing Form 7200.

Late Determinations

What if an employer doesn't realize until a later date that it should have paid qualified leave wages to an employee? According to IRS FAQ 43, the employer can claim the credits once it has paid the employee for the period of paid leave, as long as the qualified leave wages relate to leave taken during the period starting April 1, 2020 and ending on December 31, 2020.

Documentation Required

An employer must retain records and documentation on each employee's leave to support the credit claim and must retain Forms 941 and 7200 and any other filings requesting the credit. To substantiate it is eligible for tax credits for qualified leave wages, employers must provide detailed documentation; see the following for more information:

- IRS FAQs 44–46 at https://www.irs.gov/newsroom/covid-19-related-tax-credits-how-to-substantiate-eligibility-and-periods-of-time-for-which-credits-are-available-faqs#substantiate_eligibility.
- DOL FAQs 15 and 16 at https://www.dol.gov/agencies/whd/pandemic/ffcra-questions

Litigation on DOL Rules Issued April 6, 2020

In April 2020, the New York Attorney General filed an action against the U.S. Department of Labor. This suit challenged some provisions in the DOL rules issued April 6, 2020 (85 Fed. Reg. 19,326). One of these rules was the requirement that an employer have work for an employee to do in order to qualify for paid sick or family leave. The court ruled that the DOL was incorrect in providing this requirement. Be sure to see the opinion issued August 3, 2020 for the details of all four issues and why the court ruled for the State of New York.

Also, be sure to monitor actions by the Department of Labor and IRS in response to this case. As of mid-August 2020, it is not known if the DOL will file an appeal, limit the application to employers and employees in the Southern District of New York, seek clarification from Congress, or something else. [*State of New York v. U.S. Dept. of Labor*, 20-CV-3020 (SD NY, 8/3/20)]

Summary of FFCRA Paid Leave Credits

Reference Table of FFCRA Paid Leave Tax Credits			
Reason for Worker's Leave	**Duration**	**Amount of Pay**	**Other**
1. Is subject to a federal, state, or local quarantine or isolation order related to COVID-19.	Full-time employee eligible for up to 80 hours of leave, and a part-time employee eligible for number of hours of leave that employee works on average over a two-week period.	Employees taking leave shall be paid at either their regular rate or applicable minimum wage, whichever is higher, up to $511/day and $5,110 in aggregate (over a two-week period).	Additional reminders: • Who is eligible for the leave? Employees of *covered employees* who meet a reason for sick and or family/medical leave. *All employees* of covered employers are eligible for two weeks of paid sick time for specified reasons related to COVID-19, regardless of how long they have been with the employer. *Employees employed for at least 30 days* are eligible for up to an additional 10 weeks of paid family leave to care for a child under certain circumstances related to COVID-19. • The maximum amount of leave ties to reasons 1–6. • Employees must provide documentation to prove the reason for the leave. Employers need to be sure to obtain the required documentation to qualify for the credits. They also need to show how the credits are calculated and claimed.
2. Has been advised by a healthcare provider to self-quarantine related to COVID-19.			
3. Is experiencing COVID-19 symptoms and is seeking a medical diagnosis.			
4. Is caring for an individual subject to an order described in (1) or self-quarantine as described in (2).		Employees taking leave shall be paid at two-thirds their regular rate or two-thirds the applicable minimum wage, whichever is higher, up to $200/day and $2,000 in the aggregate (over a two-week period).	

Reason for Worker's Leave	Duration	Amount of Pay	Other
5. Is caring for a child whose school or place of care is closed (or childcare provider is unavailable) for reasons related to COVID-19.	Full-time employee eligible for up to 12 weeks of leave at 40 hours a week, and part-time employee eligible for leave for number of hours that employee is normally scheduled to work over that period.	Employees taking leave shall be paid at two-thirds their regular rate or two-thirds the applicable minimum wage, whichever is higher, up to $200 per day and $12,000 in the aggregate (over a 12-week period)—two weeks of paid sick leave followed by up to 10 weeks of paid expanded family and medical leave).	
6. Is experiencing any other substantially similar condition specified by the Secretary of Health and Human Services, in consultation with the Secretaries of Labor and Treasury.	Full-time employee eligible for up to 80 hours of leave, and a part-time employee eligible for number of hours of leave that employee works on average over a two-week period.	Employees taking leave shall be paid at two-thirds their regular rate or two-thirds the applicable minimum wage, whichever is higher, up to $200/day and $2,000 in the aggregate (over a two-week period).	

STUDY QUESTIONS

3. Which of the following employers would be eligible for the FFCRA paid leave refundable credits?

a. ABC Company, which has 100 full-time employees and 50 part-time employees

b. State Government X, which has 650 full-time employees

c. National Drug Store Chain, which employs a total of 590 part-time employees

d. Non-Profit Entity Z, which has 850 employees

4. The Emergency Family and Medical Leave Expansion Act (EFMLEA):

a. Was created by the CARES Act.

b. Covers employees who are unable to work or telework because of one of six reasons.

c. Provides up to 10 weeks of paid leave to certain employees.

d. Offers a refundable credit equal to 100 percent of the qualified family leave equivalent amount

5. According to IRS Notice 2020-21, payroll and self-employment tax credits can first be claimed for qualified leave starting on:

a. April 1, 2019

b. April 1, 2020

c. July 15, 2020

d. December 31, 2020

¶ 505 CARES ACT PAYROLL TAX BENEFITS

The CARES Act sections that outline payroll tax benefits are:

- Sec. 2301, Employee Retention Credit for Employers Subject to Closure Due to COVID-19
- Sec. 2302, Delay of Payment of Employer Payroll Taxes

Employee Retention Credit for Employers Subject to Closure Due to COVID-19

The employee retention credit (ERC) is outlined in the CARES Act; it is not covered in an Internal Revenue Code section. The ERC amount is 50 percent of the qualified wages of an employee, limited to $10,000 of wages/employee (so, $5,000 credit/employee).

For purposes, of this credit, ***qualified wages*** include cash wages and compensation and qualified health plan expenses properly allocable to the wages. The identification of qualified wages differs if an employer has more than 100 full-time employees versus 100 or fewer. The credit is for wages paid after March 12, 2020, and before January 1, 2021, but not if the wages are for paid leave eligible for paid leave credits (under the FFRCA, discussed earlier).

The credit applies where an eligible employer is paying wages despite:

1. Having to fully or partially suspend operations due to government orders, *or*
2. Experiencing over a 50 percent decline in gross receipts compared to same quarter of 2019

The ERC is fully refundable; it is applied against the employer portion of Social Security taxes (or railroad taxes) but is fully refundable via a reduction to payroll taxes owed. Employers can use Form 7200 to request a credit greater than its payroll taxes owed for the quarter.

Eligible employers. Employers eligible for the credit are those that are:

- Carrying on a trade or business during 2020, and
- Paying wages, despite for any quarter:
  1. Having to fully or partially suspend operations due to government orders, or
  2. Experiencing over a 50 percent decline in gross receipts compared to the same quarter of 2019.

Employer's gross receipts are measured per the Code Sec. 448(c) definition. They must be less than 50 percent of gross receipts for the same calendar quarter of 2019, and ending with the quarter following the first quarter where gross receipts exceed 80 percent of the gross receipts for the corresponding 2019 quarter. See IRS FAQs 39 through 46; https://www.irs.gov/newsroom/covid-19-related-employee-retention-credits-determining-when-an-employer-is-considered-to-have-a-significant-decline-in-gross-receipts-and-maximum-amount-of-an-eligible-employers-employee-retention#gross_receipts.

EXAMPLE: MEASURING IF THE REDUCED GROSS RECEIPTS REASON APPLIES: Jane's Grocery Store, an essential business, is not subject to the government shutdown for the COVID-19 pandemic. The store is eligible for the ERC only if its current quarter gross receipts are below 50 percent of the comparable 2019 quarter's gross receipts.

	2019 Gross Receipts	2020 Gross Receipts
Q1	$100x	$100x
Q2	$100x	$40x
Q3	$100x	$90x
Q4	$100x	$100x

Jane's Grocery Store meets the gross receipts test for Q2 and Q3.

Although there is no employer size limitation for the credit, qualified wages are measured differently if an employer has more than 100 full-time employees. The credit is for business and tax-exempt organization employers, and not for household employees. Code Sec. 501(c) tax-exempt organizations other than state and local governments and their instrumentalities can qualify under either test.

The ERC is not available to employers who receive a Paycheck Protection Program (PPP) loan. Governments and their agencies are *not* eligible for the ERC, and it is not available for self-employment income and taxes.

Employment tax reduction. Applicable employment taxes are reduced by:

- The Code Sec. 3111(e) credit for employment of qualified veterans by qualified tax-exempt organizations
- The Code Sec. 3111(f) credit for research expenditures of qualified small businesses
- FFCRA paid leave credits

Any excess is treated as an overpayment refundable under Code Sec. 6402(a) (authority to make credits or refunds) and Code Sec. 6413(b) (overpayments of certain employment taxes). *Applicable employment taxes* equal the employer's 6.2 percent Old-Age, Survivors, and Disability Insurance (OASDI) (or equivalent railroad tax).

Qualified wages. Qualified wages are limited to $10,000 per employee for all four quarters combined. Qualified wages include cash wages and employer-provided health-care expenses properly allocable to the wages. (The IRS is to provide rules on how to allocate to wages the costs for group health plans where the benefit is excludable by an employee under Code Sec. 106(a)).

According to IRS FAQ 63: "The amount of qualified health plan expenses taken into account in determining the amount of qualified wages generally includes both the portion of the cost paid by the Eligible Employer and the portion of the cost paid by the employee with pre-tax salary reduction contributions. However, the qualified health plan expenses should not include amounts that the employee paid for with after-tax contributions."

The IRS modified the following FAQs on qualified wages on May 7, 2020 (https://www.irs.gov/newsroom/covid-19-related-employee-retention-credits-amount-of-allocable-qualified-health-plan-expenses-faqs):

- FAQ 64: May an Eligible Employer that averaged 100 or fewer full-time employees in 2019 treat its health plan expenses as qualified wages for purposes of the Employee Retention Credit?
- FAQ 65: May an Eligible Employer that averaged more than 100 full-time employees in 2019 treat its health plan expenses as qualified wages for purposes of the Employee Retention Credit?

The IRS now allows health plan expenses as qualified wages even if no wages are paid such as because employees were furloughed, or for a large employer, hours were reduced but it is still paying the same health insurance amount for its employees. The term *qualified wages* does *not* include:

- Wages for which paid leave credits are claimed under the FFRCA
- Severance pay because there is no retention
- Wages paid by an employer to employees who are related individuals
- Wages pursuant to a preexisting vacation, sick, or other personal leave policy

Wages generally constitute all remuneration, including the value of taxable benefits per Code Secs. 3121(a) and 3231(e).

Qualified wages measure depends on size of the employer's workforce in 2019. For eligible employers for which the average number of full-time employees in 2019 was 100 or less, qualified wages are wages paid during such quarter described by reasons 1 or 2 to any employee.

EXAMPLE OF SMALL EMPLOYER: A1 Fitness Center closes but continues to pay its full-time employees for 30 hours per week. Those wages are qualified wages (30 hours per week per employee) not to exceed $10,000 per employee in aggregate for qualifying quarters.

For eligible employers for which the average number of full-time employees in 2019 exceeded 100, qualified wages are only the wages paid for when the employee is *not* providing services due to reasons (1) or (2)—that is, wages paid for not working.

EXAMPLE OF LARGE EMPLOYER: A restaurant employee works 15 hours but is paid for 40. Twenty-five hours equals qualified wages. If the employee is only paid for 15 hours, he has no qualified wages.

Qualified wages may not exceed the amount the employee would have been paid for working an equivalent duration during the 30 days immediately preceding the economic hardship period. For salaried workers, employers should use a reasonable method to measure the wages paid for not working. A drop in productivity is not an appropriate measure of time not worked.

Counting Employees: "Average Number of Full-Time Employees"		
Text of CARES Act Sec. 2301(c)(3)	**Joint Committee on Taxation (JCX-12R-20 (4/23/20), footnote 145)**	**IRS FAQ 49**
"the average number of full-time employees (within the meaning of section 4980H of the Internal Revenue Code of 1986)" [Code Sec. 4980H, Shared responsibility for employers regarding health coverage]	Includes full-time equivalents as referred to in Code Sec. 4980H(c)(2)(E): "(E) Full-time equivalents treated as full-time employees. Solely for purposes of determining whether an employer is an applicable large employer under this paragraph, an employer shall, in addition to the number of fulltime employees for any month otherwise determined, include for such month a number of full-time employees determined by dividing the aggregate number of hours of service of employees who are not full-time employees for the month by 120."	"The term 'full-time employee' means an employee who, with respect to any calendar month in 2019, had an average of at least 30 hours of service per week or 130 hours of service in the month (130 hours of service in a month is treated as the monthly equivalent of at least 30 hours of service per week), as determined in accordance with Code Sec. 4980H." Compute for each month of 2019, total and divide by 12.
Per Code Sec. 4980H: Applicable large employer (ALE) = for a calendar year, an employer who employed on average at least 50 full-time employees on business days in prior year (includes FTEs). Full-time "means, with respect to any month, an employee who is employed on average at least 30 hours of service per week"	Compute for each month of 2019, total, and divide by 12 to get the average for 2019.	The IRS does not include full-time equivalent employees as the Joint Committee on Taxation suggests.

Note: Neither the Joint Committee on Taxation report nor the IRS FAQs are binding.

Counting employees: Aggregation rule. Under the single-employer aggregation rule, all persons treated as a single employer under Code Sec. 52(a) or (b) or Code Sec. 414(m) or (o) are treated as one employer for purposes of this section. This rule is the same as the gross receipts aggregation rule of Code Sec. 448(c).

What if a related entity a business needs to aggregate with received a PPP loan? Are all parties treated as single employer ineligible for the ERC? IRS FAQ 26 answers that if one entity received a PPP loan, no employer in the group may claim the ERC. Employers must be aggregated for purposes of the following rules applicable to the ERC:

- Determining whether the employer has a trade or business operation that was fully or partially suspended due to orders related to COVID-19 from an appropriate governmental authority
- Determining whether the employer has a significant decline in gross receipts
- Determining whether the employer has more than 100 full-time employees

According to IRS FAQ 27, if an eligible employer is a member of an aggregated group, the amount of the ERC must be apportioned among members of the aggregated group on the basis of each member's proportionate share of the qualified wages giving rise to the credit.

Additional limitations in claiming the ERC. According to Code Sec. 51(i)(1), wages paid to certain related individuals are ineligible for the credit, such as an employee who owns over 50 percent of a corporate employer and certain relatives at Code Sec. 152(d)(2)(A) to (G) or dependent (H), member of the household. For example, wages paid to a child is not eligible.

As defined by Code Sec. 51(i)(1), a related individual is any employee who has any of the following relationships to the employee's employer who is an individual:

- A child or a descendant of a child
- A brother, sister, stepbrother, or stepsister
- The father or mother, or an ancestor of either
- A stepfather or stepmother
- A niece or nephew
- An aunt or uncle
- A son-in-law, daughter-in-law, father-in-law, mother-in-law, brother-in-law, or sister-in-law
- For a corporate employer, any person that bears a relationship described above with an individual owning, directly or indirectly, more than 50 percent in value of the outstanding stock of the corporation
- For non-corporate entity employer, any person that bears a relationship described above with an individual owning, directly or indirectly, more than 50 percent of the capital and profits interests in the entity
- If the employer is a trust or estate, a related individual includes a grantor, beneficiary, or fiduciary of the estate or trust, or any person that bears a relationship described above with an individual who is a grantor, beneficiary, or fiduciary of the estate or trust.

Under Code Sec. 280C(a), a wage deduction is reduced by the amount of the credit. The following example is from the Joint Committee on Taxation.

> **EXAMPLE:** An eligible employer pays $2,500 in qualified wages during a quarter. The ERC is $1,250. The OASDI on the $2,500 paid is $155.
>
> The employer reduces its payroll tax expense by $155 and only deducts $1,405 of qualified wages. $2,500 – ($1,250 – $155) = $1,405
>
> So the employer loses the wage deduction equal to credit but also gets to deduct OASDI on the total wages paid (arguably because it is already reducing the wages by amount of the ERC).
>
> $2,500 paid + $155 tax paid – $1,250 ERC = $1,405

An employee is not taken into account for any period in which the employer is allowed a work opportunity tax credit (WOTC) under Code Sec. 51. Is the employee removed from the employer's employee count or just the ERC? Just the latter is likely, but the guidance is not clear. According to IRS FAQ 83, "an Eligible Employer may not claim the Employee Retention Credit and the WOTC for the same employee for the same period of time." There is no double benefit; wages used to compute the ERC may not be used to compute the Code Sec. 45S employer credit for paid family and medical leave (added by the TCJA).

Additional rules for the ERC. Certified professional employer organizations (CPEOs) are allowed any ERC treated as a credit described in Code Sec. 3511(d)(2).

> **OBSERVATION:** Since the ERC is a non-Code provision, these types of rules might be easily overlooked today and in a later audit.

An employer can elect to not have the credit apply for any quarter. The IRS is to provide a procedure for this. According to FAQs 93 and 94, an employer can make the election by not claiming the ERC, but can claim it in a subsequent quarter in 2020; it can amend its Form 941 for an earlier quarter and claim the credit.

Getting the ERC funds. IRS FAQ 72 explains how an eligible employer can claim the refundable tax credit for qualified wages as follows:

> Eligible employers will report their total qualified wages for purposes of the Employee Retention Credit for each calendar quarter on their federal employment tax returns, usually Form 941, *Employer's Quarterly Federal Tax Return*. Employers also report any qualified sick leave and qualified family leave wages for which they are entitled to a credit under FFCRA on Form 941. The Form 941 is used to report income and social security and Medicare taxes withheld by the employer from employee wages, as well as the employer's share of social security and Medicare tax.
>
> In anticipation of receiving the Employee Retention Credit, Eligible Employers can fund qualified wages by: (1) accessing federal employment taxes, including withheld taxes that are required to be deposited with the IRS, and (2) requesting an advance of the credit from the IRS for the amount of the credit that is not funded by accessing the federal employment tax deposits, by filing Form 7200, *Advance Payment of Employer Credits Due to COVID-19*.

The IRS issued a reminder to taxpayers that they should not include the ERC on their first quarter Form 941. Taxpayers cannot claim the ERC until the second quarter of 2020.

New Form 7200 for Paid Leave Credits and ERC

Form 7200, *Advance Payment of Employer Credits Due to COVID-10*, is filed to obtain a refundable payroll credit if the following credits exceed the amount of payroll taxes owed:

- Paid leave credits of FFCRA
- Employee retention credit of CARES Act

The form can be filed by faxing it to 855-248-0552. See the form instructions for more information.

Signing Form 7200 for refundable payroll tax credits. A reporting agent (RA) can sign Form 7200 for a client for which it has the authority, via Form 8655, *Reporting Agent Authorization*, to sign and file the employment tax return (e.g., Form 941, *Employer's Quarterly Federal Tax Return*). The signatory must be the principal or responsible official listed on the RA's e-file application. The signatory may sign with ink on paper or use the alternative signature method (rubber stamp, mechanical device, or computer software program; for details and required documentation, see Rev. Proc. 2005-39, 2005-28 IRB 82. The RA will submit the form via fax and must obtain written authorization from the client (paper, fax, or e-mail) to perform these actions. The RA does not need to submit that authorization to the IRS but should retain it in its files so that the RA can furnish it to the IRS upon request. For a client for which the RA does not have a Reporting Agent Authorization, the RA may complete and print the form, or it may provide the client with a means to complete and print the form, but the client will have to sign it.

Common Form 7200 errors. According to the IRS's COVID Tax Tip 2020-47, dated April 29, 2020: "Using a reputable tax preparer—including certified public accountants, enrolled agents or other knowledgeable tax professionals—can also help avoid errors.

Mistakes can result in a processing delay, which means it may take longer to get the advanced payment."

To avoid common errors, the IRS suggests the following:

- **Make sure to include an accurate Employer Identification Number.** Each EIN should be exact. Taxpayers must complete this box.
- **Check only one box for the applicable calendar quarter.** Only one box should be checked for the correct quarter.
- **Check only one box for Part 1, Line A.**
- **Make sure to complete Part 1, Line B.** In Part 1, Line B, check either Yes or No.
- **Complete Part II, Lines 1–8 using actual dollar amounts.** Part II should be completed using dollar amounts, not the number of eligible employees. All lines in Part II should be completed with an actual dollar amount.
- **Check the math.** Taxpayers should make sure they check the math on Lines 4, 7 and 8.
- **Sign the form.** Taxpayers should remember to sign the form. Failure to sign it will result in an automatic rejection.

ERC Recordkeeping

As of July 1, 2020, there was no official guidance on ERC recordkeeping. However, there seems to be a great deal of information to prove, including:

- A government order that fully or partially suspended operations or proof of a required decline in gross receipts compared to the same quarter in the prior year
  — Or both; perhaps a government order exists for the second and third quarters, or there is no government order but the business experiences a significant decline in gross receipts.
- The number of full-time employees in 2019 (particularly if the number is close to 100)
  — Determine if the aggregation rule applies.
- If the entity has more than 100 employees, it must provide proof of the hours paid for not working and that the amount was not more than the amount the employee would have been paid for working an equivalent duration in the 30 days immediately preceding the hardship period.
- Qualified health plan expenses (although wages might be enough to reach the $10,000 maximum per employee).

OBSERVATION: It might not be easy to show that a person is working fewer hours, such as due to work-from-home interruptions. It is unclear what type of documentation would be needed in this case.

Taxpayers and practitioners should watch for guidance from the IRS on recordkeeping and other developments. According to CARES Act Sec. 2301(l), the IRS is to provide forms, instructions, regulations, and guidance as necessary:

- To allow advance payment of the ERC, subject to the limitations in Sec. 2301
- To provide for reconciliation of an advance payment with the amount advanced at the time of filing a return of tax for the applicable quarter or year

- To provide for recapture of the ERC if the employer receives a PPP loan
- For application of the gross receipts test for any employer not carrying on a business for all or part of the same calendar quarter in 2019

EXAMPLE: PPP VERSUS ERC: Bert's Restaurant has been in business since 2009. It had an average of 10 full-time employees in 2019, and its 2019 payroll costs were $453,000. The restaurant partially closed on March 26, 2020, due to the state's shelter-in-place order, and switched to pick-up orders only. As a result, Bert's saw a 60 percent drop in its gross receipts.

Its PPP loan amount is determined as follows:

$453,000 ÷ 12 × 2.5 = $94,375 maximum loan amount

There is a possibility that all or part of the loan is forgiven and not taxable. According to IRS Notice 2020-32, there is no deduction of expenses paid via a forgiven PPP loan.

The ERC is calculated as follows:

10 employees × maximum credit of $5,000 each = $50,000

This assumes $10,000 of qualified wages are paid to each of the 10 employees in the second, third, and fourth quarters combined.

What If an Employer Cannot Measure Gross Receipts Until a Later Period?

The following question and answer are from IRS FAQ 42:

> **If an Eligible Employer does not determine that it had a significant decline in gross receipts in 2020 until after January 1, 2021, may it still be eligible for ERC on qualified wages paid in 2020?**
>
> Yes. The employer may claim ERC on qualified wages paid in 2020 if it determines that a significant decline in gross receipts occurred in 2020 even if it does not make the determination until after January 1, 2021. In this case, the employer may claim the credit by filing the appropriate form to report adjustments to its employment taxes, typically Form 941-X, Adjusted Employer's Quarterly Federal Tax Return or Claim for Refund.

If an employer fails to claim the ERC and realizes later that it was entitled to the credit, it should amend its Form 941 for the appropriate quarter of 2020 (but any Q1 ERC is claimed in Q2).

What Is the Effect on the Federal Old-Age and Survivors Insurance Trust Fund?

The credit is against the employer share of the OASDI (6.2 percent), plus the refundable amount beyond that has to come from somewhere. CARES Act Sec. 2301(i) states that amounts not deposited due to the ERC are to be transferred from the general fund "at such times and in such manner as to replicate *to the extent possible* the transfers which would have occurred to such Trust Fund or Account had this section not been enacted" [emphasis added].

Sec. 2302 Delay of Payment of Employer Payroll Taxes

Employers (businesses and non-profits) may defer the deposit and payment of their share of FICA, and self-employed individuals may defer payment of 50 percent of the FICA portion of their self-employment taxes (1/2 of 12.4 percent tax). No deferral of Medicare tax is allowed. This deferral is effective for applicable employment taxes for the period beginning March 27, 2020, and ending December 31, 2020 ("payroll tax deferral period").

The deferral applies to all employers (not only those eligible for payroll credits under the CARES Act). An employer may defer the payment before it knows if it is entitled to the credits or amounts.

Deferred deposits of employers and the self-employed must be deposited by the following dates (the "applicable dates") to be treated as timely (and avoid a failure to deposit penalty):

- On December 31, 2021, 50 percent of the deferred amount; and
- On December 31, 2022, the remaining amount.

OBSERVATION: The year 2020 is the last year (under CARES Act changes) to carry back a net operating loss for five years, so the taxpayer might not want to defer the payment.

¶ 506 EXAMPLE, SUMMARY CHARTS, AND RESOURCES

Let's look at an example of the ERC with and without an OASDI deferral. An employer (ER), a gym with 100 or fewer employees, is shut down due to the COVID-19 pandemic and has just a few employees working for security and maintenance purposes. (The gym is a non-essential business and an eligible employer for the ERC.) The employer continues to pay its four employees 80 percent of their normal pay. Since there are 100 or fewer employees, all wages paid due to the government shutdown in the second quarter are qualified wages, subject to the aggregate wage limit of $10,000 per employee. None of these wages is for the FFCRA required paid leave (so there are no payroll leave credits). Assume ER has no healthcare costs.

Employee	Q2 wages	Federal Income Tax (FIT)	EE OASDI + HI (7.65%)	ER OASDI (6.2%)	ER HI (1.45%)	ERC
Amy	$15,000	$1,500	$1,148	$930	$218	$5,000
Bob	$9,000	$1,000	$689	$558	$131	$4,500
Cara	$16,000	$2,000	$1,224	$992	$232	$5,000
Duoc	$20,000	$2,800	$1,530	$1,240	$290	$5,000
Total taxes		$7,300	$4,591	$3,720	$871	
ERC						$19,500

The total taxes owed for the quarter are $16,482 [$7,300 + $4,591 + $3,720 + $871].

	Scenario 1: ER opts to defer payment of $3,720, so its tax owed in 2020 is $12,762* [$7,300 + $4,591 + $871] * Also see IRS ERC FAQ 74 and Deferral FAQ 6.	**Scenario 2: ER does not defer its share of OASDI ($3,720), so its total payroll tax of $16,482 is owed in 2020. ER is confident in its Q2 ERC amount, so it sees no reason to defer its OASDI tax.**
ERC	$19,500	$19,500
Excess ERC over tax owed; claim on Form 7200	$6,738	$3,018
Deferred ER OASDI owed at 12/31/21 (50%)	$1,860	$0
Balance of ER OASDI deferral due 12/31/22	$1,860	$0

	Scenario 1: ER opts to defer payment of $3,720, so its tax owed in 2020 is $12,762* [$7,300 + $4,591 + $871] * Also see IRS ERC FAQ 74 and Deferral FAQ 6.	**Scenario 2: ER does not defer its share of OASDI ($3,720), so its total payroll tax of $16,482 is owed in 2020. ER is confident in its Q2 ERC amount, so it sees no reason to defer its OASDI tax.**
Cash flow reconciliation	Q2 payroll receives/keeps $11,891 [$7,300 + $4,591] from employee withholding Q2 941 pays zero Form 7200 receives $6,738 12/31/21 pays $1,860 12/31/22 pays $1,860 NET $14,909	Q2 payroll receives/keeps $11,891 [$7,300 + $4,591] from employee withholding Q2 941 pays zero Form 7200 receives $3,018 NET $14,909
Strategy	Obtain $3,720 more funds for 2020 but need to pay it to the government ratably at 12/31/21 and 12/31/22	Less funds for 2020 but no need to worry about payments of the 2020 ER OASDI in 2021 and 2022

For both scenarios in the preceding chart, the employer must reduce its wages deduction on its 2020 income tax return by the ERC of $19,500.

Comparisons

The following charts compare several aspects of the employment tax provisions of the FFCRA and CARES Act.

Provision	**Source***	**Effective Dates**	**How to Claim**	**PPP Connection**	**Interaction with Other Rules**
Paid leave credits for employers with <500 employees and for self-employed	FFRCA Secs. 7001–7005	For required paid leave taken starting 4/1/20 and ending on 12/31/20	Fully refundable. Apply against payroll taxes owed; Form 7200 for refundable credit greater than payroll taxes owed.	Okay to also receive PPP loan, but qualified leave wages are not eligible as a "payroll cost" for loan forgiveness.	Employer increases gross income by amount of credit. Wages for credit cannot be used for Code Sec. 45S credit.
Employee retention credit for employers of any size; not for self-employed	CARES Act Sec. 2301	Wages paid after 3/12/20 and before 1/1/21		Not available if receive PPP loan.	Not applicable for wages used for paid leave credits. Related party limit (Code Sec. 51(i)(1)). Reduce wage deduction by credit (Code Sec. 280C(a)). Wages for credit cannot be used for Code Sec. 45S credit.

Provision	Source*	Effective Dates	How to Claim	PPP Connection	Interaction with Other Rules
Delay payment of employer and self-employed OASDI 6.2 percent tax; no employer size limit	CARES Act Sec. 2302	For applicable employment taxes for period beginning 3/27/20 and ending 12/31/20	Defer 50 percent to 12/31/21; balance to 12/31/22. Look for changes to Form 941.	P.L. 116-142 (6/5/20) modified the CARES Act to allow an employer with a forgiven PPP loan to also defer payroll taxes.	
* These provisions are only in the Public Law; no changes were made to the Internal Revenue Code. Documentation is needed for each provision; watch for more IRS guidance.					

Provision	Counting Employees
Paid leave credits for employers with <500 employees and for self-employed	FMLA 101(4) is modified to read: Any person engaged in commerce or in any industry or activity affecting commerce who employs fewer than 500 employees Interim temporary rules under Code Sec. 826.40(a): Count all full-time and part-time employees working in the United States at the time leave would be taken (headcount, not FTE). Includes employees on leave, employees jointly employed, and day laborers supplied by temp placement agency. Excludes independent contractors and furloughed/laid off employees. Includes employees of integrated employers per FLSA. If one corporation owns an interest in another, the two are separate employers unless they are joint employers under the FLSA.
Employee retention credit for employers of any size; not for self-employed	All employers (except certain government employers) are eligible. Number of employees is relevant in measuring qualifying wages. If employer has 100 or fewer employees, all wages paid due to reason 1 or 2 are qualified wages. If it has over 100 employees, qualified wages are only those paid while the employee is not working. Per the Joint Committee on Taxation report, count the number of employees as including full-time equivalent employees. Per the IRS, only count full-time employees (per Code Sec. 4980H, those working on average 30 or more hours per week or 130 hours of service in the month). Employer must apply the aggregation rules of Code Sec. 52(b) and (b) and Code Sec. 414(m) or (o). Note: The definition of FT between the IRS and JCT is significantly different.
Delay payment of employer and self-employed OASDI 6.2 percent tax; no employer size limit	N/A

Provision	Meaning and Relevance of Full-Time and Part-Time Employees
Paid leave credits for employers with <500 employees and for self-employed	Full-time for EPSLA is an employee normally scheduled to work 40 or more hours per week (otherwise the employee is part-time). Full-time employee can get up to 80 hours of paid sick leave. Part-time employees get the number of hours they work on average over a two-week period. For EFMLEA there is no relevance between full-time and part-time employees, although the number of hours normally worked affects amount of paid leave the employee is eligible to receive.
Employee retention credit for employers of any size; not for self-employed. Number of FT employees is relevant to know what are "qualified wages" for the employer.	IRS FAQ 49: "Full-time employee" is an employee who for any calendar month in 2019 had an average at least 30 hours of service per week or 130 hours of service in the month as determined per Code Sec. 4980H. An employer that operated for all of 2019 measures the number of FT employees by taking the sum of the number of full-time employees each month and dividing by 12. See FAQ 49 if the employer is not in business for all of 2019. JCT CARES Act Report (JCX-12R-20; 4/23/20): Include full-time equivalent in counting number of FT employees; FT means 30 or more hours per week. See Code Sec. 4980H. IRS and JCT: Aggregation rule same as under Code Sec. 448 for measuring gross receipts applies in counting full-time employees.
Delay payment of employer and self-employed OASDI 6.2 percent tax	N/A No employer size limit or relevance of FT versus PT

Provision	Does the Benefit Apply to Household Employees?
Paid leave credits for employers with <500 employees and for self-employed	Applies to an employer that is considered an employer under the Fair Labor Standards Act (FLSA). Example: Full-time nanny working in a home is economically dependent on the employer. Also may apply to an employer who files Schedule H (Form 1040) for the worker. Not required for a worker who is self-employed or working for an agency/employer.
Employee retention credit for employers of any size; not for self-employed Number of FT employees is relevant to know what are "qualified wages" for the employer.	No. It is only available to employers who are a trade or business or non-profit entity.
Delay payment of employer and self-employed OASDI 6.2 percent tax	Appears to apply as the CARES Act doesn't limit this to an employer in a trade or business.

COVID-19 Tax Resources

Consult the following resources for information on COVID-19 tax implications:

- Text of public laws
  - — PL 116-127, FFCRA: https://www.congress.gov/bill/116th-congress/house-bill/6201
  - — PL 116-136, CARES Act: https://www.congress.gov/bill/116th-congress/house-bill/748
- IRS guidance website: https://www.irs.gov/coronavirus/coronavirus-and-economic-impact-payments-resources-and-guidance

- Joint Committee on Taxation, Description of the Tax Provisions of Public Law 116-136, The Coronavirus Aid, Relief, And Economic Security ("CARES") Act: https://www.jct.gov/publications.html?func=startdown&id=5256
- Joint Committee on Taxation, Technical Explanation of Division G, "Tax Credits For Paid Sick and Paid Family and Medical Leave," of H.R. 6201, The "Families First Coronavirus Response Act": https://www.jct.gov/publications.html?func=startdown&id=5251

CAUTION: Remember that the IRS FAQs and form instructions are not binding. Hopefully, binding guidance will be issued and tie to the extensive FAQs released.

¶ 507 SAMPLING OF PAYROLL-RELATED COVID-19 LEGISLATIVE PROPOSALS

The following are just some of the proposed legislative acts introduced in connection with the COVID-19 pandemic.

- H.R. 6776, Jumpstarting Our Businesses' Success Credit (JOBS) Act
  - Would increase the ERC from 50 percent to 80 percent of qualified wages.
  - Would increase the $10,000 wage maximum to $15,000 per quarter and $45,000 maximum.
  - Would increase the threshold for large employer from over 100 full-time employees to over 1,500 and over $41.5 million of gross receipts.
  - Also includes other changes.
- S. 3779 would create a tax credit for training services received by individuals unemployed due to the pandemic.
- H.R. 6695, Excluding Pandemic Unemployment Compensation from Income Act
- H.R. 6396, Responsible Relief for Americans Act
  - Eliminates the paid leave mandate.
  - Increases the Code Sec. 199A deduction from 20 percent to 43 percent (47 percent after 2025).
  - Repeals the Code Sec. 199A specified service trade or business exclusion.
  - States there is no taxable event if a corporation changes to another entity form with the same owners and interests.
  - Repeals estate tax and retains the basis step-up.
  - Includes PPP changes.
- S.3793
  - Amends the CARES Act to modify the ERC to secure the paychecks and benefits of workers, to provide a refundable credit against payroll taxes for operating costs of employers, to provide a small business rebate, and for other purposes.
- H.R. 6567, GROCER Act of 2020
  - Excludes from gross income, compensation, and other income up to $25,000 paid to certain retail grocery and gasoline service station employees between February 15, 2020, and June 15, 2020, who are working in a county that has at least one confirmed case of COVID-19. The period may be extended for an additional three months if the Treasury determines that the COVID-19 emergency is likely to be ongoing during such extended period.

- H.R. 6484, Hazard Pay for Health Care Employees During Public Health Emergencies
  - Requires employers to pay specified healthcare workers 125 percent of such workers' regular rate of pay during a federal public-health emergency. Generally, healthcare workers who provide direct and essential services are eligible for such hazard pay. Workers not eligible for such pay include, among others, dentists, optometrists, physical therapists, and other therapists and related technicians.
  - Employers receive a payroll tax credit for up to 100 percent of the hazard wages paid each calendar quarter.

¶ 508 RELATED STATE AND LOCAL LAWS

Some states, such as California, already had required sick leave laws before the pandemic. Some states and local governments added required sick leave in response to COVID-19, such as to cover employers with 500 or more employees, but they likely do not provide any tax credits.

The COVID employment tax credits are not in the Internal Revenue Code. Therefore, there is likely no automatic state conformity. Practitioners should check how a particular state treats the addition of paid leave credits to gross income or the reduction to the wage deduction for the ERC. They should also determine if any special state or local tax provision is allowed.

STUDY QUESTION

6. Which of the following statements about the employee retention credit (ERC) is true?

a. The ERC amount is 50 percent of the qualified wages of an employee, subject to a certain limitation.

b. The ERC is partially refundable.

c. There is an employer size limitation for the ERC.

d. The ERC applies to state government agencies.

CPE NOTE: When you have completed your study and review of chapters 3-5, which comprise Module 2, you may wish to take the Final Exam for this Module. Go to **cchcpelink.com/printcpe** to take this Final Exam online.

MODULE 3: DEBT—Chapter 6: Tax Issues Involving Troubled Borrowers

¶ 601 WELCOME

Troubled borrowers face numerous tax issues, and sometimes tax surprises, in the context of debt workouts and bankruptcy. This chapter addresses the creation and exclusion of cancellation of indebtedness income, debt modifications, tax attribute reduction, the treatment of tax claims in bankruptcy, and the taxation of the bankruptcy estate.

¶ 602 LEARNING OBJECTIVES

Upon completion of this chapter, you will be able to:

- Explain the difference in tax treatment between cancellation of recourse debt and foreclosures of property securing non-recourse debt
- Identify situations when cancellation of indebtedness income may be excluded under Code Section 108
- Describe which types of debt modifications are treated as exchanges, and the tax consequences
- Explain the tax treatment of claims in bankruptcy and the taxation of the bankruptcy estate
- Identify what is considered first in the order of basis reduction

¶ 603 CANCELLATION OF INDEBTEDNESS INCOME

Cancellation of indebtedness (COD) income, also called *discharge of indebtedness income*, occurs when a debt that a taxpayer owed has been reduced, cancelled, or forgiven in some way (e.g., the creditor accepts less than full balance) and the taxpayer is creating income by virtue of that cancellation, forgiveness, or reduction.

According to Code Sec. 61(a)(12), discharge of indebtedness is included in gross income. There is an accession "to wealth" under two theories:

- **Freeing of assets theory:** A decrease in the taxpayer's liabilities increases the taxpayer's net worth.
- **Loan proceeds theory:** The taxpayer received "something for nothing." A debtor who receives funds in the form of a loan has an offsetting obligation to repay those funds. Therefore, the funds are not included in income and are tax-free. If the taxpayer does not repay the funds, however, the taxpayer must include them in income. Borrowing is treated as an "open" item until repayment or discharge, as though the taxpayer used the income to satisfy the debt.

The loan proceeds theory is the stronger of the two theories. There is no COD income if the holder has no "basis" in the obligation, for example, if the debtor did not get anything for the debt.

EXAMPLE: A corporation decided to declare a dividend to its shareholders and paid for it with bonds. Dividends are not deductible, so the corporation did not receive a tax deduction. The corporation decided to pay for that dividend by issuing bonds, and later, the corporation repurchased the bonds at a discount.

There is no COD income in this case because there is no tax effect to the borrowing and no receipt of income or property from the borrowing (the issuance of the bonds).

What Is Debt?

In order to have cancellation of indebtedness income, a taxpayer must have a valid debt. *Debt* is defined as an unconditional and legally enforceable obligation for the payment of money. A gift is not a true debt because there is no expectation of repayment. To determine what is and is not a debt, one should look to the traditional debt/equity tests and the intent of the parties (i.e., whether the borrower intended to repay and whether the lender wanted to be sure to collect).

Traditional debt/equity tests include looking for formalities that indicate that something is debt, typically a fixed obligation to repay a set amount. However, in some cases, even though something is set forth as a debt, perhaps it is disguised equity. Any loans that are made to a financially distressed party may actually be considered to be equity rather than debt. If the entity receiving the loans is severely undercapitalized, even though the loans may be called debt, there is no expectation of repayment. Under debt/equity tests, one should look at whether it would be reasonable for a lender in that situation to expect to be repaid. Similarly, consider whether a lender is getting equity participation, that is, whether it will be sharing in the equity or the growth of the business.

Disputed Debt/Contested Liability

There is no COD income if a debt is disputed or unliquidated (e.g., illegal gambling debts that were not enforceable under state law could be considered to be disputed debts). If debts are not legally enforceable, then having them forgiven will not result in cancellation of indebtedness. Similarly, if the amount of the debt has not been determined, that too would be an unliquidated debt. It will not become cancellation of indebtedness income until it is forgiven and the amount is acknowledged and fixed by either a settlement or a court order. Relief of a contingent liability does not result in COD because there was never an unconditional obligation to repay.

What Is a Discharge?

A discharge is a true cancellation or forgiveness by the lender (including in a workout where the lender reduces the amount owed). A cancellation by operation of law (e.g., a bankruptcy) also constitutes a discharge. The following are ***not*** considered discharges:

- Setoffs of amounts between debtor and creditor (counterclaims)
- A "spurious" discharge, that is, whether it is really a cancellation of debt or a disguised payment. An example is when a debt is paid off with goods or services. The parties may have some other type of income, but not COD income.

Guarantees

Guarantees are something for which the taxpayer is not the primary obligor, not the primary borrower, but just a guarantor of someone else's loan. The guarantor will not have cancellation of indebtedness income upon release from the guarantee because the guarantor did not get "something for nothing." The guarantee is a contingent liability until it is triggered by actually guaranteeing the debt and paying it off.

There cannot be a situation where there is double COD income. The main party to have COD income, of course, should be the debtor rather than the guarantor. If the guarantor pays the debt, the debtor should have income based on the fact that he was relieved of an obligation by someone else. That is not COD income.

Measuring COD Income

Generally, the amount of cancellation of indebtedness income is the difference between the adjusted issue price of the debt (remaining balance) and the holder's amount realized (what it had to give to satisfy the debt). This measurement can be more complicated in foreclosure situations, particularly in the context of nonrecourse debt.

Discharge of Indebtedness: Section 108 Exclusions

The Code Sec. 108 exclusions offer relief for certain financially troubled taxpayers. They typically allow taxpayers to exclude cancellation of indebtedness income in exchange for reducing the basis in property or giving up certain tax attributes.

The exclusions are based on the judicially created insolvency exception. Code Sec. 108 was issued to codify and broaden those exceptions. The rules under Code Sec. 108 attempt to strike a compromise between a "fresh start" for the debtor (which is the underlying theory of bankruptcy law) and tax policy, which entails raising revenue and treating taxpayers fairly. Generally, attribute and basis reduction are the "price" of excluding cancellation of indebtedness income. This preserves the income for future recognition.

The Code Sec. 108 exclusions override the income inclusion rule of Code Sec. 61(a)(12) in limited circumstances, such as situations in which the borrower is experiencing financial difficulty or for certain types of indebtedness.

Only true income can be excluded from discharge of indebtedness. A taxpayer cannot exclude ***Tufts*** type gains on the disposition of property (see ***Commissioner v. Tufts***, 461 U.S. 300 (1983)). That case involved a foreclosure of a property that was subject to nonrecourse debt. It was considered gain on the sale of the property rather than cancellation of indebtedness income.

The key Code Sec. 108 exceptions are:

- Bankruptcy
- Insolvency
- Qualified farm indebtedness
- Qualified real property business indebtedness
- Other situations that involve solvent debtors without a qualified debt (e.g., purchase price adjustment, deductible payment, contribution to capital, unamortized premium/discount in debt instrument, or partnership debt-for-equity exchanges)

Bankruptcy exception. For this exclusion to apply, the taxpayer must be subject to the jurisdiction of a bankruptcy court in a Title 11 case. The taxpayer gets a full exclusion of any cancellation of indebtedness income; it is not limited to the extent of the taxpayer's insolvency. The discharge of the debt must be granted by a court or pursuant to a plan approved by a court (i.e., this exception does not apply to individual debt workouts outside of a bankruptcy).

Insolvency exception. This is probably the most widely used Code Sec. 108 exception. In this case, the amount excluded is limited to the amount by which the taxpayer is insolvent, which equals the excess of the taxpayer's liabilities over its assets. The treatment of assets exempt from a bankruptcy estate is unclear. The treatment of contingent liabilities also is unclear, but they are probably included if it is more likely than not that they will be called upon. Nonrecourse debt is included only if it is being discharged and only to the extent that the debt is greater than the fair market value of the property securing it.

Qualified farm indebtedness. Farmers need a special rule because a farm is a non-liquid asset. Discharged debt must be incurred in connection with the operation of a farming trade or business. If the debt is secured by farmland or by equipment, it will count as debt incurred in the operation of a farming trade or business. An income test (a three-year income lookback) must be met to prove that the individual is really a farmer.

The debt must be held by a bona fide creditor. The exclusion is limited to the farmer's tax attributes (e.g., tax credits, net operating losses, capital loss carryforwards) and the basis of qualified property. The property must be used in a trade or business.

Qualified real property business indebtedness. This exclusion is meant to facilitate debt workouts for real estate by deferring recognition of gain until the property is sold. The taxpayer must elect this treatment, and the debt must be:

- Incurred or assumed in connection with real property used in a trade or business and secured by that real property. Offering the property for rent counts as a trade or business.
- Qualified acquisition indebtedness (used to acquire or substantially improve real property). Land qualifies for this.

However, there are some limitations. The taxpayer can only exclude the amount of discharged liability that exceeds the net fair market value of the property (not including discharged debt). Taxpayers cannot exclude more than the aggregate adjusted bases of depreciable real property (including real property unrelated to this debt). The "price" of this exclusion is reducing basis.

Qualified principal residence exclusion. This exclusion allows taxpayers to exclude up to $2 million, and they must reduce their basis accordingly. It must be acquisition indebtedness (acquisition, construction, or substantial improvement) on a principal residence (tied to the Code Sec. 121 definition). Home equity indebtedness is not included, and the discharge will be considered to be the first home equity amount (if any). This exclusion is covered in IRS Notice 2016-72 and has been extended through December 31, 2020.

Purchase price adjustment exclusion. The purchase price adjustment is interesting because it is both a Code Sec. 108 statutory exclusion and a judicial exception. It was initially created as a judicial exception, and the judicial exception is a bit broader. When Congress codified the Code Sec. 108 exceptions, it slightly narrowed the scope of this exclusion. If debt is reduced due to disputes over a purchase transaction or a subsequent decline in the value of a property, the reduction is treated as a purchase price reduction with a reduction in basis for the owner and a reduction in gain for the seller. Later, depreciation deductions are reduced based on the new, lower basis.

For the statutory exception, there must be purchase money debt between the buyer and seller (no third-party lending or later assignments of debt). The debtor cannot be insolvent or in bankruptcy, and the amount must otherwise be COD income.

Attribute Reduction

Attribute reduction is the "price" of excluding COD income. Code Sec. 108 provides rules for reducing tax attributes and also for reducing basis. First, a taxpayer determines its tax for the taxable year of discharge, including COD income. Then, the taxpayer applies any net operating loss (NOL) carryovers and Code Sec. 108 exclusions that may reduce COD income.

> **EXAMPLE:** Taxpayer P has $7,000 of cancellation of indebtedness income and is insolvent by $3,000. She has a $5,000 NOL carryforward and $1,000 of other gross income during the year. Taxpayer P will use the NOL against $5,000 of income. She will exclude the remaining $3,000 under the insolvency exception and

has no more tax attributes to reduce. Her COD income will disappear because she has used all of her tax attributes and does not have any basis to reduce.

Code Sec. 108(b)(2) specifies the order of attribute reduction as follows:

- NOLs
- Certain tax credits (reduced $1 for every $3 of COD income)
- Capital losses and capital loss carryovers
- Basis in property (first depreciable, then nondepreciable)
- Passive activity loss carryovers
- Foreign tax credits

The order for basis reduction is:

- Real property used in a trade or business (other than inventory) that secured the discharged debt
- Personal property used in a trade or business (other than inventory) that secured the discharged debt
- Remaining property used in a trade or business (other than inventory and accounts receivable)
- Inventory, accounts receivable, and real property held as inventory
- Property not used in a trade or business or investment

There are other considerations for reducing tax attributes and limitations that may apply to basis reduction. Other suspended losses or tax benefits to be used in the future would be subject to tax attribute reduction because those suspended losses or other types of miscellaneous credits to be used in the future also have to be wiped out. According to commentators, if something is not specifically listed in the rules, the general consensus is that it does not have to be reduced. There is no general requirement to reduce other types of tax attributes that are not listed. Taxpayers should be able to sell their assets to satisfy their liabilities and not have gain, so they cannot reduce basis in property below the amount of the nondischarged debt that remains.

The idea is to balance tax policy, making people pay their fair share with a fresh start for the debtor. Therefore, any excess COD income disappears. For qualified farm indebtedness, taxpayers can reduce the basis of only qualified property. For qualified real property business indebtedness, they will reduce only depreciable property. The amount of any basis reductions will later be recaptured as ordinary income when the property is sold.

STUDY QUESTIONS

1. Which of the following is the strongest theory related to wealth and gross income?

a. Freeing of assets theory
b. Loan proceeds theory
c. Cash proceeds theory
d. Debt cancellation theory

2. Which of the following identifies an unconditional and legally enforceable obligation for the payment of money?

a. Debt
b. Liability
c. Mortgage
d. Recourse

3. Which of the following key Code Sec. 108 exceptions relates to the excess of liabilities over assets?

a. Bankruptcy

b. Qualified farm indebtedness

c. Qualified real property business indebtedness

d. Insolvency

¶ 604 DEBT MODIFICATION RULES

Debt modification occurs in situations where it does not appear that the debt is being canceled; it does not appear that anything is being forgiven. There is no kind of foreclosure. Instead, the lender agrees to work with the borrower in the context of a debt workout so that the borrower has a better chance of paying back the lender.

When Modifying a Debt Instrument Results in a Deemed Exchange Under Code Sec. 1001

An exchange results when the taxpayer has a change in legal rights or entitlements due to modifying a debt instrument. One must examine whether the modified debt instrument results in "legally distinct entitlements." The regulations under Code Sec. 1001 state that a "significant" modification of a debt instrument will trigger a deemed exchange. It's important to note that all modifications to the debt instrument will be considered together to determine if the overall changes are significant.

Which "modifications" or changes to terms of debt instruments constitute deemed exchanges, and what are the consequence of a deemed exchange? The regulations under Code Sec. 1001 provide many examples of which modifications are significant. For the holder (lender), it is as though the "old debt" was satisfied or paid off by the debtor's giving a "new" debt instrument. The holder should compare the basis in the old debt instrument (generally the amount loaned/given plus any accrued interest, minus any repayments) with the amount realized (issue price, or fair market value, of the "new" debt instrument, depending on if it is publicly traded) (Treas. Reg. Sec. 1.1001-1(g)).

The issuer (debtor) may have cancellation of indebtedness income. The debtor is satisfying the old balance with the "new" debt instrument. Compare the adjusted issue price of the original debt (amount borrowed plus accrued interest minus payments) with the issue price of the new debt. Issue price may be discounted for hidden interest. Taxpayers have to be especially careful in calculating issue price with respect to contingent payment debt.

Certain changes can be made essentially for free, without triggering these consequences. Anything that occurs under the original terms of the debt instrument (e.g., an increase in interest rate if the value of the collateral drops) is not considered a modification. The only exception that could be built in automatically yet still trigger a modification is substituting an obligor, changing the co-obligor, or changing whether the debt is recourse or nonrecourse debt. It is not a modification if the issuer defaults or the holder exercises a forbearance or waiver of the remedies.

Examples of significant modifications include the following:

- Change in obligor or co-obligor on recourse debt
- Change in collateral on nonrecourse debt except fungible collateral
- Change in priority of debt
- Change from debt to equity. The debt/equity rules should be used to test for this.

- Change in yield that exceeds the greater of 25 basis points or 5 percent of the yield of the old debt instrument
- Change in timing that results in a "material deferral," such as a change in maturity date or payments

Transfers of Property Subject to Debt

The consequences for property transferred in satisfaction of debt (e.g., a foreclosure, quitclaim deed, or short sale) depend on whether the debt is recourse or nonrecourse debt. Generally, nonrecourse debt results in sale or exchange treatment under Code Sec. 1001, and recourse debt results in COD income. If the debt is partially recourse debt, the amounts paid are first allocated to the nonrecourse portion.

Transfer of property in satisfaction of nonrecourse debt. In this type of transfer, the entire balance of the debt is treated as the amount realized and the excess over basis is treated as gain on the property transaction. This is true even if the fair market value of the property is less than the balance of the debt (see ***Tufts v. Commissioner***). This rule may change the character of what seems like it should be cancellation of indebtedness income to capital gain or Code Sec. 1231 gain if the property is a capital or Code Sec. 1231 asset. Taxpayers cannot use Code Sec. 108 to exclude this income because it is not cancellation of indebtedness income. The debt is satisfied on its own terms with the lender having agreed to particular property in exchange for the debt. However, a true cancellation/reduction of nonrecourse debt (i.e., nonpurchase money) will result in COD income (Rev. Rul. 91-31).

Transfer of property in satisfaction of recourse debt. For this type of transfer, Treas. Reg. Sec. 1.1001-2 outlines a bifurcation approach:

- First, look at the gain or loss on the property transaction. Compare the fair market value of the property and the basis of the property.
- Second, compute the cancellation of indebtedness transaction. Compare the outstanding balance of debt with the fair market value of the property.

The cancellation of indebtedness piece is true COD income (ordinary income) and eligible for the Code Sec. 108 exclusion.

¶ 605 TAXPAYERS IN BANKRUPTCY

There are several different types of individual bankruptcy:

- Chapter 7 is a basic liquidation of the taxpayer's assets to pay off debt; it is typically simple and quick.
- Chapter 13 is a "wage earner" bankruptcy, under which the taxpayer will pay off debts out of its steady income stream over three or five years.
- Chapter 11 is a reorganization. The taxpayer will continue to operate its business and control the assets, but it has to have a plan for paying its creditors.
- Chapter 13 states that the taxpayer does not have a separate bankruptcy estate with a "trustee."

According to Code Sec. 1398, for Chapter 7 and Chapter 11 bankruptcies, the bankruptcy estate is a separate entity that has to file its own tax returns. Any money earned during a Chapter 11 reorganization bankruptcy belongs to the bankruptcy estate. The bankruptcy estate has a separate taxpayer ID number and must pay tax on the income.

Filing Tax Returns

Taxpayers must file returns even if they have filed for bankruptcy. The return is filed by the trustee, debtor in possession, or other fiduciary. The bankruptcy court will act as a determinant of proper tax administration once it has jurisdiction over a tax matter. This can happen from the debtor listing the IRS as a creditor or the IRS filing a proof of claim for taxes owed. If a separate estate is created under Code Sec. 1398, the fiduciary or trustee will file Form 1041. The trustee must withhold taxes on wages if it is being paid out of the estate, and only "pre-petition" claims may be paid from the estate.

The IRS is on the lookout for pre-petition claims, based on the taxpayer's last filed tax return. It may file a motion to compel an estate or a debtor to file a return. There is a special insolvency team at the IRS that monitors bankruptcy cases to try to avoid missing out on taxes. In bankruptcy cases, a taxpayer cannot discharge any liability to the IRS for taxes that should be due on returns that the taxpayer did not file.

If a debtor did not file returns, and the IRS filed them for the taxpayer based on past data, that will not suffice to discharge liability unless the taxpayer actually signed and acknowledged the returns and agreed to the taxes owed. To take advantage of a Chapter 13 bankruptcy, a debtor must have timely filed tax returns for the last four years.

¶ 606 RECENT DEVELOPMENTS

The Tax Cuts and Jobs Act (TCJA) of 2017 included several changes relevant to troubled borrowers:

- **NOL limitations for post-2017 losses.** The rules for NOLs arising in tax years beginning after December 31, 2017, are modified such that a corporation's NOL carryover can only offset 80 percent of taxable income without regard to the new Section 199A deduction. However, these NOLs can now be carried forward indefinitely instead of being limited to 20 years. Carrybacks of these losses are no longer permitted.

- **NOL limitations for pre-2018 losses.** Rules for existing NOLs remain the same. These losses can be carried back two years and forward 20 years. There is no taxable income limit to usage of pre-2018 losses.

- **Limitation on losses for noncorporate taxpayers**. In a significant departure from prior law, the TCJA restricts the use of business losses of noncorporate taxpayers. Previously, business losses recognized by individuals could reduce nonbusiness income (such as interest, dividends, and capital gains) without limitation. Beginning in 2018 through the 2025 tax year, taxpayers can only deduct up to $500,000 (for married filing jointly taxpayers) of these losses against nonbusiness income. Amounts above the threshold are considered "excess business losses" and carried forward and treated as part of the taxpayer's NOL carryforward in subsequent taxable years. These NOL carryforwards are also subject to the new 80 percent NOL limitation.

The Coronavirus Aid, Relief and Economic Security (CARES) Act amended Code Sec. 172(b)(1), and Rev. Proc. 2020-24 provides related guidance. The CARES Act provides a five-year carryback for losses earned in 2018, 2019, or 2020, which allows firms to modify tax returns up to five years prior to offset taxable income from those tax years.

The CARES Act also suspends the NOL limit of 80 percent of taxable income. This means that firms may deduct their NOLs to eliminate all of their taxable income in a given year, instead of having to carry forward any NOL beyond 80 percent of taxable income. Pass-through business owners may use NOLs to offset their nonbusiness income above the previous limit of $250,000 (single) or $500,000 (married filing jointly) for 2018, 2019, and 2020.

STUDY QUESTIONS

4. Which of the following is first in the order of attribute reduction in accordance with Code Sec. 108(b)(2)?

a. Certain tax credits

b. Net operating losses

c. Capital losses and capital loss carryovers

d. Basis in property

5. Which of the following is last in the order of basis reduction in accordance with Code Sec. 108(b)(2)?

a. Property not used in a trade or business or investment

b. Real property used in a trade or business that secured the discharged debt

c. Personal property used in a trade or business that secured the discharged debt

d. Inventory

6. Which of the following is ***not*** an example of a significant debt modification?

a. Change in co-obligor on recourse debt

b. Change in collateral on nonrecourse debt except fungible collateral

c. Change in yield that exceeds 1 percent of yield of old debt instrument

d. Change in priority of debt

7. Which of the following types of individual bankruptcy is a simple and quick basic liquidation?

a. Chapter 7

b. Chapter 11

c. Chapter 13

d. Chapter 16

8. Which of the following changes relevant to troubled borrowers was made by the Coronavirus Aid, Relief and Economic Security (CARES) Act?

a. The use of business losses of noncorporate taxpayers is restricted.

b. There is a five-year carryback for losses earned in 2018, 2019, or 2020.

c. A corporation's carryover for net operating losses (NOLs) arising in tax years beginning after December 31, 2017, can only offset 80 percent of taxable income.

d. For Chapter 7 and Chapter 11 bankruptcies, the bankruptcy estate is a separate entity that has to file its own tax returns.

MODULE 3: DEBT—Chapter 7: Paycheck Protection Program (PPP) Loans: New Legislation and the Impact on Forgiveness

¶ 701 WELCOME

For clients who are applying for or have received Paycheck Protection Program loans, the planning has just begun. This chapter discusses practical planning ideas to maximize debt forgiveness.

¶ 702 LEARNING OBJECTIVES

Upon completion of this chapter, you will be able to:

- Recognize how to compute the amount of debt forgiveness
- Recognize how to compute the limit on nonpayroll expenses
- Develop practical steps for unused funds near the end of the 8-week covered period
- Compute the maximum loan amount for sole proprietors and partnerships
- Identify remaining areas where guidance is still lacking

¶ 703 INTRODUCTION

The Coronavirus Aid, Relief, and Economic Relief (CARES) Act authorizes the Small Business Administration (SBA) to temporarily guarantee loans under a loan program called the Paycheck Protection Program (PPP). Under the program, the SBA provides loans to small businesses to help pay up to 8 weeks of payroll costs, mortgages, rent, and utilities during the COVID-19 pandemic. All payments of principal, interest, and fees under the loans are deferred for at least six months. The loans are also forgiven for amounts of payroll costs, mortgage or rent obligations, and certain utility payments incurred between February 15, 2020, and June 30, 2020. The amount forgiven is excluded from an eligible recipient's gross income for federal income tax purposes.

The CARES Act was amended by the Paycheck Protection Program Flexibility Act of 2020 (the "Flexibility Act"), which was signed into law on June 5, 2020. The Flexibility Act gives borrowers more freedom in how and when loan funds are spent while retaining the possibility of full forgiveness. The legislation includes the following changes to the PPP:

- Extends the covered period from 8 weeks to 24 weeks;
- Reduces the 75 percent payroll ratio requirement to 60 percent;
- Extends the two-year loan repayment requirement to five years for future borrowers (existing PPP loans can be extended up to five years if the lender/borrower agree);
- Allows payroll tax deferment for PPP recipients; and
- Extends the June 30, 2020, rehiring deadline to December 31, 2020.

On June 16, 2020, the SBA issued a new forgiveness "interim final rule" that provides clarification on S corporation shareholders. And on June 17, 2020, a new forgiveness application form was released.

¶ 704 PPP FLEXIBILITY ACT OF 2020

The Flexibility Act made significant changes to several PPP provisions.

Expanded Covered Period

All taxpayers who receive PPP funds are eligible to use a 24—week covered period (as opposed to the previous 8—week period). This solves many of the problems for borrowers who were having difficulty spending the PPP funds for permissible uses in the original 8—week period. Although taxpayers who received PPP loans prior to June 5, 2020, may elect to continue using the 8—week period, almost all borrowers are expected to use the 24—week period.

Most taxpayers who choose 24-week covered period should be able to pay forgivable costs greater than the PPP loan amount in 24 weeks. A more significant issue might be avoiding the full-time equivalent (FTE) and wage reduction "haircuts," which will be discussed more fully later in this chapter. Generally, employers who do not retain employees in place before receiving a PPP Loan, as measured by percentage of payroll and percentage of full-time equivalent employees ("FTE"), can lose out on full loan forgiveness. The "haircuts" are reductions in the loan forgiveness amount, and ultimately require the employer to repay a greater amount of the PPP loan.

New Payroll Cost Percentage

Before the amendment, the amount of forgiveness was limited to payroll costs divided by 75 percent. The Flexibility Act changes the payroll percentage limit to 60 percent. Note that there is some controversy regarding the fact that as written, this provision appears to create a "cliff" whereby spending any percentage less on payroll results in the inability for all qualifying costs to be forgiven.

EXAMPLE: A borrower has $60,000 in eligible payroll costs. Prior to the Flexibility Act, total forgiveness would have been limited to $80,000 ($60,000 ÷ 75 percent). After the amendment, total forgiveness would be limited to $100,000 ($60,000 ÷ 60 percent).

New Loan Term

For loans made on June 5, 2020 or after, the new loan term is five years (for loans made before June 5, the term was two years). To extend the PPP loan repayment period to five years for loans made before June 5, 2020, the borrower and lender (and presumably the SBA as guarantor) must mutually agree to the change. This requirement will likely necessitate loan modification processes and possibly a new note.

NOTE: Loans made *before* June 5 are subject to renegotiation. Borrowers and lenders may negotiate to extend the two—year period to five years.

The "Magic Moment"

The date by which borrowers can restore FTEs or wage reductions was changed to December 31, 2020, for all borrowers. The recently released revised PPP Loan Forgiveness Application alters this to the date of the date of submission of the forgiveness application (if prior to December 31).

New Additional FTE Waivers

New waivers of the FTE "haircut" are provided if:

- Employers were unable to rehire workers or those with similar skills.
- Employers were unable to return to the same level of business due to guidelines or restrictions issued by the Centers for Disease Control and Prevention (CDC), the Occupational Safety and Health Administration (OSHA), or the Department of Health and Human Services (HHS).

Changing Emphasis Under the Flexibility Act

The focus under the Flexibility Act will shift from the prior emphasis on "pushing dollars out the door" to minimizing the effect of the FTE and wage reduction "haircuts," as illustrated in the following chart:

	Primary Emphasis	Secondary Emphasis
8-week covered period	Pushing money out the door—Prepayment, etc.	Avoiding FTE and wage reduction haircuts
24-week covered period	Avoiding FTE and wage reduction haircuts	Pushing money out the door

STUDY QUESTION

1. Which of the following allows taxpayers who receive Paycheck Protection Program (PPP) funds to use a 24—week covered period?

a. CARES Act

b. Small Business Administration (SBA)

c. Paycheck Protection Program Flexibility Act

d. IRS

¶ 705 MATURITY DATE

Under the Flexibility Act, loans "made" on June 5, 2020, or later have a five-year maturity date. The date on which the SBA assigns the loan number determines when a loan is "made." Loans made before June 5, 2020, have a two-year maturity date, but borrowers and lenders can agree to change the maturity date to five years.

EXAMPLE: Ronnie's Pizzeria, Inc., receives PPP loan proceeds on May 31, 2020. The loan term is generally two years (for loans made prior to June 5, 2020). However, Ronnie's Pizzeria can negotiate with the lender to stretch the term to five years. In fact, some lenders are automatically converting these loans to five-year terms.

The significance of five years is that it represents a second type of "forgiveness." Many small businesses fail. If a borrower used the PPP funds for proper purposes, and if it has an entity insulating it from liability, it appears the borrower will receive the second type of forgiveness.

EXAMPLE: Ronnie's Pizzeria, Inc., borrows $150,000 on a PPP loan. Only $100,000 of that amount is forgiven. A $50,000 loan balance remains. Ronnie's Pizzeria uses the funds for a permissible use. Three years later, the pizzeria goes out of business. Generally, the SBA will not pursue the shareholder (Ronnie) in this situation.

The following chart highlight the changes to PPP loans under the Flexibility Act.

	CARES	PPP Flexibility Act	Effective Date
Minimum maturity of loan	2 years (SBA)	5 years	Loans on or after June 5; banks can use for earlier loans.
Covered period	8 weeks	Earlier of: • 24 weeks or • December 31, 2020	All PPP loans. Loans prior to June 5, 2020, can elect to stay with 8 weeks.
Magic moment (FTE waiver)	June 30	December 31	All PPP loans
New additional FTE waiver	None	• Cannot hire similar workers by December 31, 2020, or • Cannot return to same level of business due to CDC, OSHA, HHS restrictions	All PPP loans
Limit on nonpayroll costs	25% (SBA)	40%	All PPP loans
Loan deferral period	6 months	Until SBA remits forgiveness → lender, not later than 10 months after the end of the covered period.	All PPP loans
Payroll tax deferral (employer's Social Security)	Ends after forgiveness	PPP loan has no effect; all employers can use	All PPP loans
Final date for SBA to approve loan	June 30, 2020	June 30, 2020	No change

STUDY QUESTION

2. Under the Paycheck Protection Program Flexibility Act:

- **a.** For loans made on or after June 5, 2020, the term is two years.
- **b.** For loans made on or after June 5, 2020, the term is five years.
- **c.** Loans made after June 5, 2020, are subject to renegotiation.
- **d.** Borrowers are greatly restricted in how they can use PPP loan funds.

¶ 706 SIXTY PERCENT PAYROLL COSTS LIMIT: CLIFF OR PHASEOUT

According to the Flexibility Act, a borrower should use at least 60 percent of a PPP loan for payroll costs, and up to 40 percent of the loan for payment of interest, rent, utilities. Partial forgiveness is granted even if less than 60 percent of the loan is used for payroll costs. This rule applies to all borrowers (before and after June 5, 2020).

> **EXAMPLE:** A borrower obtains a PPP loan for $106,000. The borrower spends $60,000 on payroll costs during the covered period and spends the remaining $46,000 on covered nonpayroll (rent, etc.). The borrower's maximum loan forgiveness is $100,000 (60,000 ÷ 60 percent).

Loan Deferral Period

Under the PPP, payments of principal and interest on a PPP loan are deferred for six months from the date the PPP loan is made. The Flexibility Act extends that time period to the date the SBA remits the PPP loan or 10 months after the end of the covered period (if the taxpayer does not apply for forgiveness).

¶ 707 THE NEW CONSTRAINTS ON FORGIVENESS

Under the new rules, taxpayers have a 24-week period to spend their PPP loan. The forgivable costs remain the same, payroll costs and covered nonpayroll costs. The maximum limit on forgiveness is payroll costs divided by 60 percent. Payroll costs are the sum of the following:

- Salary, wages, commission, and similar compensation
  - — Tips
  - — Dismissal or separation pay
  - — Vacation, sick, parental, or family leave (other than leave under the Families First Coronavirus Response Act)
  - — Bonuses
- Certain employee benefits
  - — Group healthcare benefits (including health insurance)
  - — Retirement benefits
  - — Payment of state or local tax assessed on compensation of employees (primary type is state unemployment)

Covered nonpayroll costs include covered mortgage interest (interest on mortgage on real or personal property incurred before February 15, 2020), rent (as long as the leasing agreement was in force before February 15), and utilities. See the details in the following chart:

Covered "Nonpayroll" Costs	
Covered mortgage interest	Liability of borrower; on mortgage on real or personal property incurred before February 15, 2020.
Covered rent obligation	Rent obligated under leasing agreement in force before February 15, 2020 (real and personal property). Should include car payments for business automobiles.
Covered utility payment	Payment for a service for the distribution of electricity, gas, water, transportation, telephone, or internet access for which service began before February 15, 2020. • Appears to cover fuel in business automobiles. • Should cover business cell phones.

Forgivable Costs Paid or Incurred

Forgivable costs include:

- Eligible costs paid or incurred during the 8-week or 24-week period. Taxpayers can count the costs either when they paid them or when they incurred them, but they cannot count them twice.
- Eligible costs not paid but incurred during the 8-week or 24-week period, as long as they are paid by the next pay period or, for a utility bill, the next billing date. For this option, the taxpayer must have a biweekly or more frequent payroll.

Payroll Costs Choice of Periods

Taxpayers can choose their payroll period. The regular covered period of 56 days (8 weeks) begins on the date of the PPP deposit. The same principles should apply for 24-week period if there is no 8-week election. The alternative payroll covered period (APCP) begins on the first day of the payroll period that follows disbursement. Taxpayers can choose this option only if their payroll is biweekly or more frequent. Note that the APCP does not change the timing for nonpayroll costs.

Payroll Costs Incurred or Paid

In determining when payroll costs were incurred or paid, taxpayers should be aware of the definitions of the terms. *Paid* means the date the taxpayer distributed the payroll checks/initiated an ACH transfer. *Incurred* means the date the pay was earned. If an employee has been furloughed, the employer should use the date the employee ***would*** have worked.

Under the special payment rule (detailed in the following chart), employees must be paid on or before the next regular payroll date. The *payroll date* is the date the employer usually distributes paychecks/makes direct deposits.

Incurred Rule: Special Payment Deadline		
	Incurred	**Payment Deadline**
Payroll costs	During covered period or APCP	On or before the next regular pay date
Nonpayroll costs	During covered period only	On or before the next regular billing date

Eligible nonpayroll costs include covered interest, covered rent, and covered utilities that are:

- Paid *during* the covered period (no reference to APCP), *or*
- Incurred in the covered period, *and*
- Paid on or before the *next* regular billing date (special payment rule).

EXAMPLE: COVERED UTILITIES: The covered period is 8 weeks (56 days): April 20 through June 14. Service began *before* February 15, 2020. The chart below provides an example of the eligible forgiveness amounts.

Period Water Used	Amount	Billing Date	Date Paid	Eligible Forgiveness
March (whole month)	$31	April 15	April 30	$31 ($31 paid, $0 incurred)
April (whole month)	$30	May 15	May 31	$30 ($30 paid, $11 incurred)
May (whole month)	$31	June 15	June 30	$31 ($0 paid, $31 incurred at $1/day in covered period, *and* paid by next billing date of July 15)

¶ 708 FORGIVENESS "HAIRCUTS"

There are two types of "haircut" tests that might reduce the amount of loan forgiveness available to an employer. Generally, these "haircuts" result when an employer has not "retained" employees to a sufficient degree. (Code Sec. 1106(d)(2) and (3)):

- Head count (based on FTEs)
- Wage reductions (for any employee)

For borrowers using the 24-week covered period, the objective will be to avoid "haircuts." This can be accomplished in a number of ways:

- Keeping head count levels up
- Getting a *de minimis* exemption
- Applying the "magic moment"
- Getting the new Flexibility Act exemption

The loan forgiveness application and its instructions are important. They are incorporated into the final regulations (*Federal Register* Vol. 85, No. 105, p. 33007).

FTE Headcount Haircut

Basic computations. FTEs are computed as follows: an employee working 40 hours/week or more = 1 FTE (60 hours/week = 1.5 FTE).

There are two methods for measuring part-time employees. An employer must pick one method and apply it to all of its part-time workers. Also, an employer should use one convention for both the covered period and the reference period.

- **First method:** The employee's actual hours/week ÷ 40 hours. For example, an employee who usually works four hours/week = .10 FTE.
- **Alternate method:** The rounding convention: a part-time worker = .50 FTE.

EXAMPLE: The Ritz Hotel received a PPP loan of $150,000 ($100,000 forgivable in 8 weeks).

Step 1: Determine how many FTEs it had in the covered (8-week) period: 9 FTEs.

Step 2: Pick the *lesser* number of FTEs from two "reference periods."

Average number of FTEs in the period February 15, 2019, through June 30, 2019 = 10 FTEs.

Average number of FTEs in the period January 1, 2020, through February 29, 2020 = 12 FTEs.

Step 3: Calculate the FTE percentage.

90 percent [9 FTEs (8-week period) ÷ 10 FTEs (better of the two reference periods)]

Step 4: Calculate the revised debt forgiveness.

$90,000 [90 percent (FTE quotient) × $100,000].

Under the Flexibility Act, an employer will likely use the average number of FTEs over 24 weeks. This means the employer will need to maintain FTEs for a much longer time (16 more weeks) than if it used the 8-week period. Businesses that may not be able to maintain FTEs for 24 weeks may be better off electing to stick with the 8-week period. However, opting for 24 weeks might be better for "overflowing" forgivable costs; see the discussion later in this chapter.

EXAMPLE: ABC, LLC, borrowed funds through the PPP on April 6. It has been able to maintain its number of FTEs for 8 weeks, but its funds are running low. It might have to cut back on its number of FTEs. ABC should consider electing to use the 8-week option.

EXAMPLE: The Acropolis Restaurant has two employees. George works 60 hours per week, and Frank works four hours per week. Its FTE computations are shown in the following chart:

Employee	Actual Hours	First Method	Alternate Method
George	60	1 FTE	1 FTE
Frank	4	.10 FTE	.50 FTE

Employers who use the rounding convention (.50 FTE) will likely get a break if they have many part-time workers with limited hours during the 24-week period.

EXAMPLE: A French restaurant hires 20 part-time workers, just for one day (eight hours each). The restaurant uses the rounding convention. The workers will count as 10 FTEs for the entire week, even though their total hours worked is 80 hours (which would otherwise be two FTEs). Note that the restaurant will also have to use the rounding convention for the reference period, either February 15 through June 30, 2019, or the first two months of 2020, if chosen.

There is some uncertainty surrounding these rules. Can all borrowers use the .50 part-time exemption? Or can only borrowers with "bad records" use it? The regulations are a bit unclear. They seem to say all borrowers can choose the rounding option (*Federal Register* Vol. 85, No. 105, p. 33008). But the same page states that the option may be limited to borrowers who do not keep track of employee hours. "Such borrowers" receive the flexibility to choose the rounding convention. The PPP Loan Forgiveness Application form instructions (https://home.treasury.gov/system/files/136/3245-0407-SBA-Form-3508-PPP-Forgiveness-Application.pdf) do not restrict the .50 exemption to employers without records. Therefore, it is likely that all borrowers can use rounding.

***De minimis* exemption.** This exception allows employers to count employees who have been laid off or whose hours have been reduced if:

- The employer makes a good faith, written offer to rehire or restore the employee's hours during the 8 weeks;
- The employer gives the employee an offer for same salary or wages, and same number of hours (before the change);
- The offer is rejected by the employee;
- The employer retains records that document the rejection, and
- The employer notifies the state unemployment insurance office within 30 days.

The SBA will provide future guidance on what is involved in notifying the state unemployment office.

EXAMPLE: Judy's Chocolates, Inc., lays off Paul, a full-time employee, on March 20, 2020. The company receives PPP funds on May 28, 2020, and on June 16, 2020, it makes a qualified written offer to Paul to come back to work for the same salary and same hours he worked before the layoff June 16. However, Paul rejects the offer. The company can count Paul as a FTE even though he does not work at Judy's Chocolates. However, "double counting" is not allowed; Judy's Chocolates cannot count Paul as a FTE if he is replaced by a new employee.

No FTE haircut is allowed for employees who voluntarily resign, who voluntarily request a reduction in hours, or who are fired for cause. Employers should retain records to document these situations.

There are new exceptions under the Flexibility Act. If an employer cannot rehire the same or a similar employee, it gets an exemption. If it cannot return to the same level of business because of HHS, CDC, or OSHA guidelines or requirements, it also can get a waiver.

Recap: FTE Reductions	
Basic computation	Compare "covered period" FTEs to choice of reference periods
Reference periods	Can choose either: • February 15 through June 30, 2019, or • January 1 through February 29, 2020
Computing FTEs	Full-time worker • Over 40 hours = 1 FTE Part-time workers • Actual FTE (example 4 hours/week = .10), or • Rounding (4 hours/week = .50)
Exceptions: *de minimis*	• Laid off and made good faith written offer, etc. • Quit • Voluntary reduction in hours • Terminated for cause But no double-counting if worker is replaced.
Exceptions: Flexibility Act	Cannot hire back the same or similar employee. Cannot return to same level of business (HHS, CDC, etc.)

Wage Reduction Haircut

The basic computation involves comparing the average wage or the average salary of employees who work during the covered (8-week) period. Employees who earned more than $100,000 in any 2019 pay period are excluded. The employer must annualize pay periods. The forgivable costs are reduced only if the wage for the 8 weeks is greater than the 25 percent average for the first quarter of 2020. Presumably, a similar computation will work for a 24-week period. Note that the employer can only include employees who were employed during the covered period or APCP; there is no wage reduction for people who did not work during the relevant covered period.

EXAMPLE: Letitia's average salary during the covered period is $700/week. Her employer elects to use the 8-week period. The average salary in 2020 Q1 was $1,000.

Salary reduction/week = $50 ($300/week – $250 [25% Q1 2020 average]).

Total forgivable costs reduction = $400 (8 weeks × $50).

The forgiveness, which would otherwise have been $10,000, is reduced to $9,600.

EXAMPLE: Paul was laid off on March 30, 2020, and does not return to work prior to the end of the covered period.

There will be no wage reduction for Paul because he did not provide services during the covered period.

Any employee who earns less than $100,000 during any pay period in 2019, even if for just one pay period, is annualized out to more than $100,000. The employer does not have to count wage reductions for such employees.

EXAMPLE: Barry's employer has a biweekly payroll. Barry receives $4,000 in total pay (including a holiday bonus) on December 31, 2019.

$4,000 (December pay period) × 26 biweekly pay periods = $104,000.

There is no wage reduction "haircut" for Barry because his pay has been annualized to more than $100,000 for a pay period.

Proportionate wage reductions are not counted. There is no "double penalty." An employer gets the wage reduction haircut *only* for a portion of the wage reduction, not related to reduced hours or reduced time.

EXAMPLE: Paul earned an average of $20/hour in the first quarter of 2020. Paul is laid off during the covered period, so his weekly pay drops from $800 to $0. There is no wage reduction haircut for Paul because his cut in pay from $20/hour to $0/hour was entirely related to his being laid off.

Recap: Wage Reduction Haircut	
Basic computation	See if reduction for covered period > 25% of 2020 Q1 wages.
Employees tested	Only those who worked during 8-week (or 24-week) period
Exclude employees	Who have > $100,000 in annualized salary, for any pay period in 2019
Don't count "proportionate" wage reductions	Don't compute wage reduction haircut to extent related to reduced hours.

The Magic Moment

There is no forgiveness haircut if an employer eliminates the FTE problem no later than the earlier of December 31, 2020, or the date it submits the loan application. This new "magic moment" applies to all borrowers.

- **FTE "magic moment."** Both the interim final rule and the PPP Loan Forgiveness Application form state that the employer must "restore"—by December 31, 2020, or the date it submits the loan application—its number of FTEs to the level it had on February 15, 2020.
- **Wage reduction "magic moment."** An employer must restore by the date of the magic moment (December 31, 2020, or the date it submits the loan application) the average annual salary or hourly wage *at* the magic moment. Employers may want to use (at a minimum) the salary or wages for an entire pay period. Payroll reports can support the restored wage or salary.

EXAMPLE: Ronnie's Pizzeria, Inc., had four FTEs during the reference period. It had a decrease in FTEs between February 15 and April 26 (*requirement*). Ronnie's workforce decreases to two employees in the payroll period that includes February 15, 2020. It has four full-time employees working on December 31, 2020. There's a reasonable argument that there is no FTE haircut in this case. The pizzeria restored its employees by the "magic moment." More cautious taxpayers may want to staff up in advance of December 31.

NOTE: Employers must *fully restore* their FTEs to meet the "magic moment" requirements. If an employer had 10 FTEs on February 15, 2020, it must restore completely to 10 FTEs. The same applies for the wage reduction "magic moment"—an employer must *fully* restore wages on December 31, 2020.

STUDY QUESTION

3. For which of the following employees would a full-time equivalent (FTE) "haircut" be allowed?

a. Mario, who works 50 hours per week

b. Emma, who voluntarily resigned from her position

c. Josef, who requested that his hours be reduced

d. Suman, who was fired for embezzling funds from her employer

¶ 709 "OVERFLOWING" FORGIVABLE COSTS

By "overflowing" forgivable loan costs, an employer can offset the .50 FTE deficiency. An employer may have to prepay to get full forgiveness. Employers can divide the loan amount by its FTE quotient to determine the amount of forgivable costs. For example, if its loan amount is $100,000 and the FTE quotient is .50, it will need $200,000 in forgivable costs in the covered period. This is much easier to do over the 24-week period if the employer maintains its FTE levels.

EXAMPLE: A borrower took a PPP loan for $100,000. It uses the 24-week covered period and has $200,000 of forgivable costs ($120,000 payroll costs + $80,000 nonpayroll costs (rent)). The borrower is subject to a 50 percent FTE haircut.

The borrower's forgiveness equals the lesser of:

- PPP loan = $100,000
- Forgivable costs × haircut percent = $100,000 ($200,000 × 50 percent)
- 60 percent of payroll costs = $200,000

Extra payroll and rent for the 24-week period offset the FTE haircut.

¶ 710 THE ARGUMENT FOR PREPAYMENTS

The PPP Loan Forgiveness Application form states eligible payroll costs include costs "paid or incurred" during the 8-week period. A prepayment means the costs are *paid* during the covered period. Prepaid costs do not include "prepayments of interest." Note that there is no such instruction for payroll costs, rent, or utilities.

The statute says that "any" payment of rent or utilities qualifies, except interest prepayments. The AICPA takes a different position—that one cannot prepay rent.

EXAMPLE: Ronnie's Pizzeria, Inc., does not have enough forgivable costs for *full* loan forgiveness. On the last day of the covered period, Ronnie's prepays the next two weeks' payroll. There is a reasonable argument that this should count toward "eligible" costs.

Cautious taxpayers may want to take the following steps:

Cautious Clients: Examples	
Forgiveness Period	Keep "pedal to the metal" for *both* 8 weeks *and* 24 weeks.
FTEs	Regular FTE test • Don't rely on .50 part-time rule (use actual) Magic moment • Use "restore" (don't just hire December 31). • Don't use "rounding convention for part-time employees.
Wage reductions	Follow "restore" rule • Don't just restore pay on December 31
Prepayments	Fund retirement contributions, etc. • Make prepayment "suspenders"

EXAMPLE: Your client DeShawn owns a restaurant. He wants to take a conservative approach to debt forgiveness. You might advise him not to prepay but just to pay bonuses. If he has a FTE haircut issue, you might encourage him to restore his FTEs to the reference period FTE level well before December 31, 2020. In addition, you might suggest that he makes sure his restaurant is well staffed on December 31, 2020 (the magic moment).

¶ 711 UPDATES

Sole Proprietors, Partners, and S Corporation Shareholders

Sole proprietors, partners, and S corporation shareholders should be able to get the maximum amount of PPP loan forgiveness as long as they paid a decent amount of wages in 2019. For example, if they choose the 8-week period, their maximum forgiveness amount is $15,385. For the 24-week period, they can get up to $20,833 in forgiveness. This is also the full amount that could have been borrowed. Employers have higher limits if they choose a 24-week period.

EXAMPLE: Mohammad is a sole proprietor and has no employees. His net profit on Line 31 of his Schedule C is $125,000. Mohammad has no rent, utilities, or interest expense. His maximum forgiveness if he chooses the 8-week period is $15,385. $100,000 limit/year × 8 weeks ÷ 52 weeks. If he chooses the 24-week period, the maximum is $20,833. $100,000 × 2.5 months ÷ 12 months (same as original loan amount). This is the full amount that he could have been borrowed.

EXAMPLE: Bob is an S corporation shareholder and the only employee of the S corporation. He uses the 24-week period (he does not elect the 8-week period). Bob received $150,000 in compensation in 2019 and made no retirement contributions. The maximum PPP loan amount (when he applied in April) was $20,833. His maximum forgiveness (2019 W-2 at 2.5 months) is $20,833.

According to the SBA Paycheck Protection Program interim final rule, sole proprietors and partners can never include contributions to their own retirement plan or payment of their own medical insurance as forgivable costs. S corporation shareholders, on the other hand, can count two and a half months of their 2019 contributions. For example, if they put $20,000 into a SEP IRA in 2019, they can prorate that for two and a half months divided by the 12 months in a year.

New Forgiveness Form

A taxpayer can use the new PPP Loan Forgiveness Application form (https://home.treasury.gov/system/files/136/3245-0407-SBA-Form-3508-PPP-Forgiveness-Application.pdf) if it:

- Is a sole proprietorship with no employees included in the original loan application
- Did not reduce the following during the covered period (8 or 24 weeks, as chosen):
  - Salaries or wages by more than 25 percent for any employee, *and*
  - The number of employees.
- Did not reduce salary or wages of any employee by more than 25 percent.
- Is unable to operate at same level of business as before February 15, 2020, due to HHS, OSHA or CDC requirements established or guidance issued

Keep an Eye Out for Developments

Practitioners should keep apprised of developments in the PPP area, as there have been a number of changes in the program already. The U.S. Department of the Treasury provides updated information on the PPP for borrowers and lenders, as well as program rules, at https://home.treasury.gov/policy-issues/cares/assistance-for-small-businesses. Future guidance will include revisions to the loan forgiveness and loan review procedures and a new forgiveness application.

STUDY QUESTION

4. The Paycheck Protection Program Flexibility Act changed the date by which borrowers can restore full-time equivalents or wage reductions (the “magic moment”) to:

a. June 30, 2020
b. July 15, 2020
c. December 31, 2020
d. December 31, 2021

CPE NOTE: When you have completed your study and review of chapters 6 and 7, which comprise Module 3, you may wish to take the Final Exam for this Module. Go to **cchcpelink.com/printcpe** to take this Final Exam online.

MODULE 4: ESTATE AND FINANCIAL PLANNING—Chapter 8: Retirement Plan Changes by Congress and the IRS in Response to COVID-19

¶ 801 WELCOME

This chapter discusses the changes to retirement plans made by Congress and the IRS shortly before 2020 and later in response to the COVID-19 pandemic. It outlines the changes implemented by the SECURE Act and CARES Act and is designed to give tax practitioners a new perspective on old retirement plan rules to better guide their clients during this uncertain time.

¶ 802 LEARNING OBJECTIVES

Upon completion of this chapter, you will be able to:

- Describe the efforts by Congress and the IRS in response to the COVID-19 pandemic
- Describe the retirement distribution changes implemented by the SECURE Act and CARES Act
- Recognize and analyze the options available to employees to use retirement funds for current liquidity needs
- Recognize recommended plan changes to employer retirement plans based on shrinking revenue and employee reductions
- Identify the impact of using government loan proceeds to contribute to retirement plans
- Recommend estate planning techniques to achieve client goals in light of modified withdrawal options

---

¶ 803 INTRODUCTION

The COVID-19 pandemic created an economic crisis, and Congress and the IRS have employed numerous tactics to alleviate the impact. Among these efforts are significant changes to retirement savings options, including increased loan options, penalty eliminations, and required minimum distribution (RMD) waivers.

Analyzing retirement plan distributions is difficult enough without the uncertainty of a global pandemic. The changes implemented by the SECURE Act and CARES Act added another layer of complexity for taxpayers nearing retirement or reevaluating distribution plans in light of current market conditions.

Regardless of whether they have been negatively impacted by coronavirus, employees should analyze their retirement plans and savings habits over the coming months to make the most of these changes to their retirement plan options. Employers must also analyze their plans to ensure employees can utilize the new rules and are not negatively affected in the event of large layoffs.

¶ 804 LEGISLATIVE HISTORY OF THE SECURE ACT AND CARES ACT

The Setting Every Community Up for Retirement Enhancement Act of 2019 (SECURE Act) was introduced in the House on March 29, 2019 (H.R. 1994). It passed in the House on May 23, 2019, and was sent to the Senate on June 3, 2019. It finally passed the Senate as part of a massive year end funding bill in December of 2019 and was signed into law on December 20, 2019 (P.L. 11694).

The SECURE Act implemented major changes, particularly to Internal Revenue Code Sec. 401. Modifications relevant to retirement plans include changes to the required beginning date, the removal of age related contribution limits, and the modification of certain beneficiary withdrawal periods. However, the act also made many quiet changes to a number of other Code sections.

The IRS has not yet issued regulations to better explain how the SECURE Act changes will interact with many of the existing reporting procedures. The hope is that these regulations will come more quickly than did the regulations related to the Tax Cuts and Jobs Act of 2017 (TCJA).

Three months after the passage of the SECURE Act and in response to significant uncertainty related to the looming pandemic, the Coronavirus Aid, Relief, and Economic Security Act (CARES Act) passed the Senate on March 25, 2020 as H.R. 748 which was originally introduced in January 2019 and used as the vehicle to pass the enormous economic stimulus package. On March 27, 2020, the CARES Act passed the House and was signed into law the same day. Offering $2 trillion of relief, it is the largest economic stimulus package ever passed in the United States. The CARES Act added to the $8.3 billion and $104 billion packages passed earlier in March 2020 to benefit vaccine research and paid sick leave and unemployment related to the coronavirus.

The retirement-related sections of the act are contained in Section 2202, detailing special rules for use of retirement funds, and Section 2203, outlining a temporary waiver of RMD rules for certain retirement plans and accounts. Since the act's passage, numerous notices have been issued by the IRS which further explain these provisions and outline their application for taxpayers.

> **CAUTION:** Tax practitioners must watch what they read and hear regarding the CARES Act, and keep in mind what constitutes legal authority during this time. For example, IRS FAQs (frequently asked questions), comments from politicians, and social media posts are *not* legal authority. New guidance is issued regularly and practitioners must stay aware of changes affecting their clients.

¶ 805 RETIREMENT PLAN CONTRIBUTION LIMITS

The SECURE Act repealed the maximum contribution age for a traditional individual retirement account (IRA). Under Code Sec. 219(d)(1), taxpayers under age 70½ before the end of the tax year were permitted to deduct contributions to their retirement accounts. The SECURE Act lifts this restriction so taxpayers can continue their deductible contributions well after age 70½. This is particularly helpful for clients who are working later in life. The change applied only to IRA plans and not 401(k) plans since 401(k) plans did not restrict participation by older employees. Employee contributions are still limited by annual contribution maximums and compensation thresholds which must be analyzed when advising clients concerning their continued ability to save toward retirement.

For 2020, the IRA contribution limits are:

- Taxpayers under age 50 = $6,000
- Taxpayers over age 50 = $7,000

For 2020, the 401(k) contribution limits are:

- Taxpayers under age 50 = $19,500
- Taxpayers over age 50 = $26,000

Since the contribution amounts are limited not only by annual contribution thresholds, but also by the taxable compensation of the taxpayer, this change only affects individuals who are still working and not those who have already retired and are living off their savings. Being able to contribute funds after age 70½ can have a dramatic impact on a taxpayer's ability to increase the size of his account even during the years in which he has to take required minimum distributions.

As the following chart illustrates, under the old rules which required RMDs at age 70½ and disallowed further contributions, if a client's retirement account has a balance of $100,000 and the client stops contributing, the account balance after 10 years will be $79,241. However, if the client continues to contribute after age 70½ and waits until age 72 to withdraw his RMDs (as shown in the following, his account will grow to $148,367.

Comparison of Post-70½ Contributions: $100,000 Account							
Single Life	**Age**	**Account Value (5%) Growth + No Contribution**	**RMD**	**Single Life**	**Age**	**Account Value (5%) Growth + $7,000 Contribution/ Year**	**RMD**
17	70	$100,000	$5,882	17	70	$100,000	
16.3	71	$98,824	$6,063	16.3	71	$112,350	
15.5	72	$97,399	$6,284	15.5	72	$125,318	$8,085
14.8	73	$95,671	$6,464	14.8	73	$130,444	$8,814
14.1	74	$93,667	$6,643	14.1	74	$135,062	$9,579
13.4	75	$91,375	$6,819	13.4	75	$139,107	$10,381
12.7	76	$88,784	$6,991	12.7	76	$142,512	$11,221
12.1	77	$85,883	$7,098	12.1	77	$142,205	$12,000
11.4	78	$82,724	$7,256	11.4	78	$147,215	$12,914
10.8	79	$79,241	$7,337	10.8	79	$148,367	$13,738
			$66,837				**$86,732**

The next chart illustrates the same concept, except the account starts at $500,000.

Comparison of Post-70½ Contributions: $500,000 Account							
Single Life	**Age**	**Account Value (5%) Growth + No Contribution**	**RMD**	**Single Life**	**Age**	**Account Value (5%) Growth + $7,000 Contribution/ Year**	**RMD**
17	70	$500,000	$29,412	17	70	$500,000	
16.3	71	$494,118	$30,314	16.3	71	$532,350	
15.5	72	$486,994	$31,419	15.5	72	$566,318	$36,537
14.8	73	$478,354	$32,321	14.8	73	$563,620	$38,082
14.1	74	$468,334	$33,215	14.1	74	$559,164	$39,657
13.4	75	$456,875	$34,095	13.4	75	$552,833	$41,256
12.7	76	$443,919	$35,954	12.7	76	$554,505	$42,874
12.1	77	$429,413	$35,498	12.1	77	$534,062	$44,137
11.4	78	$413,620	$36,282	11.4	78	$521,771	$45,769
10.8	79	$396,205	$36,686	10.8	79	$507,152	$46,959
			$334,187				**$335,722**

As these charts illustrate, the SECURE Act has little impact on the total amount of the RMDs withdrawn and therefore, is nearly tax neutral for the taxpayer. However, the savings potential is significantly increased for a taxpayer to plan for future needs or leave monies to the next generation. Lifting this savings restriction does not increase revenue production for the government and is really intended to simply encourage taxpayers to continue saving if they are able. The contribution limits are applicable for tax years starting after December 31, 2019, and will begin to apply in 2020. This means a 75-year-old taxpayer could not make a contribution in the first part of 2020 to count for the prior year like a 65-year-old taxpayer could have done under the late contribution rules.

Delayed Required Beginning Date

The SECURE Act increases the age for the required beginning date. Before the act, the term *required beginning date* meant April 1 of the calendar year following the later of:

- The calendar year in which the employee attains age 70½, or
- The calendar year in which the employee retires.

The SECURE Act replaces age 70½ with age 72. Therefore, taxpayers will be able to wait longer to start taking their required minimum distributions. If a taxpayer is still employed past age 72 and wishes to further delay withdrawals, the taxpayer must confirm that all retirement accounts are eligible for delay based on the employment exception—not all plans may permit deferral until retirement.

Most practitioners and taxpayers see this provision as a positive change. With the workforce continuing to work later in life, many taxpayers are seeing a significant increase in their income when they reach 70½ because they are still working but they also have to take withdrawals from their retirement accounts—even though they may not actually need the money to supplement their lifestyles.

The effective date for this provision is December 31, 2019. Since the effective date is based on when the taxpayer reaches 70½, there will still be some taxpayers under age 72 who need to take distributions. Those who had already reached 70½ as of the effective date were not grandfathered in.

The following charts illustrate how these changes might affect an individual taxpayer with varying balances in his account. The first chart illustrates a $500,000 account growing at 5 percent per year. Over 10 years, the total RMDs for the taxpayer who waited until age 72 are less than the taxpayer who started RMDs at age 70. From an income tax saving standpoint, this change favors the taxpayer over a 10 year period of time.

Comparing $500,000 IRA at 70½ vs. 72 (10 Years)							
Single Life	Age	Account Value (5%) Growth + No Contribution	RMD	Single Life	Age	Account Value (5%) Growth + No Contribution/ Year	RMD
17	70	$500,000	$29,412	17	70	$500,000	
16.3	71	$494,118	$30,314	16.3	71	$525,000	
15.5	72	$486,994	$31,419	15.5	72	$551,250	$35,565
14.8	73	$478,354	$32,321	14.8	73	$541,470	$36,586
14.1	74	$468,334	$33,215	14.1	74	$530,128	$37,598
13.4	75	$456,875	$34,095	13.4	75	$517,157	$38,594
12.7	76	$443,919	$35,954	12.7	76	$502,491	$39,566
12.1	77	$429,413	$35,498	12.1	77	$486,071	$40,171

Comparing $500,000 IRA at 70½ vs. 72 (10 Years)							
Single Life	Age	Account Value (5%) Growth + No Contribution	RMD	Single Life	Age	Account Value (5%) Growth + No Contribution/ Year	RMD
11.4	78	$413,620	$36,282	11.4	78	$468,195	$41,070
10.8	79	$396,205	$36,686	10.8	79	$448,482	$41,526
			$334,187				**$310,675**

If the analysis is expanded to a 15-year withdrawal period, as shown in the next chart, the total RMDs become greater for the taxpayer who waited until age 72 in comparison to the taxpayer who started withdrawing RMDs at age 70. This result is attributable to the fact that the account is able to grow larger in the beginning which then requires higher RMDs. Advisers should analyze this possible result to ensure a client's tax liability is optimized.

Comparing $500,000 IRA at 70½ vs. 72 (15 Years)							
Single Life	Age	Account Value (5%) Growth + No Contribution	RMD	Single Life	Age	Account Value (5%) Growth + No Contribution/ Year	RMD
17	70	$500,000	$29,412	17	70	$500,000	
16.3	71	$494,118	$30,314	16.3	71	$525,000	
15.5	72	$486,994	$31,419	15.5	72	$551,250	$35,565
14.8	73	$478,354	$32,321	14.8	73	$541,470	$36,586
14.1	74	$468,334	$33,215	14.1	74	$530,128	$37,598
13.4	75	$456,875	$34,095	13.4	75	$517,157	$38,594
12.7	76	$443,919	$35,954	12.7	76	$502,491	$39,566
12.1	77	$429,413	$35,498	12.1	77	$486,071	$40,171
11.4	78	$413,620	$36,282	11.4	78	$468,195	$41,070
10.8	79	$396,205	$36,686	10.8	79	$448,482	$41,526
10.2	80	$377,495	$37,009	10.2	80	$427,303	$41,892
9.7	81	$357,510	$36,857	9.7	81	$404,681	$41,720
9.1	82	$336,686	$36,998	9.1	82	$381,110	$41,880
8.6	83	$314,672	$36,590	8.6	83	$356,191	$41,418
8.1	84	$291,986	$36,048	8.1	84	$330,512	$40,804
7.6	85	$268,735	$35,360	7.6	85	$304,194	$40,025
			$533,049				**$558,415**

STUDY QUESTION

1. Gloria is an 80-year-old retiree. After the passage of the SECURE Act, how much can she contribute to her IRA?

a. $0

b. $6,000

c. $7,000

d. $26,000

¶ 806 RETIREMENT PLAN WITHDRAWAL CHANGES

As a result of the SECURE Act and the CARES Act, early withdrawal penalty waivers are expanded as detailed in the following sections.

Penalty Waiver for Childbirth and Adoption

In order to encourage taxpayers from withdrawing retirement funds prior to retirement, a 10 percent penalty is assessed on withdrawals prior to age 59½ in addition to any income tax consequences. As a result of the SECURE Act, Code Sec. 72(t) added a new early withdrawal penalty waiver for sums up to $5,000. To qualify for this waiver, the withdrawal must occur within one year *after* the birth of a child or the finalization of an adoption of a child under age 18. There is no requirement that the $5,000 be used for costs related to birth or adoption. The rule applies on a "per-taxpayer" basis, which means each parent could withdraw $5,000 penalty-free. This withdrawal waiver is available after each birth or adoption. Taxpayers may recontribute the withdrawn amount in later years according to regulations that will be drafted.

Penalty Waiver for COVID-19 Hardships

To alleviate the financial pressure felt by many as a result of the coronavirus, the CARES Act created another exception to the 10 percent early withdrawal penalty tax under Code Sec. 72(t). The terms of this penalty waiver were further explained in Notice 2020-50. Eligible employees may withdraw up to $100,000 from their IRA or 401(k) plan without penalty. A distribution will be subject to normal income taxation rules related to distributions. Employees eligible for the exception include those:

- Who are diagnosed with COVID-19;
- Whose spouse or dependent is diagnosed with COVID-19;
- Who experienced adverse financial consequences as a result of being quarantined, furloughed, laid off, having work hours reduced, having a job offer delayed or rescinded, or being unable to work due to lack of child care due to COVID-19;
- Who are the owner of a business that is closing or reducing hours due to COVID-19; or
- Who are impacted by other factors as determined by the Treasury Secretary.

Keep in mind that even though the early withdrawal penalty is waived, withdrawals are still subject to income tax. The income tax liability related to a coronavirus withdrawal may be spread over a three-year period, and withdrawn funds may be recontributed in later years without being subject to annual contribution limits.

Tax preparers should be mindful that the default treatment for these withdrawals is to recognize the taxable income over a three year tax period. Taxpayers may elect to recognize the entire distribution in 2020. Taxpayers should analyze their 2020 income tax bracket, their future income tax brackets, and their potential eligibility for any stimulus tax credits when deciding how to report these distributions.

Repayment of Withdrawals

Repayment of a retirement plan withdrawal related to the COVID-19 pandemic may be made within three years of the account withdrawal. Once it is repaid, the taxpayer must file an amended tax return to claim a refund for the income tax paid on the withdrawal. Once repaid, the withdrawal is treated as a completed rollover. Furthermore, the repayment is not subject to the annual retirement account contribution limits.

The CARES Act does not limit repayment to taxpayers of a certain age; however, since the 10 percent penalty only applies to taxpayers under age 59½, there could be an argument that the repayment exception applies only to individuals under age 59½ who would otherwise be subject to the penalty. Taxpayers should stay tuned for additional guidance on this topic.

STUDY QUESTIONS

2. A married couple suffering from COVID-19 who give birth to a child in 2020 can withdraw a maximum of _______ from their IRA accounts.

a. $5,000

b. $10,000

c. $100,000

d. $210,000

3. Under the CARES Act, eligible employees impacted by COVID-19 who take retirement distributions prior to age ____ do not have to pay the 10 percent early withdrawal penalty tax.

a. 59½

b. 62

c. 65

d. 70

4. Which of the following employees is eligible to escape the early withdrawal penalty under the new COVID-19 related withdrawal rules?

a. An employee whose sibling was diagnosed with COVID-19

b. An employee who was laid off due to COVID-19 downsizing

c. A doctor on the front line of the COVID-19 fight

d. A business owner whose business is strong and has not been affected by the COVID-19 pandemic

¶ 807 RETIREMENT PLAN LOAN CHANGES AND REPAYMENT RULES

Credit Cards

Prior to the passage of the SECURE Act, some plans offered credit cards linked to 401(k) plan loans. However, these have been eliminated. Code Sec. 72(p) was revised to prohibit loans via credit cards for 401(k) plans.

Modified Plan Loan Rules

Employer retirement plans are not required to offer loans. But if they do offer loans, the pre-pandemic rules required that total outstanding loans could not exceed the lesser of:

- $50,000, or
- Fifty percent of the employee's vested balance (once the account reaches $20,000).

Such loans were required to be repaid within five years. Employers are permitted to set their own loan limits and terms as long as they do not exceed the statutory thresholds. Note that these rules apply to employer-sponsored plans such as 401(k) plans; they do not apply to IRAs. Section 2202 of the CARES Act modified the plan loan rules. The maximum loan amount is increased to the lesser of:

- $100,000, or
- 100 percent of the employee's vested balance.

However, employers are not required to offer these increased limits for their plan participants. The increased limits are available until September 23, 2020 (180 days from enactment). Borrowers eligible for the modified loans include those:

- Who are diagnosed with COVID-19;
- Whose spouse or dependent is diagnosed with COVID-19;
- Who experienced adverse financial consequences as a result of being quarantined, furloughed, laid off, having work hours reduced, or being unable to work due to lack of child care due to COVID-19;
- Who are the owner of a business that is closing or reducing hours due to COVID-19; or
- Who are impacted by other factors as determined by the Treasury Secretary.

Repayment of New and Existing Outstanding Loans

Repayment for both COVID-19 related and otherwise outstanding loans that are due between March 27, 2020, and the end of 2020 can also be delayed for up to a year. This extension applies to qualified employees who are working, furloughed, or on a temporary leave of absence. Interest on the outstanding loan continues to accrue on any outstanding balance. The employer's plan may extend the term of the loan by up to one year, providing a six-year repayment term instead of a five-year term. The extension will not necessarily be granted automatically.

Plan sponsors are *not* responsible for confirming an employee's eligibility for loans or withdrawals based on the coronavirus factors. The employee is personally responsible to ensure their own eligibility for these programs.

STUDY QUESTION

---

5. Which of the following statements is true about the modified retirement plan loan rules under the CARES Act?

a. All employer retirement plans must now offer loans to their employees.

b. The retirement plan loan amount cannot be more than $50,000 or 50 percent of the employee's vested balance.

c. The retirement plan loan amount cannot be more than $100,000 or 100 percent of the employee's vested balance.

d. The new loan rules apply to both IRAs and 401(k) plans.

¶ 808 RETIREMENT PLAN AMENDMENTS FOR EMPLOYERS

Employer-related deadlines have been extended by the CARES Act (see Notices 2020-18 and 2020-23 and Rev. Proc. 2018-58). Deadlines falling between April 1, 2020, and July 15, 2020, were extended to July 15, 2020, including:

- Form 5500 filings for plan years that ended in September, October, or November of 2019;
- Repayment of loans from qualified retirement plans;
- The five-year deferral of recognition of employee equity grants as income;
- Distributions of deferrals in excess of the Code Sec. 402(g) limit; and
- Distributions of contributions in connection with failed nondiscrimination testing.

When updating their plan documents for the CARES Act modifications, plan sponsors (i.e. employers) should:

- Examine their plan's loan limits and consider expanding them to allow for larger loans.
- Examine the loan repayment terms to permit additional time for employees who request repayment deferrals or have outstanding loans at the time of termination.

The plan amendments to incorporate the CARES Act changes apply for calendar years beginning after December 31, 2019.

Single-Employer Defined Benefit Plan Funding Delay

Single-employer defined benefit plans have more time to meet their funding obligations by delaying the due date for any contribution, including quarterly contributions. Contributions due during 2020 can be delayed until January 1, 2021; however, they must be contributed to the plan with interest.

Employer Plan Amendment Requirements

Employers may take action to amend their retirement plans immediately to provide for the expanded COVID-19 distributions and loans. Amendment is not actually required until the last day of the plan year beginning on or after January 1, 2022. For calendar-year plans, the amendment to the plan documents must be made by no later than December 31, 2022. Government plans have until December 31, 2024, to make the necessary amendments. However, employers should consider amending plans sooners so employees can confidently take advantage of the expanded options since the loan and penalty waiver provisions do not apply indefinitely. Notice 2020-50 clarified that employees who qualify for coronavirus related relief do not have to wait for an employer to amend a plan to take advantage of the expanded relief.

Plan Loan Procedure Updates

Loan procedures should also be updated to permit suspension of loan payments during the pandemic and permit employees to apply for loans based on the increased loan amounts. Delayed loan payments should be accurately coded to prevent loans with suspended payments from going into default. Amortization schedules should also be updated accordingly. Loan procedures should be updated to account for any increased loan amounts (i.e., $100,000 or 100 percent vested balance or whatever sum is chosen by the employer).

As far as repayment, plan loans are typically repaid through payroll deductions. If an employee ceases employment, the loan balance must be repaid during the grace period specified in the plan (which is usually a few months). Plan sponsors may want to amend their plan documents or loan policies to provide added flexibility for repayment after termination. Defaults on loans are counted as distributions and will be subject to income tax and possibly the 10 percent early withdrawal penalty.

If mass layoffs are planned, plan sponsors should consider amending their plan documents or loan policies to provide added flexibility for repayment after termination. Doing so is recommended if many participants have outstanding loans and will not be able to repay them during the difficult unemployment environment.

STUDY QUESTION

6. Nongovernmental employers who decide to amend their retirement plans to provide for the expanded COVID-19 distributions and loans must make those amendments:

a. By the last day of the plan year beginning on or after January 1, 2021

b. By the last day of the plan year beginning on or after January 1, 2022

c. By December 31, 2021

d. By December 31, 2024

¶ 809 EMPLOYER USE OF PAYCHECK PROTECTION PROGRAM FUNDS FOR RETIREMENT PLANS

The Paycheck Protection Program (PPP), signed into law as part of the CARES Act, offers forgivable loans to eligible businesses. While this chapter does not provide a full discussion of the ins and outs of the PPP, there are many questions about whether an employer who receives a PPP loan can use the funds toward meeting the employer obligation on retirement contributions.

PPP loans are low-interest forgivable loans. The amount that can be borrowed is based on the business's prior payroll. The forgiveness is based on whether the business actually used the loan proceeds to meet payroll and other permissible expenses. While there are many nuances to the forgiveness, the business must essentially spend at least 60 percent of the money on payroll costs. The other 40 percent can be used for costs such as rent and utilities. Originally these percentages were set at 75 percent for payroll but were later reduced as part of the Paycheck Protection Flexibility Act signed into law on June 4, 2020.

For purposes of this chapter, the question employers should consider is whether the term *payroll costs* includes an employer's contributions to a retirement plan. The following are considered payroll costs:

- Salaries, tips, and commissions (except annual salaries over $100,000; see the next section)
- State and local employer payroll taxes
- Health insurance premiums
- Employee retirement plan contributions

The amount of the PPP loan that can be forgiven will be reduced if any of the employees who historically earned less than $100,000 per year have their salaries reduced by more than 25 percent, or if the business does not bring back all of its full-time workers. The original covered period for the PPP loan forgiveness examination (being 8 weeks compared to the later expanded 24 weeks) caused employers to worry that they could not fully utilize their PPP monies for payroll expenses. Therefore, as discussed in the following, contributions toward retirement plans have been an attractive method for employers to meet these spending thresholds.

Payroll Costs, Retirement Contributions, and $100,000 Salary Cap

According to the IRS FAQs, the CARES Act excludes from the definition of payroll costs any employee compensation in excess of an annual salary of $100,000. However, that exclusion does not apply to all employee benefits of monetary value. The exclusion of compensation in excess of $100,000 annually applies only to cash compensation, not to noncash benefits, including:

- Employer contributions to defined-benefit or defined-contribution retirement plans;
- Payment for the provision of employee benefits consisting of group health care coverage, including insurance premiums; and
- Payment of state and local taxes assessed on compensation of employees.

In order to be eligible for full loan forgiveness, at least 60 percent of the loan proceeds must be used toward those items that qualify as *payroll costs*. Since so many loan recipients have had mass layoffs and work reductions, some employers are seeking additional ways to use their PPP monies and still qualify for forgiveness in situations where their employee payroll alone does not meet the 60 percent threshold. The following chart illustrates how an employer can use a retirement plan contribution to meet the 60 percent payroll costs qualification.

Example: Using Retirement Contributions for "Payroll Costs"			
Loan Eligibility Figures		**Covered Period**	
Employee 1	$80,000	Employee 1	$8,000
Employee 2	$40,000	Employee 2	$4,000
Total	$120,000	Total	$12,000
PPP Loan (Payroll/12 × 2.5)	$25,000	Retirement Contribution	$3,000
Payroll Forgiveness Threshold 60 Percent of Loan Amount	$15,000	Total Payroll Costs	$15,000

Retirement Plan Contributions

Employers who make matching contributions on employee deferrals to certain defined contribution plans can utilize these contributions to qualify for full loan forgiveness. The guidance released to date indicates that the portion of the matching contributions allocable to and paid during the covered period can be included as a forgivable payroll cost. Other potential contributions that may qualify (pending guidance) include:

- Matching contributions allocable to the portion of 2020 *before* the covered period but *paid during* the covered period
- Contributions due for 2019 but paid in 2020 during the covered period
- Contributions for entire 2020 year made during the covered period

Profit-sharing (401(k)) matching contributions are usually made at the end of the year for the entire year instead of contributed at every pay period. It is possible that a proportionate share of the contributions made at the end of the year can be classified as "payroll costs" for calculating forgiveness. In order to maximize the chances that these contributions will be counted as payroll costs for purposes of PPP loan forgiveness, employers should make matching contributions for at least the eight-week or twenty-four-week covered period. Prepaying matching contributions for the portion of 2020 *after* the end of the covered period will likely *not* be considered a "payroll cost."

Employers wishing to make contributions during the covered period may require an amendment to the retirement plan documents since the plan document may specify the annual payment date. Such entities should check for allocation conditions, such as a last-day or hours of service requirement. Accelerating contributions can create problems. Entities should be prepared to present amendments to the board of directors or managing partners to adopt a resolution authorizing officers to make retirement contributions during the qualifying period up to a stated maximum.

Even though using PPP funds for retirement plans may be cumbersome, there are several benefits to making contributions to plans:

- By funding retirement plan contributions during the covered period, employers will increase eligible payroll costs used to determine the forgiveness of their PPP loan.
- Contributions go toward the employer's potential future obligations under the plan.
- Contributions provide additional benefits employees can access through early, penalty-free 401(k) distributions and plan loans under the hardship rules.
- Increasing eligible payroll costs may increase the amount of the employer's mortgage interest, rent, and utilities paid during the covered period that may be forgiven.

Owner-Employees and Self-Employed Persons

There are caps on the amount of loan forgiveness available for owner-employees and self-employed individuals' own payroll compensation. The amount of loan forgiveness requested can be no more than the lesser of 8/52 of 2019 compensation or $15,385 per individual, if using the eight-week covered period or 24/52 of 2019 compensation or $46,154 per individual, if using the twenty-four-week covered period. No additional forgiveness is provided for retirement or health insurance contributions for self-employed individuals, including Schedule C filers and general partners, as such expenses are paid out of their net self-employment income.

For self-employed individuals or owner-employees, adding to retirement accounts will not help them because, as was clarified by the IRS, the amount of the forgiveness for these individuals is based on their compensation in 2019. So unlike employees with salaries in excess of $100,000 who can have retirement contributions added to their eligible payroll costs, self-employed individuals do not benefit from the same rule.

¶ 810 WITHDRAWAL OPTIONS FOR RETIREMENT PLAN BENEFICIARIES

Prior to the SECURE Act, the options for withdrawing an IRA were divided into three categories—surviving spouses, named beneficiaries, and no beneficiary. Then, depending on whether the decedent had already reached their required beginning date, there were varying distribution options that would apply to the post-death withdrawals.

Subsection (B) of Code Sec. 401(a)(9) laid out the three options for the Code as it was written before the SECURE Act changes:

> (B) Required Distributions Where Employee Dies Before Entire Interest is Distributed
>
> (i) For a participant's death **after the required beginning date**, the plan must distribute at least as quickly as it would have distributed to the plan participant.

(ii) For a participant's death **before the required beginning date**, the plan must distribute within 5 years.

(iii) If the participant **names a beneficiary**, then the plan can distribute over the beneficiary's life expectancy instead of under the (i) and (ii) rules.

The following chart provides a summary of the old rules for account owners who died *after* their RMDs had begun, meaning that they died after the required beginning date of April 1 after reaching age 70½.

	Options *After* Minimum Distributions Begin
Spouse Beneficiary	Spouse can receive distributions over the surviving spouse's remaining single life expectancy as recalculated using the single life table. Spouse can rollover the plan balance to an IRA in the surviving spouse's name and delay distributions until the spouse is age 70½. Spouse can receive distributions over the deceased owner's remaining single life expectancy reduced by one year each year after death.
Nonspouse Beneficiary	Beneficiary can rollover the plan balance to an inherited IRA and distribute over the longer of the remaining single life expectancy of the beneficiary *or* the remaining life expectancy of the participant.
No Named Beneficiary (Payable to Estate)	Distribution may continue over the remaining distribution period of the deceased owner. The remaining distribution period is reduced by one each year.

The following chart is a summary of the rules for taking distributions if the account owner died *before* reaching his or her required beginning date. As explained in further detail below, the changes instituted by the SECURE Act provide a better result for taxpayers who fail to name a beneficiary. Unfortunately, for named beneficiaries who do not qualify as Eligible Designated Beneficiaries, the new withdrawal rules are much more restrictive.

	Options *Before* Minimum Distributions Begin
Spouse Beneficiary	Spouse can receive distributions over the surviving spouse's remaining single life expectancy as recalculated using the single life table beginning when the deceased owner would have turned age 70½. Spouse can rollover the plan balance to an IRA in the surviving spouse's name and delay distributions until the spouse is age 70½. Fully distribute plan within five years.
Nonspouse Beneficiary	Distribute deceased owner's account within five years. Beneficiary can roll over the plan balance to an inherited IRA and distribute over the remaining single life expectancy of the beneficiary.
No Named Beneficiary (Payable to Estate)	Distribute deceased owner's account within five years.

The SECURE Act adds a new Subsection H, which provides as follows:

(H) SPECIAL RULES FOR CERTAIN DEFINED CONTRIBUTION PLANS.—In the case of a defined contribution plan, if an employee dies before the distribution of the employee's entire interest—

(i) IN GENERAL.—Except in the case of a beneficiary who is not a designated beneficiary (i.e. no beneficiary or estate or non-see thru trust), subparagraph (B) (ii)—

(I) shall be applied **by substituting '10 years'** for '5 years', and

(II) **shall apply whether or not distributions of the employee's interests have begun** in accordance with subparagraph (A).

(ii) EXCEPTION FOR ELIGIBLE DESIGNATED BENEFICIARIES.—Subparagraph (B) (iii) shall apply only in the case of an eligible designated beneficiary.

This new subsection negates the effectiveness of (i) by making (ii) apply to both pre-required beginning date and post-required beginning date deaths. Second, it replaces the five-year payout term for deaths before the required beginning date with a 10-year payout term. For participants who failed to name a beneficiary, this change actually provides welcome relief from the compressed five-year withdrawal period. Unfortunately, (B)(iii) which previously provided the "stretch IRA" option to any named beneficiary has now been limited to apply only to eligible designated beneficiaries as defined by statute.

Since the passage of the SECURE Act, the distribution options can be divided into four categories: (1) spouses, who still have a range of distribution options; (2) eligible designated beneficiaries, who have the old "stretch IRA" options; (3) individuals or trusts that were actually named as a beneficiary on the participant's form (the 10-year rule); and (4) the no beneficiary category with the five-year or remaining life expectancy rule.

Post-SECURE Act Distribution Options	
Spouses	Spouse can receive distributions over the surviving spouse's remaining single life expectancy as recalculated using the single life table. Spouse can rollover the plan balance to an IRA in the surviving spouse's name and delay distributions until the spouse reaches their required beginning date. Spouse can receive distributions over the deceased owner's remaining single life expectancy reduced by one year each year after death.
Eligible Designated Beneficiary (Disabled, Ill, and Minors)	Beneficiary can rollover the plan balance to an inherited IRA and distribute over the longer of the remaining single life expectancy of the beneficiary *or* the remaining life expectancy of the participant.
Designated Beneficiaries	Fully withdraw account by the end of the 10th year following the decedent's date of death.
No Beneficiary	Fully withdraw account by the end of the 5th year following the decedent's date of death or over the decedent's remaining life expectancy depending on whether the decedent died before or after his required beginning date.

The new category of "eligible designated beneficiary" who are not subject to the 10-year payout includes:

- The surviving spouse of the employee (the account owner)
- A child of the employee who has not reached majority (Note that the exception is not for all minors; instead, the exception is for *children* of the employee who are minors. A taxpayer cannot name grandchildren as beneficiaries in hopes of qualifying for the longer payout term.)
- Disabled beneficiaries in accordance with the Code Sec. 72(m)(7) definition
- A chronically ill individual (Code Sec. 7702B(c)(2))
- Any other individual who is less than 10 years younger than the decedent

STUDY QUESTION

7. Which of the following is ***not*** an eligible designated beneficiary under Subsection H of the SECURE Act?

- **a.** The employee's adult son
- **b.** An individual suffering from a chronic illness
- **c.** A disabled beneficiary
- **d.** The employee's surviving spouse

¶ 811 WAIVER OF 2020 REQUIRED MINIMUM DISTRIBUTIONS

To alleviate market concerns of retired investors, the CARES Act implemented an RMD "holiday" for 2020. The reasoning behind offering such a holiday include:

- Additional decreases in account balances add to the already traumatic psychological toll of decreasing account balances.
- Stocks purchased during a market boom must be sold at bargain prices.
- The 2020 RMD is based on last year's account balance as of December 31, 2019, resulting in a potentially significant balance decrease.
- The 2009 economic crisis stimulus package included a similar waiver.

The 2020 RMD "holiday" waives the 2020 RMD requirement, including the 2019 RMD due by April 1, 2020. No COVID-19 related hardship is required for a taxpayer to skip the RMD. This rule affects taxpayers whose 70th birthday was prior to July 1, 2019. Taxpayers whose 70th birthday was after July 1, 2019, are covered by the SECURE Act and are not required to begin RMD withdrawals until April 1 of the year following their 72nd birthday. Those taxpayers who did not take their 2019 RMD and planned to take it by April 1 essentially got to skip two RMDs, because without this rule, they would have had to take two RMDs (both 2019 and 2020). Plans covered by this waiver include:

- IRAs
- Roth IRAs
- 401(k)s
- 403(a)s
- 403(b)s
- 457(b)s
- SEP IRAs
- SIMPLE IRAs
- TSPs

The following plans are not covered by the RMD holiday provisions: defined benefit plans, nongovernmental Sec. 457(b) plans, annuitized annuities in retirement accounts, and Sec. 72(t) "substantially equal payment" distribution schedules.

The waiver is particularly beneficial for the following taxpayers:

- 2020 RMD payments for individuals who already are withdrawing annual distributions (individuals who reach age 70½ before 2019).
- 2020 RMD payments for individuals who turned age 70½ or retired (if later) in 2019, and the 2019 RMD if not already withdrawn.

- 2020 RMD payments for individuals who have a required beginning date of April 1, 2021, as a result of their retirement in 2020.
- 2020 RMD payments for beneficiaries of an inherited IRA who would have been required to withdraw a distribution based on their own life expectancy.

Estate of a Deceased Employee on Five-Year Plan

According to Code Sec. 401(a)(9)(B), if an employee dies before his required beginning date and does not name a beneficiary (i.e., the plan is payable to the estate), then the account must be withdrawn within five years of the date of death. The CARES Act extends this by one year by eliminating 2020 from the five-year calculation. This applies to the estates of individuals dying in 2015–2019.

Qualifications for the six-year plan (extending the deadline for withdrawal of the account by one year) include the following:

- The employee died before January 1, 2020.
- The employee died before the required beginning date and was under age 71 as of July 1, 2019.
- The five-year rule was elected by the beneficiary (i.e., not a lump-sum payout) or was applied under the terms of the governing document.

EXAMPLE: Alberto passed away in 2017. The five-year withdrawal period would have ended in 2022. Alberto's estate now has until the end of 2023 to fully withdraw the retirement account. The account is not required to be withdrawn ratably over the five-year period; Alberto's estate may wait until the end of the fifth year to fully deplete the account.

Beneficiaries on the 10-Year Plan

The SECURE Act abolished the "stretch IRA" and requires most beneficiaries to withdraw an inherited IRA account within 10 years after the date of death. That means the 10-year clock starts ticking in the year *after* the decedent's death. Because 2020 is the first year this rule applies, there is essentially no effect to beneficiaries governed by the 10-year rule. The estate of a decedent dying in 2020 will not have to withdraw any remaining RMD on behalf of the decedent prior to releasing the funds to the beneficiary.

Inherited IRAs

For designated beneficiaries who inherited IRA accounts prior to 2020 and are using the "stretch IRA" rules, no RMD is required during 2020. Similarly, for non-designated beneficiaries using the deceased owner's life expectancy, no distribution is required during 2020. However, in 2021, the remaining life expectancy must be reduced by two years to account for the lapse in time (since the normal annual reduction is one year).

Benefits to the Taxpayer of Skipping the RMD

Taxpayers who decide not to take a RMD can keep their monies invested and allow their retirement accounts to more fully recover from negative market volatility. Taxpayers can also reduce their 2020 income tax burden and possibly qualify for the economic stimulus credit on their 2020 tax return.

Under the CARES Act, economic impact payments were made to taxpayers based on their 2018 or 2019 returns. Married taxpayers filing jointly with annual income under $150,000 qualified for a $2,400 stimulus check. The amount was phased out up to an income of $198,000. Single taxpayers with annual income below $75,000 qualified for a $1,200 payment; the amount was phased out up to income of $99,000. Taxpayers subject to these limitations who did not receive a full stimulus check can claim a credit on their

2020 Form 1040 if their 2020 earnings are within the threshold. If a previously schedule RMD can be cancelled to enable the taxpayer's income to fall within these thresholds, this could be an added benefit for the taxpayer.

A taxpayer who is considering skipping a RMD should consider several questions:

- Can I afford to skip it?
- What is my tax bracket?
- Should I consider taking a partial RMD to push myself up to the edge of the next tax bracket?
- Am I eligible for a stimulus payment?
- What is my anticipated future income?

Qualified Charitable Distributions

Taxpayers are still allowed to take qualified charitable distributions (QCDs) at age 70½ even after the SECURE Act change in the required beginning date age. Making a QCD during 2020 will not offset any 2020 RMD because none is owed. However, a taxpayer can still make a QCD from his or her IRA and send money directly to a qualified charity. Because no RMD is owed in 2020, the QCD will not offset any future RMDs, but the QCD will further reduce the taxpayer's account balance and reduce the total taxable income on future RMDs.

STUDY QUESTIONS

---

8. A taxpayer may skip his 2019 required minimum distribution (RMD) if he turned ___ years old in 2019.

a. 59½

b. 70½

c. 71

d. 72

9. Which statement about the RMD "holiday" is true?

a. A taxpayer must provide he or she has experienced a hardship related to the COVID-19 pandemic to qualify.

b. A taxpayer can skip making RMDs for up to five years.

c. A RMD is not required during the time an employee is on vacation.

d. The 2020 RMD requirement is waived.

¶ 812 REPAYMENT OF WITHDRAWN RMDs

For taxpayers who already took their 2020 RMD, there is no provision in the CARES Act that explicitly allows repayment of the RMD. The typical method of recontribution to an IRA is through a rollover; however, RMDs are not eligible for rollover. Because 2020 has no RMD withdrawal requirement, withdrawals that have been made are technically not RMDs. Therefore, employees may roll back such withdrawals into the same account or into a different IRA account if they meet the 60 day rollover window.

Most taxpayers may not act quickly enough to qualify for the 60 day rollover. In the months following the passage of the CARES Act, practitioners guessed at alternate methods for recontribution. As discussed in the following, authority has since been issued which clarifies taxpayers' options for recontributing RMDs withdrawn by unknowing taxpayers earlier in the year.

Recontribution under Notice 2020-51

Notice 2020-51 was finally issued by the IRS which provides explicit guidance to taxpayers who withdrew a RMD prior in the year and want to return it to their retirement account. The Notice permits taxpayers to recontribute withdrawn funds withdrawn at any time during 2020 to their account before August 31, 2020.

Previously, the IRS had permitted taxpayers to recontribute RMDs taken after February 1, 2020 until July 15, 2020 under Notice 2020-23. The IRS second notice broadens the recontribution to any 2020 withdrawals and specifically applies to any individual who turned 70½ after December 31, 2019 who withdrew a RMD without realizing that the SECURE Act changed the required beginning age to 72. Key too is the ability of a beneficiary of an inherited IRA to recontribute any withdrawn funds to their inherited IRA which has never previously been allowed.

Coronavirus Recontribution Rules

Under CARES Act Section 2202(a), distributions related to coronavirus complications may be rolled over to another retirement account within three years of the date of receipt. This rule applies to distributions taken anytime during 2020. To qualify, an individual must experience a COVID-19 related hardship during 2020 (even if it is after the withdrawal). This recontribution rule may also help clients recontribute RMD withdrawals after the August 31, 2020 deadline passes.

> **EXAMPLE:** Cynthia is a 74-year-old IRA owner who took what she believed to be her 2020 IRA RMD in January of 2020. Fortunately, Cynthia is in excellent financial shape and does not need (or want) to take any money out of her IRA.
>
> Upon hearing about the RMD relief in the CARES Act, Cynthia called her tax advisor to see if she could roll back the RMD. Her adviser recommends returning the withdrawal before August 31, 2020. Cynthia does not complete the recontribution paperwork by the deadline.
>
> Suppose, however, that in September 2020, Cynthia is diagnosed with COVID-19. As a result of that diagnosis, Cynthia can (retroactively) classify her January 2020 distribution as a coronavirus-related distribution. In doing so, the rollover deadline for that distribution becomes three years from the date of receipt, thus allowing her to replace the would-be RMD in her account to avoid taxation of the distribution.

Self-Certification for Late Recontribution

As a method of potential last resort, Rev. Proc. 2016-47 permits employees to self-certify that they qualify for a late rollover if they meet one of the following criteria:

- An error was committed by the financial institution.
- The distribution was misplaced and never cashed.
- The distribution was deposited in an account the taxpayer mistakenly thought was an eligible retirement plan.
- The taxpayer's principal residence was severely damaged.
- A member of the taxpayer's family died.
- The taxpayer or a member of the taxpayer's family was seriously ill.
- The taxpayer was incarcerated.
- Restrictions were imposed by a foreign country.
- A postal error occurred.

- The distribution was made on account of a levy under Code Sec. 6331.
- There is a delay in the provision of necessary information to the taxpayer.

Taxpayers may be able to rely on this "catch all" rule to explain their inability to recontribute their withdrawn RMD within the permitted timeframe.

¶ 813 ESTATE PLANNING WITH RETIREMENT ACCOUNTS

Ever since the SECURE Act was introduced in March 2019, planners have been trying to come up with ideas to help clients avoid the unfortunate 10-year withdrawal period for non-eligible designated beneficiaries. There are two main concerns for clients. The first is the accelerated payment of tax. Some of these suggestions will help alleviate that concern. However, clients also worry about giving their children or beneficiaries the unfettered ability to access funds. Historically, clients name trusts as beneficiaries to address this issue. While this is still feasible, it can create some unintended consequences if a client's estate planning documents are not drafted to accommodate the new withdrawal rules. The next sections discuss several planning ideas.

Using IRA Funds During Life

Withdrawing funds over the owner's lifetime may very well be the best option for a client who is in a lower income tax bracket. Of course, analysis should be done to ensure this is the best option for the client. Such withdrawals might benefit clients who are in a lower tax bracket than their children, or those who incur significant medical expenses later in life, especially after they move into assisted living. A client who has carryover losses that can shelter additional income might also opt to withdraw funds over their lifetime. Clients who are already charitably inclined should consider using these funds and make qualified charitable contributions instead of writing checks or cashing in non-qualified funds.

Converting an IRA to a Roth IRA

Clients might also consider converting their IRA to a Roth IRA. This requires income tax analysis similar to medical expenses, tax rates, losses, etc. Of course, this may not be ideal for every client depending on their current income tax bracket, but with tax rates at historical lows right now, conversion to a Roth IRA may be an idea that some clients want to consider.

Naming Multiple Non-Spouse Beneficiaries

Another simple planning recommendation is to name multiple beneficiaries of a retirement account instead of just a single. By doing this, the taxpayer can spread out the 10-year withdrawal payments among multiple taxpayers instead of conglomerating all the income onto one beneficiary's tax return.

> **EXAMPLE:** If a taxpayer's son is the beneficiary of a $500,000 IRA, at a minimum, the son's income increased by $50,000 per year. If a taxpayer's three grandchildren are the beneficiaries of a $500,000 IRA, each grandchild's income only increased by $16,666 per year—they are also likely in lower tax brackets than their parents.

If the taxpayer does not get around to making this decision, the beneficiary can consider disclaiming the inherited IRA, if by doing so it would pass down to his children. Caution must be exercised when using disclaimers to avoid accounts being payable to the estate and then being subject to the shorter five-year payout schedule.

Accumulation Trusts

To address control issues when clients are worried that their children will cash out the entire retirement account and spend it foolishly, planners historically recommend accumulation trusts. With an accumulation trust, the trust is named as the beneficiary instead of the irresponsible child. The benefit of a trust is that the trustee can time the withdrawals from the IRA and dole out the money to the beneficiaries as needed. However, the disadvantage of accumulation trusts is that any income that is not distributed to a beneficiary is taxed to the trust at the trust's income tax rates, which are draconian in comparison to individual income tax rates.

See-through (or conduit) trusts. In the past, estate planners have avoided the problem of significant income tax by requiring that the trustee distribute the "RMD" to the beneficiaries annually. Since the passage of the SECURE Act, there is no longer a definition for a RMD during the 10-year payout term. Technically, there is no RMD until the final year when the trustee would be required to withdraw the entire account.

Clients who have retirement accounts for which they have named their trust as the beneficiary should meet with their estate planner to review the language in their documents and ensure they are not creating a tax time bomb. Some of these account owners may want to consider naming the individuals as direct beneficiaries on their accounts if those individuals are old enough to responsibly manage the funds.

Discretionary trusts. With a discretionary trust, the trustee is given discretion to make distributions to the beneficiaries as needed. Oftentimes these trusts include language which directs the trustee to withdraw only the bare minimum from a taxable retirement account and to only take withdrawals from the retirement funds if no other assets are available. Additionally, if beneficiaries do not actually need monies, there is no impetus on the trustee to withdraw funds. Again, this might result in a situation where the trustee is prevented from taking a withdrawal until the tenth year and triggering a significant amount of income tax.

Naming a Testamentary Charitable Remainder Trust as Beneficiary

Naming a charitable remainder trust as a beneficiary of an IRA might achieve tax deferral similar to the stretch IRA and maintain control over the monies so the beneficiaries do not receive everything at once. A charitable remainder trust can be effected in the following manner:

- Testamentary charitable remainder trust language is included in the participant's estate plan.
- The participant names the charitable remainder trust as the beneficiary of the plan.
- The charitable remainder trust claims the account at the participant's death.
- The charitable remainder trust can withdraw from the account now or over the 10-year period.
- Distributions are made over a lifetime or period of years to named beneficiaries.

Careful analysis must be done to ensure a charitable remainder trust achieves the client's goals. Unlike an accumulation or discretionary trust, the terms of a charitable trust are less flexible to accommodate future changes for the beneficiary. A charitable trust can ensure continued fund management and delayed taxable for clients who are especially concerned with these issues.

¶ 814 RECOMMENDATIONS FOR EMPLOYEES AND EMPLOYERS

In light of the CARES Act penalty waivers and loan expansion, employees might wonder whether they should take a retirement account distribution or take advantage of the expanded loan options. The chart below provides a comparison of these options.

Retirement Account Distributions vs. Loan	
Distribution	**Loan**
No early withdrawal penalty	No penalty
No repayment obligation	Must be repaid with interest
Income tax due	No income tax

For most borrowers, continued retirement savings get put on hold until the 401(k) loan is repaid. Payroll deductions for 401(k) loan repayment typically eliminate or greatly reduce 401(k) contributions during the five year payback period. Losing five years of retirement savings, and likely forfeiting the employer's matching contributions, is potentially a significant setback in the retirement savings process. The following analyzes an employee who takes a loan and then uses his $10,000 annual contribution to repay the loan versus the employee who takes a withdrawal but continues contributing as normal.

Loan vs. Withdrawal			
Employee earns $200,000, contributes 5% ($10,000), 2.5% match ($5,000)		**COVID Loan**	**COVID Withdrawal**
IRA balance 2020		$200,000	$200,000
COVID loan/withdrawal		$(50,000)	$(50,000)
Post-loan balance		$150,000	$150,000
Annual repayment ($10,000 + 5% growth)	Year 1	$167,500	$172,500
	Year 2	$185,875	$196,125
	Year 3	$205,169	$220,931
	Year 4	$225,427	$246,978
MFJ tax liability on withdrawal ~$12,500	Year 5	$246,699	$274,327

Another client might wonder whether he should take a withdrawal or just stop his contributions. As reflected in the following chart, mathematically, the options are about equal for an employee who withdraws $10,000 versus an employee who skips two years of $5,000 contributions. However, the tax liability on the withdrawal must also be considered in comparison to the income tax savings on pre-tax contributions to the account. This comparison has much less drastic differences for the employee.

Withdrawal vs. Stopping Contributions			
Employee earns $50,000, contributes 10% ($5,000), 2.5% match ($2,500)		**Stop Contributions**	**COVID Withdrawal**
IRA balance 2020		$75,000	$75,000
COVID loan/withdrawal		—	$(10,000)
Post-loan balance		$75,000	$65,000
Annual repayment ($10,000 + 5% growth)	Year 1	$78,750	$75,750
	Year 2	$82,688	$87,038
	Year 3	$94,322	$98,889
	Year 4	$106,538	$111,334
Single tax liability on withdrawal $2,200	Year 5	$119,365	$124,401

The new rules related to retirement plans also pose questions for employers. Some might wonder if they should reduce their retirement plan contributions. They should keep in mind that freezing or reducing future benefit accruals under a defined benefit plan requires them to provide plan participants with written notice at least 45 days before the effective date of the reduction. The reduction may also require a plan amendment. Safe harbor plans are subject to additional restrictions that may prohibit reductions.

Employers who are considering cancelling their retirement plan should note the following:

- A reduction in force of 20 percent or more of a qualified retirement plan's participants in a particular plan year can result in the partial termination of the plan.
- Partial plan termination provides immediate and full vesting to all affected participants.
- Full termination of a plan fully vests *all* participants, plus a new plan may not be opened within 12 months following the termination, with some exceptions.

Employers must analyze whether a cancellation is desirable given all the facts and circumstances.

The impact of the COVID pandemic is extensive, and there are no quick fixes. Employers must think long-term and consider all their fiscal responsibilities. Amending a retirement plan to help employees may be advisable. Employers should also consider the impact of any decisions on employee morale during this difficult time.

When making retirement plan decisions, employees also need to think long-term, taking into account their future tax obligations and income changes. They should consider lifestyle changes instead of savings reductions, and calculate the differences between the options available to them.

CPE NOTE: When you have completed your study and review of chapter 8, which comprises Module 4, you may wish to take the Final Exam for this Module. Go to **cchcpelink.com/printcpe** to take this Final Exam online.

¶ 10,100 Answers to Study Questions

¶ 10,101 MODULE 1—CHAPTER 1

1. a. *Correct.* This is the first step in determining if an expenditure is deductible by a business. If yes, the next step to consider is if there is any such limit under any subsection Code Sec. 162 (i.e., such as a penalty disallowed by Code Sec. 162(f)).

b. *Incorrect.* This is not the first step in determining if an expenditure is deductible by a business. Instead, this is considered for entertainment, meal and certain travel expenses once the expense is determined to be ordinary and necessary and there is not a Code Sec. 162 subsection limit.

c. *Incorrect.* This is not the first step in determining if an expenditure is deductible by a business. Instead, this is considered only for charitable contributions.

d. *Incorrect.* This is not the first step in determining if an expenditure is deductible by a business. Instead, this is considered after an ordinary and necessary expense is determined to be entertainment or meal related.

2. a. *Incorrect.* Compensation for services is included within gross income. However, note that gross income does not include most fringe benefits such as ones that meet the definition of a qualified transportation fringe (Code Sec. 132(f)).

b. *Incorrect.* Commissions are included within gross income similar to salary and wages.

c. *Correct.* Gross income means all income from whatever source derived. However, exclusions for many types of fringe benefits includes *de minimis* fringe benefits as defined at Code Sec. 132(e).

d. *Incorrect.* The value of season tickets to the local sports team are included within gross income when given to an employee.

3. a. *Incorrect.* This is the incorrect percentage reduction amount. Instead, for meals that are a *de minimis* fringe or for the convenience of the employer, the amounts incurred after December 31, 2017, and before January 1, 2026, are reduced by a higher percentage amount.

b. *Correct.* In accordance with the TCJA changes to Code Sec. 274(n), this provision generally applies to amounts paid or incurred after December 31, 2017.

c. *Incorrect.* This is the incorrect percentage reduction. For these types of meals, they are reduced by a lower percentage amount. This provision generally applies to amounts paid or incurred after December 31, 2017.

d. *Incorrect.* For meals that are a *de minimis* fringe or for the convenience of the employer, the amounts incurred after December 31, 2017, and before January 1, 2026, are reduced by a lower percentage amount.

4. a. *Incorrect.* This is the incorrect date. Instead, meals provided for the convenience of the employer are 50 percent deductible for a limited time period after December 31, 2022.

b. *Incorrect.* Meals provided for the convenience of the employer are 50 percent deductible for a limited time period after December 31, 2023. However, after a certain date, they are no longer deductible.

c. ***Incorrect.*** Meals provided for the convenience of the employer are deductible for a limited time period after December 31, 2024. In general, they are 50 percent deductible in accordance with Code Sec. 274.

d. ***Correct.*** **After December 31, 2025, meals provided for the convenience of the employer are no longer deductible. However, it is possible that this provision may be changed before this date.**

5. a. ***Incorrect.*** Food and beverages for employees are not excepted from either the employee/taxpayer lavish or extravagant provision or the 50 percent disallowance.

b. ***Incorrect.*** Meetings of business leagues are not excepted from either the employee/taxpayer lavish or extravagant provision or the 50 percent disallowance. An example of expenses that are excepted from both are expenses for items made available to the public.

c. ***Correct.*** **Expenses treated as compensation are also excepted from both the employee/taxpayer lavish or extravagant provision and the 50 percent disallowance. This is also the case for reimbursed expenses.**

d. ***Incorrect.*** Employee business meetings are not excepted from either the employee/taxpayer lavish or extravagant provision or the 50 percent disallowance. An example of expenses that are excepted from both are expenses includible in income of persons who are not employees.

6. a. ***Correct.*** **Publication 463 covers travel, entertainment, gift and car expenses.**

b. ***Incorrect.*** Publication 535 does not relate to travel, gift, and car expenses. Instead, this publication relates to business expenses.

c. ***Incorrect.*** Publication 15-B does not relate to travel, gift, and car expenses. Instead, this publication is the *Employer's Tax Guide to Fringe Benefits*.

d. ***Incorrect.*** Publication 5137 does not relate to travel, gift, and car expenses. Instead, this publication is a *Fringe Benefit Guide*. Also note that there are IRS training materials for employee meals in the hospitality industry.

¶ 10,102 MODULE 1—CHAPTER 2

1. a. ***Incorrect.*** The deduction is 20 percent for QBI.

b. ***Incorrect.*** The deduction is available to taxpayers other than C corporations. This includes Schedule C and Schedule E businesses.

c. ***Correct.*** **The 20 percent deduction for QBI is limited to 20 percent of taxable income without regard to net capital gain income.**

d. ***Incorrect.*** The deduction may be phased out if taxable income exceeds a threshold amount.

2. a. ***Incorrect.*** The general 20 percent deduction applies to the taxpayer's combined business income. Therefore, Marty's QBID is based on $60,000 of QBI.

b. ***Correct.*** **If a taxpayer has an overall QBI profit but one or more loss activities, the loss(es) are apportioned among the profitable operations. The apportionment is done by relative business income of the profitable operations.**

c. ***Incorrect.*** Since Marty has an overall QBI profit, there is no loss to carry forward to the next tax year.

d. ***Incorrect.*** Even though Company A has the highest income of the three companies, Company C's loss is not entirely apportioned to Company A.

3. a. ***Incorrect.*** The maximum QBID is 20 percent of the taxpayer's QBI.

b. ***Incorrect.*** The deduction is based on the taxpayer's QBI. When a taxpayer's taxable income exceeds certain thresholds, the deduction may be limited.

c. ***Incorrect.*** The QBID limit is based on the wages of the business, not the taxpayer's wages.

d. ***Correct.*** **If the taxpayer's taxable income exceeds the threshold, the deduction may be limited to the greater of 50 percent of W-2 wages for the business or 25 percent of W-2 wages plus 2.5 percent of the unadjusted basis of depreciable business assets.**

4. a. ***Incorrect.*** Even though the taxpayer is over the taxable income threshold, his QBI is from a non-service business. Therefore, as long as other criteria are met, such as wages from the business, the taxpayer will have at least some QBID.

b. ***Incorrect.*** This is the wage/capital limit (25 percent of wages plus 2.5 percent of UBIA). This amount is compared to the wage limit, and the greater of those two limits are then compared to the maximum QBID to determine the deduction allowed.

c. ***Correct.*** **The normal QBID is 20 percent of the QBI. Since the taxpayer is over the taxable income threshold, he must compare this amount to the greater of the wage and wage/capital limits. His deduction will be the lesser of those two amounts. In this case, the wage limit of $100,000 ($200,000 × 50%) is the greater of the wage and wage/capital limits. Therefore, his deduction is limited to the lesser amount of 20 percent of his QBI, $350,000 × 20% = $70,000.**

d. ***Incorrect.*** This is the taxpayer's wage limit. This amount is greater than the normal QBID.

5. a. ***Incorrect.*** This is the wage/UBIA limit. This is the lower of the wage and wage/UBIA limits so it is not the QBID amount.

b. ***Correct.*** **The normal QBID is $70,000. However, because taxable income is greater than $421,400, the deduction is limited to $50,000, which is a full reduction to the wage limit.**

c. ***Incorrect.*** This is the normal QBID. However, since taxable income is over $421,400, the normal QBID is limited to the wage or wage/UBIA limits.

d. ***Incorrect.*** The QBID cannot exceed 20 percent of taxable income. However, the normal QBID is below this amount.

6. a. ***Incorrect.*** Although the taxpayer's taxable income is over the threshold and there are no wages from the qualified business, there is UBIA that should be considered when computing the QBID.

b. ***Correct.*** **The wage limit is zero and the wage/UBIA limit is $1,000,000. Therefore, the deduction is the lower amount of $600,000 ($3,000,000 × 20%).**

c. ***Incorrect.*** This is the wage/UBIA limit ($0 wage limit + $40,000,000 × 2.5%).

d. ***Incorrect.*** The taxable income limit does not apply because 20 percent of the QBI limit is less than the wage or wage/UBIA limit.

7. a. ***Incorrect.*** Although the taxpayer's QBI is from a service business, her taxable income is below the threshold of complete phaseout of the QBID. Since she has wages and UBIA, some QBID is available.

b. ***Correct.*** **Since the taxpayer's QBI is from a service business and her taxable income is above the threshold of $321,400, she must reduce each component of the QBID by the applicable percentage (100% – [($391,400 – $321,400)/ $100,000] = 30%). Her QBID ceiling is $18,000 ($300,000 × 30% × 20%). Her QBID floor is $9,000 ($60,000 × 30% × 20%).**

c. ***Incorrect.*** This is the deduction ceiling.

d. ***Incorrect.*** This would be the taxpayer's QBID if the qualified business was a non-service business.

8. a. ***Incorrect.*** Section 162 has been used as a test for determining whether an activity is a trade or business under both Section 1411 and 199A. However, Section 162 does not identify any specific activities as rising to a level of trade or business.

b. ***Incorrect.*** Whether an activity is a trade or business is important for many reasons. For instance, when a trade or business asset is sold at a loss, the loss can offset ordinary income under Section 1231. Section 1231 does not, however, define a trade or business.

c. ***Correct.*** **Section 162 does not clearly define a trade or business, so case law is often looked upon for guidance. The level of taxpayer activity may determine whether an activity is a trade or business. Cases such as *Hazard v. Commissioner*, 7 TC 372, have determined that a single rental may be a trade or business.**

d. ***Incorrect.*** Although both Sections 199A and 1411 point to Section 162 for the definition of trade or business, Section 162 does not in fact have a clear definition. Case law positions are frequently cited for the definition.

9. a. ***Correct.*** **To be able to aggregate businesses, the businesses must have the same year end and have common direct or indirect ownership of 50 percent or more. The businesses must also meet two of the following three criteria: (1) the same product or service is offered together, or the nature of the product service and the product is such that they are commonly offered together, (2) the businesses share facilities or business elements, (3) the businesses are operated in coordination or with reliance on one another.**

b. ***Incorrect.*** Although not in the regulations, the preamble does point out that the businesses must have the same year end.

c. ***Incorrect.*** Aggregation of SSTB with non-SSTB is not allowed unless the service business is incidental to the non-service business.

d. ***Incorrect.*** Common ownership must be 50 percent or more to aggregate.

10. a. ***Incorrect.*** Because there is common ownership, the rental activity is not automatically considered a non-service business.

b. ***Incorrect.*** Taxpayers cannot segregate the non-service portion of a business if there is 50 percent or more of common ownership and the non-SSTB income is earned from providing services or products to the SSTB and 80 percent or more of the gross receipts are from the service business.

c. ***Correct.*** **The law firm and the rental have greater than 50 percent common ownership and 100 percent of the gross receipts of the rental comes from an SSTB. Therefore, these two businesses will be aggregated.**

d. ***Incorrect.*** A law firm is a service business, so it is not a non-SSTB.

11. a. ***Incorrect.*** Architects and engineers are specifically excluded from the definition of a service business.

b. ***Incorrect.*** Brokerage services do not include insurance agents/brokers or real estate agents/brokers.

c. ***Incorrect.*** Performing arts includes actors, directors, musicians, athletes, and coaches. It does not include others that may contribute to the performance, such as lighting and sound technicians.

d. ***Correct.*** **State licensing is not relevant in determining whether a service is considered a service business for purposes of Section 199A. Bookkeeping services are considered accounting and paralegal services are considered law.**

12. a. ***Incorrect.*** This information is not reported to an owner because the owner's QBID is based on factors beyond those included in the pass-through entity, such as the taxpayer's taxable income and other sources of QBI. The QBI is reported, however.

b. ***Incorrect.*** The owner's share of W-2 wages of the business is reported to the owner to calculate the QBID.

c. ***Correct.*** **The determination of whether the entity is or is not an SSTB is made at the entity level and is reported to the owners. If the entity is classified as an SSTB, the owner cannot then aggregate the entity with other entities for purposes of Section 199A.**

d. ***Incorrect.*** Pass-through entities generally do not aggregate. However, if they do, it should be reported to the owners. A pass-through entity would not make recommendations to owners, so that is not reported.

¶ 10,103 MODULE 2—CHAPTER 3

1. a. ***Correct.*** **COVID-19 postponement applies to all taxpayers including individuals, trusts and estates, corporations, and other non-corporate tax filers. However, it is unlikely to apply to partnerships.**

b. ***Incorrect.*** COVID-19 postponement applies to all taxpayers including individuals. The postponement also applies to corporations.

c. ***Incorrect.*** COVID-19 postponement applies to all taxpayers including trusts. An affected taxpayer for COVID-19 relief means any person with a federal income tax return due on April 15, 2020.

d. ***Incorrect.*** COVID-19 postponement applies to all taxpayers including estates. The postponement also applies to other non-corporate tax filers. However, note that the coverage is very narrow.

2. a. ***Incorrect.*** The filing of estate and gift tax returns was not postponed due to COVID-19. However, note that IRA contributions due April 15, 2020, were in fact postponed.

b. ***Incorrect.*** The filing of employment and excise tax returns was not postponed due to COVID-19. However, HSA contributions due April 15, 2020, were in fact postponed.

c. ***Correct.*** **Income tax returns due April 15, including, but not limited to, Forms 1040, 1120, and 1041, were postponed due to COVID-19. However, income tax returns due May 15 or June 15 were not postponed.**

d. ***Incorrect.*** Withdrawing excess elective deferrals was not postponed due to COVID-19. Additionally, filing information returns were not postponed.

3. a. ***Incorrect.*** Even though the time for funding IRAs has been extended, you should fund IRAs now. In fact, you can fund 2019 tax year and 2020 tax year IRAs now.

b. ***Correct.*** **This is an incorrect statement. Instead, you should consider converting a traditional IRA to a Roth IRA.**

c. ***Incorrect.*** You should consider wash loss rules. Additionally, it's important to note that IRS Publication 564 says that ordinarily, shares issued by one mutual fund are not substantially identical to shares issued by another mutual fund.

d. ***Incorrect.*** This is a planning idea related to the current stock market decline. Gifting is another area to consider. However, be sure to keep in mind the potential for step-up on assets included in the estate.

¶ 10,104 MODULE 2—CHAPTER 4

1. a. ***Incorrect.*** It is available to individuals who, as determined by the applicable state unemployment agency, meet the state's usual criteria to receive UI benefits.

b. ***Incorrect.*** It does not require states to increase the amount regularly available for unemployment under state law. The states continue to pay the amounts that apply to those that meet their criteria. FPUC is a federal program.

c. ***Correct.*** **It provides an increase of a flat payment of $600 per week to the amount regularly available for unemployment under state law and is funded by the federal government.**

d. ***Incorrect.*** It applies to weeks of unemployment beginning after the state agrees to participate in the program through July 31, 2020.

2. a. ***Incorrect.*** Qualified improvement property refers to any improvement made by a taxpayer to an interior portion of a building.

b. ***Correct.*** **Qualified improvement property refers to any improvement to an interior portion of an existing building. Examples include installation or replacement of drywall, ceilings, interior doors, fire protection, mechanical, electrical, and plumbing.**

c. ***Incorrect.*** Qualified improvement property refers to improvements made to an existing building.

d. ***Incorrect.*** Qualified improvement property refers to improvements of nonresidential real property.

3. a. ***Incorrect.*** The CARES Act changes how NOLs arising in 2018, 2019, and 2020 are treated.

b. ***Incorrect.*** Prior to the CARES Act, NOL carryforwards could only offset 80 percent of taxable income in a given year. The CAREs Act changed this rule.

c. ***Incorrect.*** The $250,000/$500,000 limitation on the use of losses applied to individual taxpayers under the TCJA.

d. ***Correct.*** **NOLs arising in 2018, 2019, and 2020 may now be carried back five years, and continue to be carried forward indefinitely.**

4. a. ***Correct.*** **The TCJA limited the amount of flow-through business loss that can be used to offset nonbusiness income to $250,000 ($500,000 if filing jointly). The CARES Act eliminated this limitation for tax years 2018, 2019, and 2020.**

b. ***Incorrect.*** The CARES Act did not change that business losses from flow-through entities can be used to offset nonbusiness income, such as wages or investment income.

c. ***Incorrect.*** The CARES Act has not changed carryforward provisions of unused NOLs. It did change how the losses can be used in the current period, however.

d. ***Incorrect.*** The CARES Act changed the way business losses can be used for losses incurred in 2018, 2019, and 2020.

5. a. ***Incorrect.*** The new law states that early withdrawal is allowed without penalty up to $100,000 for qualified individuals.

b. ***Incorrect.*** Qualified individuals include not only those who have been diagnosed with the virus, but also family members, as well as those who are unable to work or had their work reduced.

c. ***Correct.*** **Penalty relief is available to qualified individuals that need the early withdrawal due to the coronavirus. Most individuals who have not been diagnosed with the coronavirus, do not have family members that were diagnosed, or did not suffer complete or partial job loss will not qualify for the penalty relief.**

d. ***Incorrect.*** Distributions from retirement plans are still included in gross income. The CARES Act only provides penalty relief.

6. a. ***Incorrect.*** The TCJA resulted in dips of charitable giving because many taxpayers were no longer benefiting from itemized deductions.

b. ***Correct.*** **Under the new law, for 2020 only, qualified contributions are disregarded in applying the 60 percent AGI limitation on cash contributions to qualifying charitable organizations.**

c. ***Incorrect.*** Deductible charitable contributions must be made to qualifying charities. Donor advised funds and supporting organizations are not included.

d. ***Incorrect.*** Even those who do not elect to itemize deductions can still benefit from the new above-the-line deduction.

7. a. ***Incorrect.*** The paid sick leave and expanded family and medical leave provisions of the FFCRA apply to certain public employers and private employers with fewer than 500 employees.

b. ***Correct.*** **Small businesses with fewer than 50 employees may qualify for exemption from the requirement to provide leave due to school closings or child care unavailability if the leave requirements would jeopardize the viability of the business as a going concern.**

c. ***Incorrect.*** Up to an additional 10 weeks of paid expanded family and medical leave may be available where an employee has been employed at least 30 calendar days.

d. ***Incorrect.*** An employee qualifies for paid sick time if the employee is unable to work or telework.

8. a. ***Incorrect.*** The deferral does not pertain to Medicare tax. It only applies to Social Security.

b. ***Correct.*** **Under the CARES Act, employers can defer paying their share of Social Security tax; 50 percent of the deferred amount must be paid by December 31, 2021, and the remaining 50 percent is due by December 31, 2022.**

c. ***Incorrect.*** Employers are generally required to withhold Social Security tax at 6.2 percent from their employees' wages, up to the annual wage limit. The annual wage limit of $137,700 for 2020 was not changed under the CARES Act.

d. ***Incorrect.*** Under the CAREs Act, employers can defer paying their share of Social Security tax. Social Security tax for employees and self-employed individuals must be paid as normal.

9. a. ***Incorrect.*** The EIDL is available to small businesses within the SBA size standards, small agricultural cooperatives and aquaculture businesses, and private non-profit organizations. However, it is not available to religious organizations, charitable organizations, and gambling concerns.

b. ***Incorrect.*** Interest rates on the EIDL are 3.75 percent for small businesses and 2.75 percent for non-profit organizations.

c. ***Correct.*** **Terms of up to 30 years are available, with the first payment due 12 months after funds are issued.**

d. ***Incorrect.*** Eligible entities may qualify for loan amounts up to $2 million.

10. a. ***Correct.*** **Applicants can apply for a loan for a maximum of $10 million from participating lenders. Loan amounts are based on payroll and covered cost amounts. It is calculated as 2.5 times the average total monthly payroll costs, up to $10 million.**

b. ***Incorrect.*** The interest rate on the PPP loan is 1 percent per annum with a term of two years.

c. ***Incorrect.*** Entities must have been operational by February 15, 2020, had payroll, and paid taxes.

d. ***Incorrect.*** Loan amounts are based on payroll and covered cost amounts.

11. a. ***Incorrect.*** If a business keeps all of its employees, the entirety of the loan will be forgiven.

b. ***Incorrect.*** If employees have been laid off, the forgiveness will be reduced by the percent decrease in the number of employees.

c. ***Correct.*** **If the employees are laid off employees, the forgiveness will be reduced by the percent decrease in the number of employees.**

d. ***Incorrect.*** Payroll costs are among several expenses that can be included in the PPP loan forgiveness amount.

12. a. ***Incorrect.*** The employee retention credit is a refundable tax credit against certain employment taxes.

b. ***Incorrect.*** The employee retention credit is equal to 50 percent of qualified wages.

c. ***Incorrect.*** The credit is based on wages paid after March 12, 2020, and before January 1, 2021.

d. ***Correct.*** **For each employee, wages, including certain health plan costs, up to $10,000 can be counted to determine the amount of the 50 percent credit.**

¶ 10,105 MODULE 2—CHAPTER 5

1. a. ***Incorrect.*** The FFCRA introduced new refundable paid leave payroll and self-employment tax credits tied to labor law changes for required sick and family/medical leave.

b. ***Correct.*** **The CARES Act introduced the PPP, which was later enhanced by other legislation.**

c. ***Incorrect.*** The TCJA was signed into law in December 2017 and included sweeping tax law changes.

d. ***Incorrect.*** P.L. 116-123 represents the first phase of legislation related to COVID-19 and did not include the PPP.

2. a. ***Incorrect.*** This waiver was included in Notice 2020-35, not Notice 2020-23.

b. ***Incorrect.*** There is no filing extension for payroll returns in Notice 2020-23; they are not included as specified forms in that notice.

c. ***Incorrect.*** This credit is detailed in Notice 2020-21, not Notice 2020-23.

d. ***Correct.*** **Notice 2020-23 extends to July 15, 2020, filing due dates that were originally due on or after April 1, 2020.**

3. a. ***Correct.*** **ABC Company is eligible for the refundable credits because it has fewer than 500 total employees.**

b. ***Incorrect.*** Government entities are typically not eligible for the refundable credits, and neither are entities with more than 500 employees.

c. ***Incorrect.*** This employer is not eligible for the credits. Part-time employees are counted for purposes of the refundable credits, and employers with more than 500 employees do not qualify.

d. ***Incorrect.*** Non-profit entities are not eligible for the credit if they employ more than 500 employees.

4. a. ***Incorrect.*** The EFMLEA is part of the FFCRA, not the CARES Act.

b. ***Incorrect.*** This statement pertains to the Emergency Paid Sick Leave Act (EPSLA), not to the EFMLEA.

c. ***Correct.*** **The EFMLEA generally allows up to 10 weeks of paid leave to employees who need a leave to care for their child under the age of 18 if the school or place of care has been closed, or the childcare provider of such child is unavailable, due to a public health emergency.**

d. ***Incorrect.*** This credit is offered for family leave for certain self-employed individuals; it is not offered under the EFMLEA.

5. a. ***Incorrect.*** The payroll and self-employment tax credits can be claimed for qualified leave beginning on a specified date in 2020, not in 2019.

b. ***Correct.*** **Payroll and self-employment tax credits can be claimed for qualified leave beginning April 1, 2020, and through the last day of 2020.**

c. ***Incorrect.*** This is not the qualified leave starting date for which the credits can be claimed. Rather, July 15, 2020, is the extended due date for certain filings and payments in Notice 2020-23.

d. ***Incorrect.*** December 31 is the ending date for qualified leave for which the credits can be claimed; it is not the starting date of the qualified leave.

6. a. ***Correct.*** **The ERC amount is 50 percent of the qualified wages of an employee, limited to $10,000 of wages/employee ($5,000 credit/employee).**

b. ***Incorrect.*** The ERC is fully refundable; it is applied against the employer portion of Social Security taxes (or railroad taxes) but is fully refundable via a reduction to payroll taxes owed.

c. ***Incorrect.*** There is no employer size limitation for the credit; however, qualified wages are measured differently if an employer has more than 100 full-time employees.

d. ***Incorrect.*** Governments and their agencies are *not* eligible for the ERC.

¶ 10,106 MODULE 3—CHAPTER 6

1. a. ***Incorrect.*** This is one of the two theories as it relates to wealth and the discharge of indebtedness. However, this is not the stronger of the two theories.

b. ***Correct.*** **Discharge of indebtedness is included in gross income based on two theories. This includes the freeing of assets and the loan proceeds theory (i.e., something for nothing).**

c. ***Incorrect.*** This is not one of the theories as it relates to wealth and the discharge of indebtedness. The two theories include freeing of assets and the loan proceeds theory.

d. ***Incorrect.*** This is not one of the theories as it relates to wealth and the discharge of indebtedness. One of the theories is the loan proceeds theory. This theory relates to the fact that something was given for nothing.

2. a. ***Correct.*** **Debt is the unconditional and legally enforceable obligation for the payment of money. It's important to look to the traditional debt/equity tests and intent of the parties.**

b. ***Incorrect.*** A liability does not explicitly mean an unconditional and legally enforceable obligation for the payment of money. Also note that a gift is not a true debt.

c. ***Incorrect.*** This is not the general term for an unconditional and legally enforceable obligation for the payment of money. Note that a debt must be true debt to produce cancellation of debt income.

d. ***Incorrect.*** Note that there is no cancellation of debt income if the debt is disputed or unliquidated. For example, this can relate to unenforceable gambling debts.

3. a. ***Incorrect.*** In order to qualify for a bankruptcy exception, the taxpayer must be subject to jurisdiction of bankruptcy court in a Title 11 case.

b. ***Incorrect.*** Qualified farm indebtedness is one of the key Code Sec. 108 exceptions. Farmers need special rules because a farm is a non-liquid asset.

c. ***Incorrect.*** This is one of the key Code Sec. 108 exceptions. It is meant to facilitate debt workouts for real estate and defer recognition until the property is sold.

d. ***Correct.*** **This is an important exclusion. The amount excluded is limited to the amount by which the taxpayer is insolvent. It's also important to note that the treatment of assets exempt from a bankruptcy estate is unclear.**

4. a. ***Incorrect.*** Certain tax credits are not considered first in the order of attribute reduction. Instead, they are considered second. They are reduced $1 for every $3 of COD income.

b. ***Correct.*** **Net operating losses are the first in the order of attribute reduction in accordance with Code Sec. 108(b)(2). After net operating losses, then certain tax credits are considered.**

c. ***Incorrect.*** Capital losses and capital loss carryovers are not considered first in the order of attribute reduction. Instead, they are considered third.

d. ***Incorrect.*** Basis in property is not considered first in the order of attribute reduction. Instead, it is considered fourth. Note that when considering the basis, depreciable property is considered first and then non-depreciable property.

5. a. *Correct.* In a basis reduction, this type of property is last. Taxpayers should keep in mind that there are other considerations for reducing tax attributes and limitations that may apply to basis reduction.

b. ***Incorrect.*** Real property used in a trade or business (other than inventory) that secured the discharged debt is first, not last, in the order of basis reduction.

c. ***Incorrect.*** Personal property used in a trade or business (other than inventory) that secured the discharged debt is second in a basis reduction, not last.

d. ***Incorrect.*** Inventory, accounts receivable, and real property held as inventory are not last in a basis reduction; rather, they are second to last.

6. a. ***Incorrect.*** A change in co-obligor on recourse debt is an example of a significant debt modification. Another example is a change from debt to equity.

b. ***Incorrect.*** A change in collateral on nonrecourse debt except fungible collateral is an example of a significant debt modification. Another example is a change in timing that results in a "material deferral" such as a change in maturity date or payments.

c. *Correct.* This is not an example of a significant debt modification. Instead, a significant debt modification is a change in yield that exceeds greater of 25 basis points or 5 percent of yield of the old debt instrument.

d. ***Incorrect.*** A change in priority of debt is an example of a significant debt modification. Another example is if there is a change in the obligor on recourse debt.

7. a. *Correct.* Chapter 7 is a type of individual bankruptcy that is a simple and quick basic liquidation. This compares to a Chapter 11, which is a type of reorganization where the individual continues to operate a business and control assets.

b. ***Incorrect.*** Chapter 11 is not a simple and quick basic liquidation. Instead, Chapter 11 is a type of individual bankruptcy that is a reorganization.

c. ***Incorrect.*** Chapter 13 is not a simple and quick basic liquidation. Chapter 13 is a "wage earner" bankruptcy where the individual pays off debts out of a steady income stream over three or five years.

d. ***Incorrect.*** This is not one of the forms of individual bankruptcy. Instead, the forms of individual bankruptcy include Chapter 7, Chapter 11, and Chapter 13.

8. a. ***Incorrect.*** This change was made by the Tax Cuts and Jobs Act (TCJA). Previously, business losses recognized by individuals could reduce nonbusiness income without limitation.

b. *Correct.* The CARES Act provides a five-year carryback for losses earned in 2018, 2019, or 2020, which allows firms to modify tax returns up to five years prior to offset taxable income from those tax years.

c. ***Incorrect.*** The NOL limitations for post-2017 losses were provided by the TCJA, not by the CARES Act. The CARES Act suspends the NOL limit of 80 percent of taxable income

d. ***Incorrect.*** This is not a change provided by the CARES Act; rather, it describes the guidance under Code Sec. 1398.

¶ 10,107 MODULE 3—CHAPTER 7

1. a. ***Incorrect.*** Although the CARES Act authorizes the Small Business Administration to temporarily guarantee loans under the Paycheck Protection Program, it does not outline a 24-week period in which to use the PPP funds.

b. ***Incorrect.*** The SBA provides loans to small businesses under the Paycheck Protection Program, but it does not specify that taxpayers are to use the funds in a 24-week covered period.

c. ***Correct.*** **All taxpayers who receive PPP funds are eligible to use a 24—week covered period, as opposed to the previous 8—week period. Most borrowers are expected to opt for the 24-week period, although they still can choose the 8-week period.**

d. ***Incorrect.*** The IRS has not specified a 24-week period in which taxpayers must use such funds.

2. a. ***Incorrect.*** Loans made before (not after) June 5, 2020, have a two-year maturity date; there is a different maturity date for loans made on or after June 5, 2020.

b. ***Correct.*** **Under the PPP Flexibility Act, the maturity date for a PPP loan made on June 5, 2020, or later is five years.**

c. ***Incorrect.*** The opposite is true; loans made *before* June 5 are subject to renegotiation. Borrowers and lenders may negotiate to extend the maturity date.

d. ***Incorrect.*** The Flexibility Act offers borrowers more freedom in how and when they can spend their PPP loan funds.

3. a. ***Correct.*** **An employee who works 40 hours/week or more equals one FTE, so a "haircut" would be allowed.**

b. ***Incorrect.*** No FTE haircut is allowed for employees who voluntarily resign.

c. ***Incorrect.*** A FTE haircut is not allowed for employees who voluntarily request a reduction in hours.

d. ***Incorrect.*** No FTE haircut is allowed for employees who are fired for cause.

4. a. ***Incorrect.*** June 30, 2020, represents the "magic moment" under the CARES Act, not the new date under the PPP Flexibility Act.

b. ***Incorrect.*** The CARES Act changed the original April 15, 2020, filing date for tax returns to July 15, 2020; this is not the new "magic moment" under the PPP Flexibility Act.

c. ***Correct.*** **The PPP Flexibility Act changed the date for the FTE employee and wage reduction safe harbors to December 31, 2020.**

d. ***Incorrect.*** The "magic moment" is in 2020, not in 2021.

¶ 10,108 MODULE 4—CHAPTER 8

1. a. ***Correct.*** **Even though taxpayers can continue their deductible contributions well after age 70½, Gloria still must have earned income to contribute to her IRA.**

b. ***Incorrect.*** The $6,000 IRA contribution limit applies to taxpayers under the age of 50 who are still working.

c. ***Incorrect.*** The $7,000 IRA contribution limit applies to taxpayers over the age of 50 who are still working.

d. ***Incorrect.*** Taxpayers over the age of 50 who are still working are limited to a $26,000 contribution to their 401(k) plan. Therefore, this limit does not apply to Gloria.

2. a. ***Incorrect.*** Each of the parents in this situation would be eligible to take a $5,000 IRA withdrawal penalty-free for the birth of the child plus another amount for their COVID-19 hardship.

b. ***Incorrect.*** Under Code Sec. 72(t), each parent can withdraw $5,000 from their IRA for the child, which totals $10,000. However, under the CARES Act they can withdraw more because they have been affected by COVID-19.

c. ***Incorrect.*** This amount does not reflect the couple's maximum IRA withdrawal under the SECURE Act and CARES Act.

d. ***Correct.*** **Both taxpayers can withdraw $100,000 if either of them tests positive for COVID-19, and both can take a $5,000 withdrawal for the birth of the child, for a total of $210,000.**

3. a. ***Correct.*** **Distributions taken by eligible employees before they turn 59½ years old are not subject to the early withdrawal penalty but are subject to normal taxation rules regarding distributions.**

b. ***Incorrect.*** Some taxpayers can take their Social Security retirement benefits as early as age 62, but this is not the age before which eligible employees must take retirement plan distributions to be excepted from the early withdrawal penalty.

c. ***Incorrect.*** Eligible employees are those who take retirement distributions at a younger age and meet other requirements.

d. ***Incorrect.*** Seventy is not the age before which an eligible employee could take a retirement distribution and be excepted from the early withdrawal penalty.

4. a. ***Incorrect.*** The exception for the early withdrawal penalty is not available to employees whose siblings have been diagnosed with coronavirus. However, the exception does apply to an employee who has been diagnosed with coronavirus or whose spouse has been diagnosed.

b. ***Correct.*** **The exception applies to employees who have experienced adverse financial consequences as a result of being quarantined, furloughed, laid off, having work hours reduced, or being unable to work due to lack of child care due to COVID-19.**

c. ***Incorrect.*** Doctors on the front lines are not automatically excepted from the early withdrawal penalty. They would have to meet other requirements, such as being diagnosed with COVID-19.

d. ***Incorrect.*** The owner of a business that is closing or reducing hours due to COVID-19 is excepted from the early withdrawal penalty, but a business owner who has not been affected by COVID-19 does not qualify for the exception.

5. a. ***Incorrect.*** The CARES Act does not include a requirement that an employer must provide such loans.

b. ***Incorrect.*** This was the maximum loan amount in place before the CARES Act was enacted.

c. ***Correct.*** **Section 2202 of the CARES Act modified the plan loan rules to reflect this maximum loan amount.**

d. ***Incorrect.*** The modified rules under the CARES Act apply to employer-sponsored plans such as 401(k) plans; they do not apply to IRAs.

6. a. ***Incorrect.*** Nongovernmental employers must make the plan amendment by a date later than the last day of the plan year beginning on or after January 1, 2021.

b. ***Correct.*** **Under the CARES Act, amendment is not required until the last day of the plan year beginning on or after January 1, 2022.**

c. ***Incorrect.*** This is not the deadline for making the necessary plan amendments for expanded COVID-19 distributions and loans.

d. ***Incorrect*** Government plans have until December 31, 2024, to make the necessary amendments. The date for nongovernmental plans is earlier.

7. a. ***Correct.*** **For purposes of Subchapter H, an employee's *minor* child is considered an eligible designated beneficiary; therefore, an adult son is not.**

b. ***Incorrect.*** Chronically ill individuals are eligible designated beneficiaries per Code Sec. 7702B(c)(2).

c. ***Incorrect.*** A disabled beneficiary is an eligible designated beneficiary as long as he or she meets the definition under Code Sec. 72(m)(7).

d. ***Incorrect.*** The surviving spouse of the employee (the account owner) is an eligible designated beneficiary and not subject to the 10-year payout.

8. a. ***Incorrect.*** The age at which a taxpayer can skip his RMD for 2019 is over age 59½.

b. ***Correct.*** **This is true because the taxpayer technically was able to wait until April 1, 2020, to take the RMD.**

c. ***Incorrect.*** This taxpayer should have taken an RMD; if he missed it, he will be subject to the penalty.

d. ***Incorrect.*** A taxpayer who turned 72 in 2019 should have taken the distribution. The taxpayer will be subject to the penalty if he did not do so.

9. a. ***Incorrect.*** There is no hardship requirement to qualify for the RMD "holiday."

b. ***Incorrect.*** The RMD "holiday" does not relieve a taxpayer of making RMDs for this period of time.

c. ***Incorrect.*** The RMD "holiday" allows taxpayers to skip a RMD in certain circumstances; however, a vacation has nothing to do with the "holiday."

d. ***Correct.*** **The 2020 RMD "holiday" waives the 2020 RMD requirement, including the 2019 RMD due by April 1, 2020.**

Index

References are to paragraph (¶) numbers.

¶ 10,200 Glossary

Adjusted taxable income (ATI) limitation: ATI is calculated by taking the taxable income for the taxable year as if Code Sec. 163(j) does not limit any interest deduction, and then adding and subtracting from it certain amounts for the taxable year:

- Additions: business interest expense; net operating loss deduction; deduction for qualified business income under Section 199A; depreciation, amortization, or depletion deduction; capital loss carrybacks or carryovers; and any deduction or loss not properly allocable to a non-excepted trade or business.
- Subtractions: business interest income; floor plan financing interest expense; the lesser of (i) gain realized on sale or disposition of property or (ii) deductions for depreciation, amortization, or depletion taken for such property during a tax year beginning after 2017 (and similar adjustments for sales or dispositions of property held by a partnership or member of a consolidated group upon the sale or other disposition of the partnership interest or stock of the member); and any income or gain that is not properly allocable to a non-excepted trade or business.

Aggregation: An election that may be made when certain criteria are met. The criteria are:

- The same person or group of persons, directly or indirectly, owns 50 percent or more of each trade or business to be aggregated;
- The ownership described above exists for a majority of the tax year, including the last day of the tax year, in which the items attributable to each trade or business to be aggregated are included in income;
- All of the items attributable to each trade or business to be aggregated are reported on returns with the same tax year;
- None of the trades or businesses to be aggregated is a specified service trade or business (SSTB); and
- The trades or businesses to be aggregated satisfy at least two of the following factors:
  - — The trades or businesses provide products, property, or services that are the same or customarily offered together;
  - — The trades or businesses share facilities or share significant centralized business elements;
  - — The trades or businesses are operated in coordination with, or reliance upon, one or more of the businesses in the aggregated group.

Bankruptcy: A legal process through which people or other entities who cannot repay debts to creditors may seek relief from some or all of their debts.

Business associate: According to Code Sec. 274, a person whom a taxpayer could reasonably expect to engage or deal in the active conduct of a trade or business, such as the taxpayer's customer, client, supplier, employee, agent, partner, or professional advisor.

CARES Act: The Coronavirus Aid, Relief, and Economic Security (CARES) Act (P.L. 116-136) was passed by Congress and signed into law on March 27, 2020. The CARES Act provides fast and direct economic assistance for American workers, families, and small businesses, and preserves jobs for American industries.

Charitable contribution: For tax deduction purposes, a cash or non-cash contribution made to a qualified organization. Contributions to individuals are never deductible.

COVID-19: An infectious disease caused by severe acute respiratory syndrome coronavirus 2.

***De minimis* fringe:** According to Code Sec. 132, any property or service whose value is so small as to make accounting for it unreasonable or administratively impracticable.

Debt: Unconditional and legally enforceable obligation for the payment of money.

Deemed exchange: When the taxpayer has a change in legal rights or entitlements due to modifying a debt instrument.

Discharge of indebtedness income: Debt is forgiven or cancelled and the creditor accepts less than full balance.

Early retirement account withdrawals: Generally, the amounts an individual withdraws from an individual retirement account (IRA) or retirement plan before reaching age 59½.

Economic Injury Disaster Loan (EIDL): A Small Business Administration program that can provide up to $2 million of financial assistance (actual loan amounts are based on amount of economic injury) to small businesses or private, nonprofit organizations that suffer substantial economic injury as a result of the declared disaster, regardless of whether the applicant sustained physical damage.

Emergency Family and Medical Leave Expansion Act (EFMLEA): Part of the Families First Coronavirus Response Act (FFCRA) that allows leave for employees who are unable to work (or telework) due to a need for leave to care for their son or daughter under the age of 18 if the school or place of care has been closed, or the childcare provider of such son or daughter is unavailable, due to the COVID-19 public health emergency.

Emergency Paid Sick Leave Act (EPSLA): Part of the Families First Coronavirus Response Act (FFCRA) that requires eligible employers to provide a specified amount of paid sick leave (generally, two weeks) to the employees who are unable to work or telework because of one of six specified reasons related to the COVID-19 pandemic.

Employee retention credit (ERC): An incentive under the CARES Act that encourages businesses to keep employees on their payroll. The refundable tax credit is 50 percent of up to $10,000 in wages paid by an eligible employer whose business has been financially impacted by COVID-19.

Families First Coronavirus Response Act (FFCRA): Legislation (P.L. 116-127) issued in response to the COVID-19 pandemic that includes funding for coronavirus testing as well as paid sick leave and family medical leave for workers affected by the pandemic.

Flow-through entity: A legal business entity that passes income on to its owners of the business. S corporations, partnerships, and sole proprietorships are examples of flow-through entities. Also known as a *pass-through entity.*

Freeing of assets theory: A theory that discharge of indebtedness income is realized when a decrease in the taxpayer's liabilities increases the taxpayer's net worth.

Gross income: According to Code Sec. 61, all income from whatever source derived, including compensation for services, such as fees, commissions, fringe benefits, and similar items.

Guarantee: Something for which the taxpayer is not the primary obligor, not the primary borrower, but just a guarantor of someone else's loan.

Income threshold limitation: A limitation on the qualified business income deduction that begins to phase out when a taxpayer's taxable income exceeds certain amounts.

For 2019, the income thresholds were $321,400 for married filing joint and $160,700 for all others.

Incurred: In determining when payroll costs were incurred or paid, *incurred* means the date the pay was earned.

Insolvency: Excess of liabilities over assets.

Loan proceeds theory: A theory that a debtor who receives funds in the form of a loan has an offsetting obligation to repay those funds. The taxpayer received "something for nothing." Therefore, the funds are not included in income and are tax-free. If the taxpayer does not repay the funds, however, the taxpayer must include them in income. Borrowing is treated as an "open" item until repayment or discharge, as though the taxpayer used the income to satisfy the debt.

Net operating loss (NOL): Occurs when certain tax-deductible expenses exceed taxable revenue for a tax year. A loss from operating a business is the most common reason for an NOL.

Paid: In determining when payroll costs were incurred or paid, *paid* means the date the taxpayer distributed the payroll checks/initiated an ACH transfer.

Paycheck Protection Program (PPP): A loan designed to provide a direct incentive for small businesses to keep their workers on the payroll. The Small Business Administration will forgive loans if all employees are kept on the payroll for eight weeks and the money is used for payroll, rent, mortgage interest, or utilities.

Paycheck Protection Program Flexibility Act of 2020: Legislation that amends the Paycheck Protection Program (PPP) and gives borrowers more freedom in how and when PPP loan funds are spent while retaining the possibility of full forgiveness.

Payroll costs: For purposes of the Paycheck Protection Program, payroll costs include salaries, tips, and commissions (except annual salaries over $100,000); state and local employer payroll taxes; health insurance premiums; and employee retirement plan contributions.

Payroll tax: Taxes imposed on an employer or employee. Employer payroll taxes are paid by the employer; employee payroll taxes are generally withheld from wages. Examples include Social Security, Medicare, and federal unemployment tax.

Pension: A fund into which a sum of money is added during an employee's employment years and from which payments are drawn to support the person's retirement from work in the form of periodic payments.

Qualified business income (QBI): The net amount of qualified items of income, gain, deduction, and loss with respect to any qualified trade or business of the taxpayer.

Qualified business income deduction (QBID): Allows eligible taxpayers to deduct up to 20 percent of their qualified business income (QBI), plus 20 percent of qualified real estate investment trust (REIT) dividends and qualified publicly traded partnership income. Income earned through a C corporation or by providing services as an employee is not eligible for the deduction.

Qualified improvement property: Any improvement to a building's interior. However, improvements do not qualify if they are attributable to: the enlargement of the building, any elevator or escalator, or the internal structural framework of the building.

Recourse debt: Debt backed by collateral from the borrower.

Relevant pass-through entity: A partnership (other than a publicly traded partnership) or S corporation owned by at least one person, trust, or estate.

Roth IRA: A retirement plan under U.S. law that is generally not taxed upon distribution, provided certain conditions are met.

Section 6662 penalty: An accuracy-related penalty imposed due to a substantial underpayment of tax.

SECURE Act: The Setting Every Community Up for Retirement Enhancement Act of 2019 (P.L. 116-94), which was signed into law on December 20, 2019. The act implemented major changes, particularly to Internal Revenue Code Sec. 401.

Specified service trade or business (SSTB): Any trade or business in the fields of accounting, health, law, consulting, athletics, financial services, or brokerage services, or any business where the principal asset of the business is the reputation or skill of one or more of its employees.

Tax Cuts and Jobs Act (TCJA): P.L. 115-97, major tax reform legislation that was signed into law on December 22, 2017, and amended the Internal Revenue Code of 1986. Major elements of the changes include reducing tax rates for businesses and individuals; and a personal tax simplification by increasing the standard deduction and family tax credits, but eliminating personal exemptions and making it less beneficial to itemize deductions.

Taxable income: The gross income of an individual or corporation, minus any allowable tax deductions. In other words, the amount of income that is subject to taxation by the government.

Trade or business: Any activity carried on for the production of income from selling goods or performing services.

Traditional IRA: A form of individual retirement plan provided by many financial institutions that provides tax advantages for retirement savings.

Unadjusted basis immediately after acquisition (UBIA): The basis of a property on the placed-in-service date by the relevant pass-through entity.

Unemployment compensation: A benefit paid by the state to an unemployed worker who has lost his or her job due to layoffs or retrenchment.

Wage limitation: Fifty percent of the W-2 wages with respect to the qualified trade or business.

Wage/UBIA (or wage/capital) limitation: The sum of 25 percent of the W-2 wages with respect to the qualified trade or business plus 2.5 percent of the unadjusted basis, determined immediately after acquisition, of all qualified property.

Working condition fringe benefit: According to Code Sec. 132, property or services provided by an employer to an employee that the employee could deduct under Code Sec. 162 if the employee had paid for them on their own.

¶ 10,300 Final Exam Instructions

To complete your Final Exam go to **cchcpelink.com/printcpe,** click on the title of the exam you wish to complete and add it to your shopping cart (you will need to register with CCH CPELink if you have not already). Click **Proceed to Checkout** and enter your credit card information. Click **Place Order** to complete your purchase of the final exam. The final exam will be available in **My Dashboard** under **My Account.**

This Final Exam is divided into four Modules. There is a grading fee for each Final Exam submission.

Online Processing Fee:	**Recommended CPE:**
$129.00 for Module 1	6 hours for Module 1
$129.00 for Module 2	6 hours for Module 2
$89.00 for Module 3	4 hours for Module 3
$79.00 for Module 4	3 hours for Module 4
$426.00 for all Modules	19 hours for all Modules
IRS Program Number:	**Federal Tax Law Hours:**
Module 1: 4VRWB-T-03783-20-S	6 hours for Module 1
Module 2: 4VRWB-T-03784-20-S	6 hours for Module 2
Module 3: 4VRWB-T-03785-20-S	4 hours for Module 3
Module 4: 4VRWB-T-03786-20-S	3 hours for Module 4
	19 hours for all Modules
CTEC Program Numbers:	
Module 1: 1075-CE-1975	
Module 2: 1075-CE-1976	
Module 3: 1075-CE-1977	
Module 4: 1075-CE-1978	

Instructions for purchasing your CPE Tests and accessing them after purchase are provided on the **cchcpelink.com/printcpe** website. **Please note, manual grading is no longer available for Top Federal Tax Issues. All answer sheets must be submitted online for grading and processing.**

Recommended CPE credit is based on a 50-minute hour. Because CPE requirements vary from state to state and among different licensing agencies, please contact your CPE governing body for information on your CPE requirements and the applicability of a particular course for your requirements.

Expiration Date: December 31, 2021

Evaluation: To help us provide you with the best possible products, please take a moment to fill out the course Evaluation located after your Final Exam.

Wolters Kluwer, CCH is registered with the National Association of State Boards of Accountancy (NASBA) as a sponsor of continuing professional education on the National Registry of CPE Sponsors. State boards of accountancy have final authority on the acceptance of individual courses for CPE credit. Complaints regarding registered sponsors may be submitted to the National Registry of CPE Sponsors through its website: www.learningmarket.org.

Additional copies of this course may be downloaded from **cchcpelink.com/printcpe.** Printed copies of the course are available for $4.50 by calling 1-800-344-3734 (ask for product 10024491-0008).

¶ 10,301 Final Exam Questions: Module 1

1. Once it is determined that an expenditure is both ordinary and necessary, the next consideration is whether:

a. It is charitable.
b. Any limit under Code Sec. 162 applies.
c. It is entertainment related and certain meals.
d. Any limit under Code Sec. 170 applies.

2. Which of the following is the first step in the general framework for the treatment of cash and non-cash items given to employees?

a. Determine whether it is a reimbursement for expenses incurred by employees.
b. Assess whether any exclusions apply.
c. Identify what was given and its value.
d. Assess if there are any restrictions on the employer deducting the amount.

3. Which of the following cash or non-cash items given to employees is taxable and withholding is generally required?

a. A holiday party primarily for employees other than highly compensated ones
b. Meals furnished for the convenience of the employer
c. An Amazon gift card
d. Tools for working at home

4. Which of the following means all remuneration for employment, including the cash value of all remuneration (including benefits) paid in any medium other than cash?

a. Bonuses
b. Wages
c. Commissions
d. Gross income

5. Provisions relating to disallowance of entertainment expenses generally apply to amounts paid or incurred after what date?

a. December 31, 2014
b. December 31, 2015
c. December 31, 2016
d. December 31, 2017

6. IRS Notice 2018-76 notes that meals are 50 percent deductible if how many specific requirements are met?

a. Three
b. Four
c. Five
d. Six

7. Which Code Sec. 274(e) exception below is ***not*** excepted from the employee/taxpayer lavish or extravagant provision or the 50 percent disallowance?

- **a.** Food and beverages for employees
- **b.** Expenses treated as compensation
- **c.** Recreational expenses for employees
- **d.** Entertainment sold to customers

8. Regarding recreational expenses for employees, businesses cannot discriminate in favor of highly compensated employees, officers, shareholders, or others who own ____ percent or greater interest in the business.

- **a.** 1
- **b.** 2
- **c.** 5
- **d.** 10

9. Which of the following schedules is the same as for 2017 despite new book–tax differences starting in 2018?

- **a.** Schedule M-1
- **b.** Schedule M-2
- **c.** Schedule M-4
- **d.** Schedule M-10

10. A(n) ______ fringe means any property or service whose value is so small as to make accounting for it unreasonable or administratively impracticable.

- **a.** Immaterial
- **b.** *De minimis*
- **c.** Inconsequential
- **d.** Unsubstantial

11. The Section 199A deduction for qualified business income (QBI) is:

- **a.** 10 percent
- **b.** 20 percent
- **c.** 30 percent
- **d.** 40 percent

12. How are net losses from qualified businesses treated for purposes of Section 199A?

- **a.** They must be carried back to the previous year.
- **b.** They are deducted from ordinary income.
- **c.** They are carried to the next tax year and will reduce an otherwise allowed QBI deduction (QBID).
- **d.** They are ignored for purposes of the QBID.

13. For 2019, the income threshold limitation for married filing jointly begins at:

- **a.** $160,700
- **b.** $210,700
- **c.** $321,400
- **d.** $421,400

14. Company A purchased equipment for $10,000 during 2019 and expensed the entire amount under Section 179. What is the unadjusted basis immediately after acquisition (UBIA) of the equipment?

- **a.** $0
- **b.** $5,000
- **c.** $8,000
- **d.** $10,000

15. A taxpayer is married filing jointly and reports taxable income of $300,000. Her QBI is $100,000, and the qualified business has no wages or UBIA. What is the taxpayer's QBID?

- **a.** $0
- **b.** $20,000
- **c.** $60,000
- **d.** $100,000

16. A taxpayer is married filing jointly and reports taxable income of $500,000. Her QBI from a non-service business is $200,000. Wages from the business are $100,000 and UBIA is $50,000 What is the taxpayer's QBID?

- **a.** $0
- **b.** $26,250
- **c.** $40,000
- **d.** $50,000

17. A taxpayer is married filing jointly and reports taxable income of $500,000. Her QBI from a non-service business is $200,000. Wages from the business are $50,000 and UBIA is $50,000 What is the taxpayer's QBID?

- **a.** $0
- **b.** $15,000
- **c.** $25,000
- **d.** $40,000

18. A taxpayer is single and has taxable income over the minimum taxable income threshold, but below the maximum threshold. His QBI is from a non-service Schedule C business. The business has no wages or UBIA. What can he do to increase his QBID with no changes to the structure of the business?

- **a.** Pay himself wages and issue a W-2.
- **b.** Classify his business as a service business.
- **c.** Increase his income from the Schedule C business.
- **d.** Reduce taxable income, such as by making a retirement contribution.

19. A taxpayer is married filing jointly and reports taxable income of $500,000. His QBI from a service business is $200,000. Wages from the business are $50,000, and UBIA is $50,000 What is the taxpayer's QBID?

- **a.** $0
- **b.** $15,000
- **c.** $25,000
- **d.** $40,000

20. The Section 6662 substantial underpayment penalty caused by the Section 199A deduction is reduced to understatements of _____ of proper liability.

a. 5 percent

b. 10 percent

c. 20 percent

d. 35 percent

21. Ann owns 100 percent of ABC Co., an S corporation, and a building that is rented to ABC Co. Which of the following statements regarding the rental is true?

a. The rental is not considered a trade or business under Section 162.

b. If ABC Co. is an SSTB, Ann can increase her QBID by shifting income to the rental.

c. The rental is considered a trade or business.

d. The rental is considered non-SSTB even if ABC Co. is an SSTB.

22. The case of *Hazard v. Commissioner*, 7 CT 372 (1946), proved that a single rental:

a. Is never a trade or business.

b. May be a trade or business.

c. Justifies the taxpayer as real estate professional.

d. Is a trade or business if the taxpayer materially participates in the rental activity.

23. In *Vandeyacht*, TC Memo 1994-148, the rental was considered investment property because:

a. The property was only rented to vacationers.

b. The taxpayer only had a single rental.

c. The taxpayer only owned the property to generate a profit.

d. The property was only rented to children or friends and not to the general public.

24. In order to aggregate, the businesses must have direct or indirect common ownership of at least:

a. 20 percent

b. 40 percent

c. 50 percent

d. 80 percent

25. Jeff owns 100 percent of his S corporation law practice. Jeff formed another S corporation to segregate the call center portion of the law firm. The call center primarily services Jeff's law firm and also earns 10 percent of its gross receipts for services performed to an unrelated office supply store. Which of the following statements regarding Jeff's businesses is true?

a. The call center is a non-SSTB.

b. The call center is an SSTB.

c. The call center is 90 percent an SSTB and 10 percent a non-SSTB.

d. The call center could be a non-SSTB if Jeff sold at least 5 percent of his call center ownership to another party.

26. Which of the following is true regarding relevant pass-through entity (RPE) aggregation?

a. If the RPE aggregates, the partner or shareholder may disaggregate.

b. The RPE is required to aggregate if it meets the criteria.

c. A QBID is not allowed unless the RPE aggregates.

d. The partner or shareholder may further aggregate other RPEs with the aggregated RPE.

27. Which of the following is true regarding service businesses under Section 199A?

a. High-income taxpayers will want to contend that their business is a service business.

b. Consulting is not considered a service business.

c. Engineers are excluded from the definition of service business.

d. Physical therapists are not in a service business.

28. On a partnership return, for purposes of Section 199A, W-2 wages are allocated:

a. Evenly among the number of partners.

b. Based on how the wage deduction is allocated.

c. Based on their profit and loss allocation.

d. In the most tax advantageous way.

29. Section 707(a) and 707(c) payments are:

a. Not part of QBI.

b. Always part of QBI.

c. Part of QBI if appropriately elected.

d. Part of QBI if payments are required by the partnership agreement.

30. Partner A and Partner B are 50/50 owners of AB Partnership. Partner A is a high-income taxpayer; Partner B is not. Partner A would like to use special allocations to shift wage and depreciation deductions to his Schedule K-1, but keep the overall deductions allocated to each partner the same. Which of the following statements is true regarding the special allocation?

a. It is an acceptable shifting allocation.

b. Since it has an effect on the partners' Section 704(b) capital, it is acceptable.

c. It is debatable whether this shifting allocation is acceptable.

d. It may be possible with an income chargeback funded by the sale of partnership property.

¶ 10,302 Final Exam Questions: Module 2

1. The first step in a disaster declaration is the president declaring a disaster under the _____ Act.

a. Stafford
b. Freedom
c. Adversity
d. COVID-19

2. An affected taxpayer for COVID-19 means any person with a federal income tax return due on:

a. April 1, 2020
b. April 15, 2020
c. May 15, 2020
d. June 30, 2020

3. Which of the following payment acts was postponed due to COVID-19 legislation?

a. Estimated tax payments due June 15, 2020
b. Income tax payments due April 15, 2020
c. Estimated tax payments for the 2019 tax year
d. Depositing employment and excise taxes

4. If you properly estimate your 2019 tax liability using information available to you and file an extension form by July 15, 2020, your return will be due on:

a. August 15, 2020
b. September 15, 2020
c. October 15, 2020
d. December 15, 2020

5. Which of the following IRAs can be funded now?

a. Both 2019 and 2020
b. Only 2019
c. Neither 2019 nor 2020
d. Only 2020

6. The supplemental unemployment amount funded by the federal government provides an increase of a flat payment of:

a. $100 per week
b. $600 per week
c. $1,000 per month
d. $1,200 per month

7. Pandemic Emergency Unemployment Compensation, which is available to unemployment insurance (UI) recipients that have exhausted all of their regular state UI benefits, provides an additional _____ weeks of state UI benefits.

a. 6
b. 10
c. 13
d. 20

8. Qualified improvement property:

a. Provides a 39-year life.

b. Is not eligible for interior improvements.

c. Is now eligible for bonus depreciation.

d. Is retroactive to January 1, 2017.

9. Under the CARES Act, corporate NOLs arising from 2018, 2019, and 2020:

a. Are suspended.

b. Can offset up to 75 percent of taxable income.

c. Can be carried forward up to five years.

d. Can be carried back five years.

10. Under the CARES Act, non-corporate taxpayers with business losses in 2018, 2019, and 2020:

a. Can carry back losses up to 10 years.

b. Are no longer subject to the $250,000/$500,000 limitation.

c. Can carry forward losses up to $250,000 to the next tax year.

d. Can use up to $3,000 of the losses to offset ordinary income each year until the losses are used.

11. The CARES Act increased the adjusted taxable income (ATI) limitation related to the interest expense deduction for 2019 and 2020 to:

a. 10 percent

b. 30 percent

c. 50 percent

d. 80 percent

12. Under the CARES Act, an early withdrawal from a qualified retirement plan:

a. Is not included in 2020 gross income.

b. Now does not apply to distributions for taxpayers over 45.

c. May not have the 10 percent penalty apply under certain conditions.

d. Can be reported in gross income over the next five years.

13. An above-the-line deduction for charitable contributions may be allowed up to what amount for taxpayers who do not elect to itemize deductions?

a. $300

b. $500

c. $1,000

d. $3,000

14. Under the Families First Coronavirus Response Act, an employee who is unable to work because the employee is quarantined or experiencing COVID-19 symptoms may be eligible for paid sick leave at their regular rate of pay for up to:

a. Two weeks

b. Five weeks

c. Seven weeks

d. 10 weeks

15. A plan participant who certifies that he, his spouse, or a dependent tested positive for COVID-19 or suffered adverse financial conditions due to COVID-19 can make a distribution from a retirement plan and include in income over a:

a. Three-year period
b. Five-year period
c. Seven-year period
d. 10-year period

16. An employer that wants to reduce employer contributions to its safe harbor retirement plans must provide employees with advance notice of:

a. One week
b. 30 days
c. 60 days
d. 90 days

17. IRS Notice 2020-18 extended the April 15 income tax return due date to:

a. June 15
b. July 15
c. September 15
d. October 15

18. Under the CARES Act, employers can defer paying their share of Social Security tax; 50 percent of the deferred amount must be paid by:

a. December 31, 2020, and the remaining 50 percent is due by June 30, 2021.
b. December 31, 2020, and the remaining 50 percent is due by December 31, 2021.
c. December 31, 2021, and the remaining 50 percent is due by June 30, 2022.
d. December 31, 2021, and the remaining 50 percent is due by December 31, 2022.

19. Under Section 1113 of the CARES Act, the Small Business Reorganization Act (SBRA) debt limit to file a bankruptcy case under Subchapter 5 has been increased to:

a. $2.7 million
b. $5 million
c. $7.5 million
d. $10 million

20. The CARES Act requires the Secretary of Education to defer federally held student loan payments through:

a. June 30, 2020
b. September 30, 2020
c. December 31, 2020
d. June 30, 2021

21. Under the EIDL provisions, eligible entities may qualify for loan amounts of up to:

a. $1 million
b. $2 million
c. $4 million
d. $5 million

22. The PPP loan is up to a maximum of $10 million or 2.5 times:

a. Average total interest costs

b. Average total expenses

c. Average total monthly revenue

d. Average total monthly payroll costs

23. What can be included in the PPP loan forgiveness amount?

a. Principal portion of loan payments

b. Rent on lease that began after February 15, 2020

c. Payroll costs

d. Inventory costs

24. An Economic Injury Disaster Loan (EIDL) received before April 3, 2020, for COVID-19 related purposes:

a. May be used for the same purpose as a PPP loan received by the same business.

b. Can be refinanced into the PPP loan forgiveness program.

c. May be completely forgiven if used the same way as PPP loan.

d. Must be repaid on the same day a PPP loan is received.

25. Which of the following statements is true regarding the employee retention credit?

a. For employers with more than 100 employees, qualified wages are wages paid to employees that are not providing services.

b. A significant decline in gross receipts occurs if gross receipts for a quarter are less than 20 percent of the gross receipts for the same quarter of the prior year.

c. The employer does not need to have experienced any decline in gross receipts in order to claim the credit.

d. The credit may be taken if the employer also received a PPP loan.

26. What administrative relief did the IRS provide in Notice 2020-23?

a. Introduction of the Paycheck Protection Program (PPP)

b. Extension of the due date for certain filings and payments to July 15, 2020

c. Correction of employment tax reporting errors using the interest-free adjustment process

d. Definitions of key terms related to paid leave under the Families First Coronavirus Response Act (FFCRA)

27. An employer can count all of the following in the number of its employees for purposes of the FFCRA refundable credits, ***except:***

a. Employees on leave

b. Independent contractors

c. Day laborers employed by a temp agency

d. Part-time workers

28. The Families First Coronavirus Response Act (FFCRA) requires employers with fewer than 500 employees to provide up to ____ week(s) of sick leave and up to ____ week(s) of family/medical leave to eligible employees.

a. 1; 3

b. 1; 10

c. 2; 6

d. 2; 10

29. Employees requesting leave under the Emergency Family and Medical Leave Expansion Act (EFMLA) must have been employed by their employer for at least:

a. 30 calendar days

b. 60 calendar days

c. Six months

d. One year

30. Under the Emergency Paid Sick Leave Act (EPSLA), eligible employers must provide paid sick leave to:

a. Full-time employees only

b. Employees who have worked a minimum of 60 calendar days

c. Employees who are unable to work because of one of six specified reasons

d. Employees who cannot work on-site but can telework

31. Which of the following statements is true about the payroll tax credit for required paid sick leave?

a. The credit is not refundable.

b. A double benefit is allowed.

c. It is based on the employee's compensation and number of hours worked.

d. An employer can require an employee to use other paid leave before paid sick leave.

32. Which of the following provides employers with relief from the penalty for failing to deposit payroll taxes?

a. Recently issued IRS regulations

b. Notice 2020-22

c. The FFCRA

d. The TCJA

33. The employee retention credit (ERC) is outlined in the:

a. CARES Act

b. FFCRA

c. Internal Revenue Code

d. Paycheck Protection Program

34. Which of the following employers is eligible for the ERC?

a. A municipal government

b. An employer that has received a loan under the Paycheck Protection Program (PPP).

c. An employer doing business in 2020 that is seeing a 50 percent decline in its gross receipts compared to the same quarter of 2019

d. Any employer with more than 1,000 full-time employees.

35. For purposes of the ERC, *qualified wages* include:

a. Wages paid by an employer to employees who are related individuals

b. Wages pursuant to a vacation, sick, or other personal leave policy

c. Wages for which paid leave credits are claimed under the FFRCA

d. Cash wages and employer-provided healthcare expenses properly allocable to the wages

---

¶ 10,303 Final Exam Questions: Module 3

1. Gross income _______ discharge of indebtedness.

a. Does not include
b. Includes
c. May include
d. Sometimes includes

2. The fact that a decrease in liabilities increases net worth describes which theory?

a. Freeing of asset accessions
b. Loan proceeds
c. Reduction of capital
d. Increase of discharge

3. Which of the following identifies a true cancellation or forgiveness by a lender (including in a workout where the lender reduces the amount owed)?

a. Reduction
b. Elimination
c. Discharge
d. Proportion

4. COD income is the difference between the adjusted issue price of (the) ______ and the holder's amount that is _______.

a. Debt; realized
b. Liability; realized
c. Debt; paid
d. Liability; paid

5. Which of the following Code Sec 108 exceptions is meant to facilitate debt workouts for real estate?

a. Bankruptcy
b. Qualified farm indebtedness
c. Insolvency
d. Qualified real property business indebtedness

6. Regarding the order of attribute reduction, after net operating losses are considered, which of the following items is next considered?

a. Capital losses and capital loss carryovers
b. Certain tax credits
c. Basis in property
d. Passive activity loss carryovers

7. Which of the following is considered first in the order for basis reduction?

a. Personal property used in a trade or business
b. Inventory, accounts receivable, and real property held as inventory
c. Real property used in a trade or business
d. Property not used in a trade or business or investment

8. A change in yield that exceeds the greater of ____ basis points or ____ percent of yield of the old debt instrument is a significant modification.

a. 25; 5
b. 50; 5
c. 25; 10
d. 50; 10

9. Which of the following is a type of wage-earner bankruptcy?

a. Chapter 7
b. Chapter 11
c. Chapter 13
d. Chapter 16

10. To take advantage of a Chapter 13 bankruptcy, the debtor must have timely filed tax returns for the last _____ years at minimum.

a. Two
b. Three
c. Four
d. Five

11. Which of the following would ***not*** be considered a discharge of indebtedness?

a. A cancellation by order of bankruptcy
b. A workout where the lender reduces the amount owed
c. Setoffs of amounts between a debtor and creditor
d. A lender's forgiveness of a loan

12. Generally, a transfer of property in satisfaction of nonrecourse debt results in:

a. A Code Sec. 108 exclusion
b. COD income
c. An insolvency exception
d. Sale or exchange treatment under Code Sec. 1001

13. With regard to discharge of indebtedness, which of the following is both a Code Sec. 108 statutory exclusion and a judicial exception?

a. Purchase price adjustment exclusion
b. Bankruptcy exclusion
c. Insolvency exception
d. Qualified principal residence exclusion

14. Under the Paycheck Protection Program Flexibility Act, the covered period for PPP funds has been expanded to:

a. 8 weeks
b. 24 weeks
c. 36 weeks
d. 52 weeks

15. With regard to forgivable costs under the Paycheck Protection Program, which of the following is a covered "nonpayroll" cost?

a. Sick leave

b. Retirement benefits

c. Employee bonuses

d. Utilities

16. Which employees are excluded for purposes of the wage reduction "haircut"?

a. Any employees who worked during the covered period

b. Any employees who earned more than $100,000 in any 2019 pay period

c. Any employees who work part-time

d. Any employees who make more than the average employee salary

17. What is the payroll cost percentage limit under the Paycheck Protection Program Flexibility Act?

a. 30 percent

b. 50 percent

c. 60 percent

d. 75 percent

18. According to the Small Business Administration's Paycheck Protection Program interim final rules, which of the following can include contributions to their retirement plan as forgivable costs?

a. S corporation shareholders

b. Partners

c. Sole proprietors

d. All of the above

19. Which of the following taxpayers can use the new Paycheck Protection Program Loan Forgiveness Application form?

a. A sole proprietorship with no employees included in the original loan application

b. A corporation that reduced several employees' salaries by 30 percent during the covered period

c. A small business that reduced its total number of employees during the covered period

d. A company that has maintained the same level of business it had before February 15, 2020

20. According to the Payroll Protection Program Flexibility Act, a borrower should use at least ____ percent of a PPP loan for payroll costs, and up to ____ percent of the loan for payment of interest, rent, utilities.

a. 50; 50

b. 30; 70

c. 60; 40

d. 70; 30

¶ 10,304 Final Exam Questions: Module 4

1. Alexis was diagnosed with coronavirus in 2020. Under the CARES Act, how much can she borrow from her $150,000 401(k) account?

a. Up to $50,000

b. Up to $75,000

c. Up to $100,000

d. Up to $150,000

2. Under the CARES Act, retirement contributions can be counted as a payroll cost to help a business qualify for:

a. A larger Paycheck Protection Program (PPP) loan

b. A smaller PPP loan

c. Full forgiveness of its PPP loan

d. More favorable loan repayment terms

3. The increased 401(k)/IRA loan limits under the CARES Act are available until:

a. July 15, 2020

b. September 23, 2020

c. December 31, 2020

d. January 15, 2021

4. Jonathan withdrew his 2020 required minimum distribution (RMD) from his retirement account in January 2020. Which of the following is his best option for recontributing the RMD to his account?

a. A 60-day rollover

b. A 90-day rollover

c. A Notice 2020-23 rollover extension

d. He cannot recontribute the RMD.

5. Which of the following individuals would be eligible for a retirement plan loan under the modified rules of the CARES Act?

a. James, whose wife was diagnosed with coronavirus

b. Stephanie, who owns a grocery store that has experienced strong sales during the coronavirus pandemic

c. Lourdes, whose best friend has been hospitalized for coronavirus

d. Dmitri, a 60-year-old man who has tested negative for coronavirus

6. Before the CARES Act was passed, Employer A's deadline for its Form 5500 filing for the plan year that ended in September 2019 was April 1, 2020. With the passage of the CARES Act, the filing date:

a. Remains April 1, 2020

b. Has been extended to July 15, 2020

c. Has been extended to December 31, 2020

d. Has been delayed until January 1, 2021

7. Which of the following is *excluded* from the definition of payroll costs for purposes of loans under the Paycheck Protection Program (PPP)?

a. State and local employer payroll taxes

b. Health insurance premiums

c. Employee retirement plan contributions

d. Annual salaries in excess of $100,000

8. Which statement is correct about retirement plan loan forgiveness for owner-employees and self-employed individuals in light of the CARES Act?

a. The limit for loan forgiveness is based on 2019 compensation only.

b. Loan forgiveness is not available for these individuals.

c. Additional forgiveness is provided for retirement contributions for self-employed individuals.

d. The amount of the forgiveness for these individuals is based on their compensation in 2020.

9. The CARES Act waiver of 2020 required minimum distributions (RMDs) does ***not*** apply to:

a. Roth IRA plans

b. Defined benefit plans

c. SEP IRA plans

d. 403(a) plans

10. At what age are taxpayers allowed to take qualified charitable distributions (QCDs)?

a. 59½

b. 62

c. 70

d. 70½

11. Maya withdraws a qualified charitable distribution of $15,000 in 2020 when no RMD is required. How much of the qualified charitable distribution (QCD) can she claim?

a. $0

b. $5,000

c. $10,000

d. $15,000

12. A retirement account owner dies at age 77 when his life expectance is 12 years and names his estate as the beneficiary of his IRA. Over how many years can the withdrawal payments be spread?

a. 5 years

b. 10 years

c. 12 years

d. 15 years

13. Which act includes a provision that waives the penalty for early retirement plan withdrawals for COVID-19 hardships?

a. CARES Act

b. Tax Cuts and Jobs Act

c. SECURE Act

d. Stimulus Act

14. The SECURE Act increases the age for the required beginning date to:

a. 70

b. 71

c. 72

d. 75

15. Under Code Sec. 72(t), the 10 percent early withdrawal penalty is waived for retirement plan withdrawals made for childbirth or an adoption up to:

a. $5,000 per married couple

b. $5,000 per taxpayer

c. $6,000

d. $7,000

¶ 10,400 Answer Sheets

¶ 10,401 Top Federal Tax Issues for 2021 CPE Course: MODULE 1

Go to **cchcpelink.com/printcpe** to complete your Final Exam online for instant results.

A $129.00 processing fee will be charged for each user submitting Module 1 to **cchcpelink.com/printcpe** for online grading.

Module 1: Answer Sheet

Please answer the questions by indicating the appropriate letter next to the corresponding number.

1. ____	9. ____	17. ____	25. ____
2. ____	10. ____	18. ____	26. ____
3. ____	11. ____	19. ____	27. ____
4. ____	12. ____	20. ____	28. ____
5. ____	13. ____	21. ____	29. ____
6. ____	14. ____	22. ____	30. ____
7. ____	15. ____	23. ____	
8. ____	16. ____	24. ____	

Please complete the Evaluation Form (located after the Module 4 Answer Sheet). Thank you.

¶ 10,402 Top Federal Tax Issues for 2021 CPE Course: MODULE 2

Go to **cchcpelink.com/printcpe** to complete your Final Exam online for instant results.

A $129.00 processing fee will be charged for each user submitting Module 2 to **cchcpelink.com/printcpe** for online grading.

Module 2: Answer Sheet

Please answer the questions by indicating the appropriate letter next to the corresponding number.

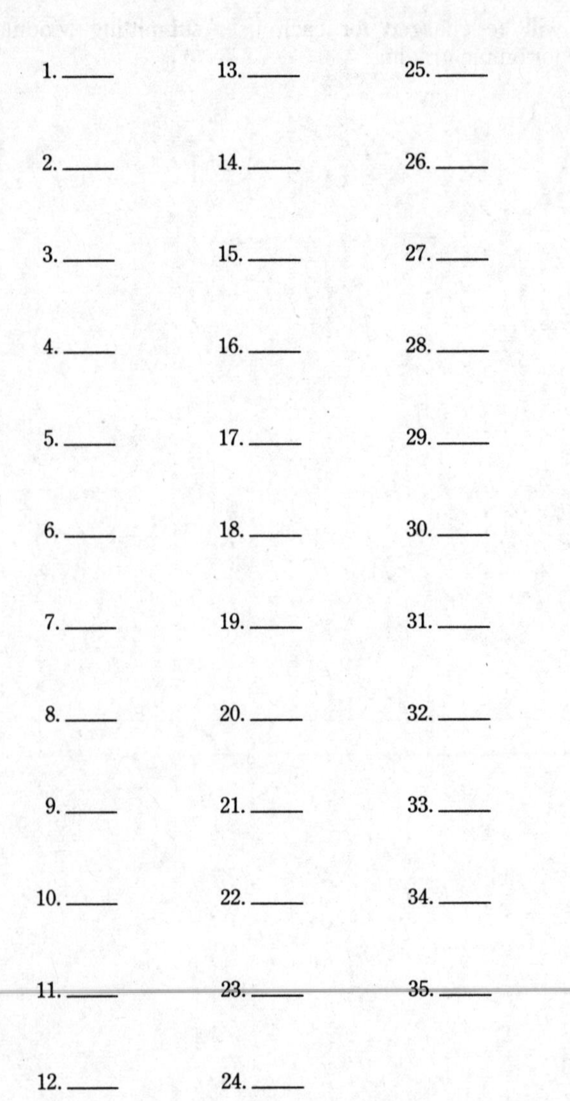
1. ____	13. ____	25. ____
2. ____	14. ____	26. ____
3. ____	15. ____	27. ____
4. ____	16. ____	28. ____
5. ____	17. ____	29. ____
6. ____	18. ____	30. ____
7. ____	19. ____	31. ____
8. ____	20. ____	32. ____
9. ____	21. ____	33. ____
10. ____	22. ____	34. ____
11. ____	23. ____	35. ____
12. ____	24. ____	

Please complete the Evaluation Form (located after the Module 4 Answer Sheet). Thank you.

¶ 10,403 Top Federal Tax Issues for 2021 CPE Course: MODULE 3

Go to **cchcpelink.com/printcpe** to complete your Final Exam online for instant results.

A $89.00 processing fee will be charged for each user submitting Module 3 to **cchcpe-link.com/printcpe** for online grading.

Module 3: Answer Sheet

Please answer the questions by indicating the appropriate letter next to the corresponding number.

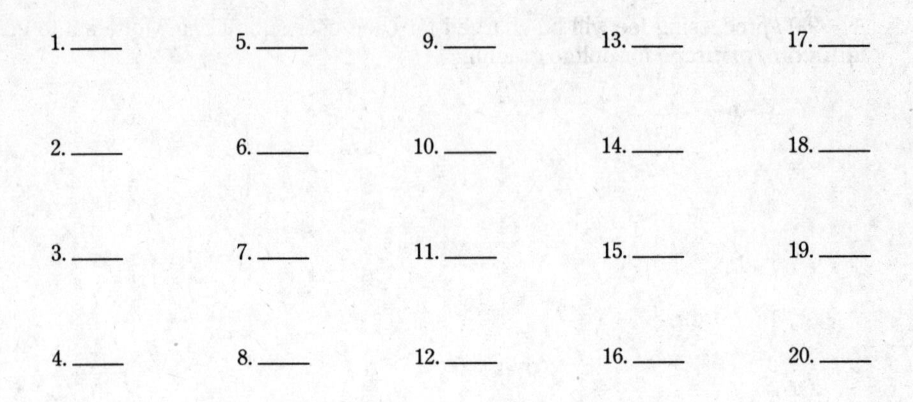

1. ____	5. ____	9. ____	13. ____	17. ____
2. ____	6. ____	10. ____	14. ____	18. ____
3. ____	7. ____	11. ____	15. ____	19. ____
4. ____	8. ____	12. ____	16. ____	20. ____

Please complete the Evaluation Form (located after the Module 4 Answer Sheet). Thank you.

¶ 10,404 Top Federal Tax Issues for 2021 CPE Course: MODULE 4

Go to **cchcpelink.com/printcpe** to complete your Final Exam online for instant results.

A $79.00 processing fee will be charged for each user submitting Module 4 to **cchcpelink.com/printcpe** for online grading.

Module 4: Answer Sheet

Please answer the questions by indicating the appropriate letter next to the corresponding number.

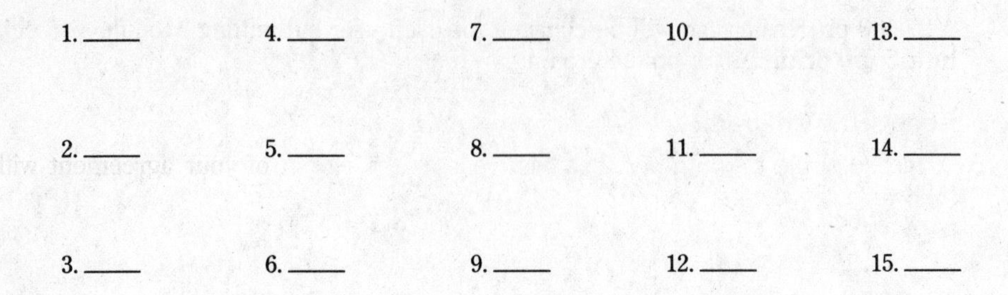

1. ____	4. ____	7. ____	10. ____	13. ____
2. ____	5. ____	8. ____	11. ____	14. ____
3. ____	6. ____	9. ____	12. ____	15. ____

Please complete the Evaluation Form (located after the Module 4 Answer Sheet). Thank you.

¶ 10,500 Top Federal Tax Issues for 2021 CPE Course: Evaluation Form

(10024491-0008)

Please take a few moments to fill out and submit this evaluation to Wolters Kluwer so that we can better provide you with the type of self-study programs you want and need. Thank you.

About This Program

1. Please circle the number that best reflects the extent of your agreement with the following statements:

		Strongly Agree				Strongly Disagree
a.	The Course objectives were met.	5	4	3	2	1
b.	This Course was comprehensive and organized.	5	4	3	2	1
c.	The content was current and technically accurate.	5	4	3	2	1
d.	This Course content was relevant and contributed to achievement of the learning objectives.	5	4	3	2	1
e.	The prerequisite requirements were appropriate.	5	4	3	2	1
f.	This Course was a valuable learning experience.	5	4	3	2	1
g.	The Course completion time was appropriate.	5	4	3	2	1

2. What do you consider to be the strong points of this Course?

3. What improvements can we make to this Course?

THANK YOU FOR TAKING THE TIME TO COMPLETE THIS SURVEY!